Foreign Direct Investment in Europe

Foreign Direct Investment in Europe

A Changing Landscape

Edited by

Klaus Liebscher

Governor of the Oesterreichische Nationalbank, Austria

Josef Christl

Member of the Governing Board of the Oesterreichische Nationalbank, Austria

Peter Mooslechner

Director of the Economic Analysis and Research Section at the Oesterreichische Nationalbank, Austria

Doris Ritzberger-Grünwald

Head of the Foreign Research Division at the Oesterreichische Nationalbank, Austria

Edward Elgar
Cheltenham, UK • Northampton, MA, USA

Published by
Edward Elgar Publishing Limited
The Lypiatts
15 Lansdown Road
Cheltenham
Glos GL50 2JA
UK

Edward Elgar Publishing, Inc.
William Pratt House
9 Dewey Court
Northampton
Massachusetts 01060
USA

Reprinted 2008

A catalogue record for this book
is available from the British Library

Library of Congress Cataloguing in Publication Data
Foreign direct investment in Europe : a changing landscape / edited by Klaus
Liebscher . . . [et al.].
    p. cm.
  Published in association with Oesterreichische Nationalbank, Austria.
  Includes bibliographical references and index.
  1. Investments, Foreign — Europe. 2. International business
enterprises — Europe. I. Liebscher, Klaus. II. Oesterreichische
Nationalbank.
  HG5422.F675 2007
  332.67'3094 — dc22   2007017588

ISBN 978 1 84720 487 5

Printed and bound in Great Britain by Biddles Ltd, King's Lynn, Norfolk

Contents

Contributors

Frank Barry, Professor of International Business and Development, Trinity College Dublin, Ireland.

Christian Bellak, Department of Economics, Vienna University of Economics and Business Administration.

Erik Berglöf, Chief Economist, European Bank for Reconstruction and Development, London.

Josef Christl, Executive Director, Member of the Governing Board, Oesterreichische Nationalbank.

Jesús Crespo Cuaresma, Professor of Economics, Department of Economics, University of Innsbruck.

René Dell'mour, Economist-statistician, Balance of Payments Division, Oesterreichische Nationalbank.

Barry Eichengreen, Professor of Economics and Political Science, University of California, Berkeley.

Samuel Fankhauser, Deputy Chief Economist and Director, Strategy and Analysis, European Bank for Reconstruction and Development, London.

Carmen Fillat Castejón, Universidad de Zaragoza, Facultad de Economía, Departamento Economía Aplicada.

Yuriy Gorodnichenko, Economics Department, University of California, Berkeley.

Andreja Jaklič, Faculty of Social Sciences, University of Ljubljana, Slovenia.

Blanka Kalinova, Senior Economist, Directorate for Financial and Enterprise Affairs, OECD.

Marcin Kolasa, Economist, Head of Macroeconomic Projections Division, National Bank of Poland.

László Kovács, European Commissioner for Taxation and Customs Union, Member of the European Commission.

Markus Leibrecht, Department of Economics, Vienna University of Economics and Business Administration.

Arjan Lejour, Programme Manager, European Analysis, CPB Netherlands Bureau for Economic Policy Analysis, the Hague, the Netherlands.

Klaus Liebscher, Governor, Oesterreichische Nationalbank.

Robert E. Lipsey, Professor Emeritus of Economics, City University of New York, and Research Associate and Director, NY Office, National Bureau of Economic Research.

Jaan Masso, Faculty of Economics and Business Administration, University of Tartu, Estonia.

Jakub Mikulasek, CzechInvest, Prague, Czech Republic.

Peter Mooslechner, Director of the Economic Analysis and Research Section, Oesterreichische Nationalbank.

Theodore H. Moran, Marcus Wallenberg Professor of International Business and Finance, School of Foreign Service, Georgetown University.

Ivan Pilip, Vice-President, European Investment Bank.

Laura Resmini, Department of Economics and ISLA, Università L. Bocconi, Milan.

Manfred Schepers, Vice President, Finance, European Bank for Reconstruction and Development, London.

Doris Ritzberger-Grünwald, Head of the Foreign Research Division, Oesterreichische Nationalbank.

Maria Antoinette Silgoner, Economist, Foreign Research Division, Oesterreichische Nationalbank.

Jürgen Stark, Member of the Executive Board and the Governing Council of the European Central Bank.

Jan Svejnar, Director of the International Policy Center at the Ford School, Everett E. Berg Professor of Business, Professor of Public Policy, Professor of Economics, University of Michigan.

Marjan Svetličič, Faculty of Social Sciences, University of Ljubljana, Slovenia.

Katherine Terrell, Professor of Business Economics and Public Policy, Stephen M. Ross School of Business, and Professor of Public Policy Analysis, Gerald R. Ford School of Public Policy, University of Michigan.

Hui Tong, Economist, International Monetary Fund.

Irina Tytell, International Monetary Fund.

Priit Vahter, School of Economics, University of Nottingham, UK.

Julia Woerz, The Vienna Institute for International Economic Studies.

Ksenia Yudaeva, Director of Research, Centre for Strategic Research, Moscow.

Katja Zajc Kejžar, Assistant Professor, Faculty of Economics, University of Ljubljana, Slovenia.

Preface

Very seldom is one so lucky to find a title for one's book that so neatly captures its central issue and the many perspectives covered. The idea of a 'changing landscape of foreign direct investment (FDI) in Europe' evokes a picture in which FDI is no longer advancing one way, flowing from higher to lower developed countries, basically from the Western to the Eastern part of Europe. Instead, we see a map of FDI routes leading in both directions, not to say in every direction, with the flow being determined less and less by borders and restrictions, but more and more by demand and supply in distant countries.

Against this backdrop this book deals with quite a broad range of topics such as global FDI trends, the effects of FDI on home and host countries, policies to attract FDI and corporate experiences with FDI, all with a special focus on the countries in Central, Eastern and South-Eastern Europe (CEECs). The book is based on the Oesterreichische Nationalbank's Conference on European Economic Integration, which took place from 20 to 21 November 2006 in Vienna. The conference was organized together with the European Bank for Reconstruction and Development, which continues to be the biggest investor/financier in Central and Eastern Europe; at the time of writing the bank was investing about USD 4 billion per year in the region.

At the very origin of the European integration project stood the hypothesis that economic – and later monetary – integration would boost trade and FDI flows, thus enhancing growth and the catching-up process. Indeed, empirical evidence and the most recent data support this hypothesis: in 2005 the European Union (EU) attracted almost half of all funds invested worldwide. The same year, FDI inflows into all ten new member states of the EU rose by 19 per cent, reaching new record levels. And the role of FDI in promoting transition is evident: FDI brings innovation, new skills and risk management techniques; it promotes competition, forces domestic incumbents to become more productive, and provides forward and backward linkages.

In this respect FDI has been and still is crucial for economic growth and the catching-up process in the countries of Central, Eastern and South-Eastern Europe. Basically, there are three channels through which FDI can influence the economic performance of a country: first, FDI increases the capital stock of an economy, which, according to the standard neoclassical growth theory, should by itself lead to higher levels of per capita output. Second, FDI contributes to productivity growth, as foreign firms tend to have better technological know-how and managing skills. Third, FDI potentially also entails a range of spillover effects to the local enterprises through labour mobility, imitation or training of suppliers. Part of the productivity increases seen in catching-up economies can also be related to multinational enterprises purchasing inputs from domestic firms.

All these effects have been at work in the CEECs, contributing to their economic convergence process with Western Europe. Not surprisingly, catching-up countries profit more from FDI than developed countries, especially in the earlier stages of their catching-up process. And – also not surprisingly – FDI seems to play a special role for industries which are capital and skill intensive, depending on the absorptive capacity of an economy. So, the prospect of reaping the benefits of FDI inflows is another reason for policy makers to promote activities that increase human capital. Concerning the negative crowding-out effect again and again attributed to FDI inflows, one should take a dynamic perspective. Even if domestic investments are crowded out in the early stage of FDI inflows, domestic investment will benefit as well once domestic demand increases due to FDI.

Competition for FDI funds is fierce, with actors and instruments having changed significantly compared with what we saw ten years ago, in the mid-1990s. Today, we no longer have different countries or large regions competing with each other – today's FDI projects pitch cities against cities, or narrow regions in one country against narrow regions in other countries. This might be partially due to agglomeration effects, which are present particularly in high-tech sectors. One of the first examples of this trend may have been Silicon Valley, the first IT cluster which attracted a lot of FDI. Today, one would immediately think of the automotive cluster that has evolved in the Slovak Republic. As a result, FDI policies may have to change or extend their mission. Nowadays local investment promotion agencies seem to be an effective instrument in spurring FDI and productivity, especially when they are combined with one-stop shops for administrative matters.

What has also changed significantly is that financial incentives in the form of subsidies have ceased to be the most efficient measures to attract FDI; what matters a lot more these days is the removal of restrictions. In addition, improving governance and creating reliable and predictable legal systems are also key, especially in early stages of transition. In fact FDI in Central and Eastern Europe led to impressive improvements at all levels of governance in the years before EU entry, although – as claimed not only by the European Commission – reform fatigue has set in since.

Overall, the main focus of the academic debate on FDI has shifted from host to home country effects recently. While there is unequivocal evidence of productivity gains by foreign producers, evidence on the crowding out of domestic players or on productivity spillovers to domestic firms is far less clear. Fears of adverse home country effects of FDI may be exaggerated, but there is no doubt that structural adjustment is necessary to move the investor's country up the skills ladder as well.

Once in a while, public opinion points out the negative effects of outward FDI flows, but empirical results do not show a drastic impact. Fears in this respect have been exaggerated, especially the off-shoring or outsourcing of intermediate input production – sometimes referred to as 'bazaar economy' developments – does not seem to be quantitatively very important. In Austria, with its high shares of FDI flows to CEECs, FDI in manufacturing industries, which are typically more likely to resort to outsourcing, only accounts for 20 per cent of total FDI. Moreover, we should not forget that the growing international division of labour benefits the home countries of FDI as well, as in some sectors they can remain competitive only if they buy cheaper intermediate inputs from abroad. Therefore, economic policy in the investors' home countries should abstain from protectionist moves.

The implications of outward investment for investors' home countries are not only an issue in developed countries; outward investment is also gaining importance in Central and Eastern European countries – classical FDI host countries, which are increasingly emerging as active investors. Currently FDI outflows from these countries are still low, but they show relatively high growth rates in recent years. For the moment the major destinations of FDI from the EU's new member states are locations in other new member states, mainly because of the narrow technological and cultural gap. But this will change in the near future as they will climb up on the technological ladder and will widen their radius of activities. Nevertheless the net investment position of the new member states will remain negative over the medium term.

Besides these many global issues, the book also covers two specific regions that may serve as a benchmark for CEECs. On the one hand, Ireland's success story and on the other hand, the newly arrived competitor, China.

The fact that Ireland has attracted substantial FDI inflows since the mid-1980s has been a key factor behind its outstanding growth performance. At the time of writing, Ireland's FDI per capita is as much as six times higher than the European average. Half of employment in manufacturing and a quarter of employment in services are in multinational firms. The absence of a language barrier and the large Irish community in the US are only two of the explanatory factors. Several other factors are equally or even more important: the favourable investment climate (since fiscal imbalances and labour market problems were sorted out in the 1980s); the low corporate taxes; institutions that provide young people with the necessary science and engineering training; the powerful influence of the Industrial Development Agency on government decisions; and the meritocratic orientation of public services.

Concerning Asia, the key question is whether recent and increasing FDI flows to China are complementary to FDI in other countries or are rather crowding them out. Empirical results suggest that FDI flows to China did not significantly influence FDI to other countries. The CEECs in particular seem to be quite resilient in this respect, as their geographical location, their still cheap but highly qualified labour, and the uniqueness of their catching-up process – which has put them into nearly the economic position they had before the Iron Curtain was built – make them attractive for FDI.

Due to its geographical location and its historical links with the CEECs, Austria has a special role in the changing landscape of FDI. Starting with the fall of the Iron Curtain and spurred by Austria's application for EU membership in 1989, Austrian companies were among the first ones to invest in the CEECs in the 1990s. As a result of this Austria became one of the leading investors in the region, rising to number one in several country rankings. As the markets and investments in the EU's new member states are maturing, Austrian companies increasingly invest in countries in South-Eastern Europe and in the CIS (Commonwealth of Independent States). In parallel, Austria became a 'bridgehead' for multinational enterprises, providing the home for many multinational companies that are active investors in Central, Eastern and South-Eastern Europe, and therefore headquartered in Austria. For them Central, Eastern and South-Eastern European countries are important markets at their doorstep as they provide excellent opportunities to expand a company's market share. This argument often dominates even the common offshoring objective of cost reduction. In some cases companies also follow their major customers or business partners already active in that region.

Overall FDI is seen as a win–win situation for both home and host countries, as Austrian firms and multinational enterprises contribute significantly to the economic development of the Central and Eastern European region. Like the earlier conference on which this book is based, this publication is meant to honour all those who have been involved in the changing landscape of FDI.

Klaus Liebscher
Josef Christl
Peter Mooslechner
Doris Ritzberger-Grünwald

Policy challenges of FDI

The changing landscape of FDI in Europe

Klaus Liebscher[1]

At first sight, foreign direct investment (FDI) may appear to be a rather narrow topic. However, a closer look at the issue quickly reveals how complex and controversial this topic really is. Robert C. Feenstra (1999), a first-rate expert on FDI, expressed it the following way: 'FDI combines aspects of both international trade in goods and international financial flows, and it is a phenomenon more complex than either of these'.

For individual businesses, FDI raises questions of ownership and location considerations. For the public, FDI raises fears of unemployment and loss of independence. For policy makers, FDI and the internationalization of business are accompanied by the challenging task of increasing the attractiveness of their country as a business location and providing the ground for positive spillovers, while at the same time responding to the fears of the public. And for international institutions there is a sheer endless list of tasks, from publishing comprehensive data on FDI and providing funds and investment insurance, to promoting an ongoing dialogue between the major nations in order to avoid the revival of protectionist and beggar-thy-neighbour policies.

International institutions such as the WTO, UNCTAD, the OECD, the IMF, the EBRD or the EIB have – each in their respective fields – contributed substantially to providing satisfactory data, best practice catalogues and a growing body of scientific research, which has laid the ground for a discussion that is based on facts rather than sentiment and prejudices.

In the past decade, the landscape of FDI has changed dramatically. Investors have extended and shifted their investment radius, entering new territory both in a geographical and a sectoral sense. Competition has increased both among investor countries and FDI host countries. At the same time, FDI has displayed its power to connect regions. Countries that appeared distant a decade ago are now perceived to be within easy reach, owing to close business relations and FDI links. In this sense, FDI is a connecting force which influences the entire business landscape.

To illustrate the complexity and the importance of foreign direct investments for the current political debate, I would like to present the topic from two perspectives: the European perspective and the perspective of Austria, a country that not only happens to be the country I am most familiar with, but that also serves as a perfect illustration of the benefits of both inward and outward FDI.

THE EUROPEAN PERSPECTIVE

Let me start with the European perspective: at the very origin of the European integration project stood the hypothesis that economic integration – and at a later stage also monetary integration – would lead to intensified trade and FDI flows, which would mutually reinforce one another. Furthermore, the more closely countries are linked through trade and FDI, the more the synchronization of their business cycles will progress. This in turn reduces the costs of a loss of customs and monetary autonomy. All these factors will ultimately lead to higher growth, promote development and stimulate the catching-up process. This line of argument is therefore essential for the assessment of the costs and benefits of removed trade barriers and monetary union.

Have these hypotheses been substantiated so far? Has the European integration process indeed stimulated trade and investment flows? And, if so: have intensified trade and investment helped to accelerate growth and the catching-up process? Empirical evidence suggests that European integration has indeed stimulated trade and FDI. In 2005, inflows and outflows of foreign direct investment funds from and to the European Union (EU) reached a level that was only topped by the record year 2000. The EU could attract almost half of all funds invested worldwide.

This brings me to the second question: have trade and investment had the desired effect of stimulating productivity and growth through knowledge and technology spillovers? How can economic policy at the national and at the EU level contribute to generating a win–win situation in which both the investors and the FDI host countries profit from capital flows? With regard to this question, I would like to emphasize two important aspects from the European integration point of view: first, the European stability architecture provides the ideal environment for trade and FDI activities. The design and the interaction of a stability-oriented single monetary policy at the euro area level, sound public finances and ambitious structural policies at the national level are all essential elements of a healthy business environment, which is conducive to FDI development. This ensures that the freedom of movement for persons, goods, services and capital can fully materialize and bring about flexible and dynamic economies.

Second, the ten new EU member states are the best example of how the FDI landscape has changed in the course of the European integration process. They have experienced trade intensification and a wave of FDI inflows, not just since May 2004 but already in the years preceding their membership. In 2005, FDI inflows into all ten countries rose by 19 per cent, reaching new record levels. I have no doubt that also Bulgaria and Romania, the new EU members as of January 2007, will increase their attractiveness as FDI locations even further in the course of aligning their legal and institutional frameworks with EU regulations.

With the eventual adoption of the euro, the EU members from Central and Eastern Europe will experience another impetus for trade and investment, just as the current euro area countries did. I would like to emphasize, however, that this next level of integration can only be successfully reached in line with the stipulations of the Maastricht Treaty. Before adopting the common currency, countries have to show sufficient stability in their monetary and fiscal policies. The two-year minimum period within the exchange rate mechanism ERM II ensures that the fixed exchange rate regime is supported by the fundamentals. Slovenia was the first country among the new EU member states to fulfil all these requirements. As part of the euro area as of January 2007, Slovenia enjoys all the benefits of the common currency.

Against the background of its stability architecture, Europe has no reason to fear the effects of globalization. Quite the contrary: Europe is well prepared to meet the new challenges and to reap the benefits of global integration. The interaction of stability-oriented monetary, fiscal and structural policies in the European context provides the optimal response to the challenges ahead within a changing business landscape. If we want to take advantage of open markets, we have to continue the implementation of the reform agenda and to advance both dimensions of integration: deepening and enlargement.

What we have achieved in Europe is today seen as giving direction to the discussions at the global level. International institutions such as the WTO, the IMF or the OECD are trying to advance worldwide trade liberalization and economic cooperation in ways that became reality at the European level years ago. At the G-7 summit 2006 in Singapore, the participant countries stressed the importance of advancing multilateral trade liberalization as an essential contribution to enhancing global growth and reducing poverty. We can therefore be confident that we are pursuing the right strategies to respond to the challenges of globalization. Defensive strategies may appear a tempting reaction to budgetary shortages and public concerns in the short run. But in the long term, such measures raise uncertainty and are not conducive to promoting investors' confidence. Only pro-active policies have the potential to sustain and support a country's role within the context of globalization.

THE AUSTRIAN PERSPECTIVE

Let me now come to the Austrian perspective. Austria can indeed be seen as the perfect example of a country that has for decades profited from outward and inward FDI flows.

On the one hand, Austria is a typical FDI host country. Starting from a relatively low stock of foreign direct investment, Austria has caught up substantially in recent years. In 2005, Austria's FDI stocks had already reached 20 per cent of GDP, which is close to the average of the developed economies. German companies are the most important source of funds, followed by British and American investors with a focus on business and financial services, retail and the chemical industries.

On the other hand, Austria is known to play an increasingly active role as an investor. In 2005, the FDI funds of Austrian companies reached a new peak. Almost half of those funds are invested in Central, Eastern and South-Eastern Europe. In the first half of 2006, Austria was the top investor country in Slovenia, Bulgaria, Croatia and Bosnia and Herzegovina.

Today, Austria is a gateway to the new and to future EU member states. If you pass through the Vienna airport, this role as a gateway becomes evident. The flight destinations and the accumulation of top managers from companies worldwide who use Austria as a stopover on their way toward the East all underline Austria's central position. But Austria is not only a stopover location. Many multinational companies today choose Austria as their operating base for expanding into Eastern markets. In my view there is no doubt that Austria has profited substantially from the opening of the former Eastern bloc and from EU enlargement.

Austrian companies' investments came in subsequent waves, both in terms of targeted regions and sectors. Starting with the neighbouring countries, Hungary and the Czech Republic, Austrian companies later on enlarged their investment radius. Investors initially focused on manufacturing and trade industries. In a second stage, banks and insurance companies entered the markets and prepared the ground for subsequent investment waves. More recently, investment projects have shifted from labour-intensive, low-skill industries to more skill-intensive industries and the service sector. This may indicate that the new EU member states have reached a new level of development. In this sense, Austria is not only confronted with a changing FDI landscape in Europe, but is actively shaping it.

The profitability of Austrian investment projects in Central and Eastern Europe is much higher than in other regions. As most projects are still young, profitability can be expected to remain above average for the years to come. By turning in this direction, Austrian companies have not only succeeded in reaping benefits for their own operational business; they have also contributed substantially to European integration and the realization of welfare gains.

However, I do not want to finish my elaborations on Austria's FDI situation without adding some words on the challenges ahead. Based on the excellent experience with investing in Austria's neighbouring countries and the wish to maintain their pioneer role, companies have begun to move farther east and south-east searching for new investment opportunities. This regional shift does not come without additional risks: Austrian companies are approaching markets that are more distant, both in a geographical sense and in their traditions and business culture. This makes a comprehensive judgement of the associated risks more difficult. At the same time, Austria increasingly faces competition from what used to be typical FDI host countries, which are now emerging as active investors in their neighbouring countries, often sharing with them a common language and a common history.

The changing FDI landscape in Europe is thus a challenge for investor countries like Austria. But Austria will also be challenged as an FDI host country. Investors constantly update their investment strategies in geographical and sectoral terms. To preserve Austria's attractiveness as a business location requires more than an appealing tax system and investment incentives. It requires a highly trained workforce and continued wage moderation in combination with flexibility and social peace, all within a general framework of stability oriented fiscal and structural policies.

NOTE

1. Maria Antoinette Silgoner, of the OeNB's staff, contributed to these remarks.

REFERENCE

Feenstra, Robert C. (1999), 'Facts and fallacies about Foreign Direct Investment', in Martin Feldstein (ed.), *International Capital Flows*, Chicago: University of Chicago Press, pp. 331–50.

FDI: a driver for and a result of private sector development

Manfred Schepers

Foreign direct investment is a topic that is close to the heart of the European Bank for Reconstruction and Development (EBRD) as the EBRD uses the tools of investment to promote entrepreneurship and help build open, market-based economies. We see FDI as an important way to promote transition.[1]

THE BENEFITS OF FDI

FDI is beneficial for the development of markets for several reasons.

First, foreign entrepreneurs bring innovation. They introduce to their host country new technologies, new products, new management practices and new skills. In the financial sector, for example, foreign banks introduced modern risk management techniques, and as a consequence they are more efficient, even today, than domestic banks. They have lower cost-to-asset ratios. They were also among the first to issue mortgage bonds and other asset-backed securities.

Second, by introducing modern production and management techniques, FDI helps to increase competition. Foreign market entrants force domestic incumbents to become more productive and adopt better ways of doing business themselves.

Third, foreign investors can also have a positive impact on their clients downstream and on their suppliers upstream – what we call forward and backward linkages. For example, Central Europe has seen a lot of investments from the world's foremost car makers. The Slovak Republic is now the world's leading car maker in per capita terms. Local suppliers are benefiting hugely from these investments but they have to be extremely competitive to remain in the game. Car makers are notoriously demanding on their suppliers in terms of quality, cost and reliability.

But not all foreign investment is FDI and not all foreign investors are strategic investors. There is also a growing number of financial investors. I am particularly thinking of private equity funds, an industry that has been growing encouragingly over the last few years. The capital raised annually for private equity funds in transition countries is fast approaching the EUR 2 billion barrier. These investors hold assets for a few years, turn the companies around and exit, often to a strategic investor or through an initial public offering. The positive impact this has on investee companies and the development of capital markets should not be forgotten when we talk about the benefit of foreign investment. Portfolio investors are also important.

THE ROLE OF EBRD

At EBRD we believe in the positive effects of FDI and indeed all forms of foreign investment. There is also clear empirical evidence that the positive spillovers described above are happening.

But EBRD also puts its money where its mouth is. We continue to be the biggest financier and investor in Eastern Europe and the former Soviet Union. Each year the Bank commits around EUR 4 billion in new financing to the transition region; in 2006 the results were in fact closer to EUR 5 billion. At the time of writing, our total portfolio stands at about EUR 16.6 billion, of which about 80 per cent is with private sector clients.

This number includes both equity and debt, so not all of it would be classified as foreign investment. In fact, our equity commitments are only just over EUR 3 billion. But of course this is only half the story. First, the EUR 3 billion in commitments has created substantial returns. If you look at our financial statements, where these investments are listed at market value, you will find a much higher number. Second, the EBRD is investing alongside its private partners who generally put in more money than we do.

I said that the EBRD is still the biggest investor in the transition region. This is true, but the market is catching up. We don't mind. We see it as part of our mandate to mobilize foreign investment and in fact measure our success partly by the amount of private capital we are able to leverage. For the same reason, we see it as a huge success that eight of our clients – the new EU members – are increasingly able to finance themselves in the market and will therefore graduate from EBRD assistance over the next five years or so. It is a tremendous achievement of which we can be proud.

FDI TRENDS

Trends in foreign direct investment are a good indicator of the tremendous economic transformation that has taken place in Central Europe and indeed in much of the transition region.

In the early days of the new millennium, transition countries attracted perhaps around USD 25 billion in FDI, and much related to the various privatization programmes. In 2005 net FDI flows reached almost USD 54 billion – a record level – and we are again predicting more than USD 50 billion in net FDI for 2006.

This is roughly the same amount of FDI as China gets. People talk a lot about the flow of FDI to China, and, yes, China as a single country attracts the same amount of investment as the 29 transition countries – the EBRD's countries of operation – together. But in per capita terms and even relative to total GDP, transition countries are actually ahead.

Perhaps more important than the overall trend is the composition of FDI. FDI flows are becoming more diverse both in terms of sectors and countries, and this is good news. However, we still have a long way to go. FDI is still heavily concentrated on Central Europe, which gets about 45 per cent of all flows. FDI to South-Eastern Europe is picking up, particularly in the EU accession countries. South-Eastern Europe now accounts for almost 40 per cent of regional net FDI. In the CIS most of the investment continues to be flows into the natural resources sectors, although in Russia at least this is beginning to change.

Increasing the flow of FDI and diversifying its regional coverage is thus an important challenge for the region. We know many of the main determinants of FDI.

Some investors look at the transition region as a new market. They are attracted to a market that is perhaps the most dynamic in Europe. Eastern Europe is growing at over 6 per cent per year – several percentage points higher than the euro area. What is more, growth is driven by consumption as wages go up, people gain access to credit, and pent-up demand is met. So clearly this is an attractive region for investors looking for new markets.

Other investors are more interested in productivity and they look at transition countries as a base from which to export. They are attracted by a well qualified, disciplined and effective work force, and the transition region still has clear advantages here. However, Central Europe at least has to make sure wages do not rise ahead of productivity gains.

Both types of foreign investors are looking for an attractive business environment and clear and predictable rules. This is also an area that is important to EBRD and one in which we invest a lot of effort in terms of policy dialogue and technical assistance. We do not do this particularly to promote FDI. The aim is much broader. A good business environment benefits not only foreign investors but the entire economy, including small and medium enterprises.

This is what the EBRD is all about – the promotion of private entrepreneurship and open, market-based economies. FDI is both a driver for and a result of private sector development.

NOTES

1. The EBRD helped to co-organize the OeNB 2006 Conference on European Economic Integration entitled 'The Changing Landscape of FDI in Europe', which provided the basis for this book. The OeNB is a very close partner of the EBRD in the transition region, and every autumn hosts the presentation of the EBRD Transition Report in Vienna. Moreover, the EBRD is a Contributing Member of the Joint Vienna Institute – primarily sponsored by Austria's central bank, its finance ministry and the IMF – which provides training to officials and managers from former centrally planned economies to assist them with the transition to market-based systems.

The contribution of taxation to European competitiveness, growth and employment

László Kovács[1]

INTRODUCTION

The focus of this chapter is on the contribution of taxation to European competitiveness, growth and employment, particularly in the area of corporate taxation. Specifically, I will mention the preparatory work on the Common Consolidated Corporate Tax Base in this domain.

Tax base harmonization is not the only instrument which can boost growth, employment and competitiveness in Europe. Soft law instruments such as co-ordination of tax policies also have a role to play, as I will discuss below.

TAXATION POLICY IN THE REVISED LISBON STRATEGY

As you know, the 2005 Spring European Council endorsed a new start for the Lisbon strategy, with a focus on growth, jobs and competitiveness.

A major priority of the European Union is to improve its competitiveness while preserving its social model, based on a high level of social protection coupled with high levels of public goods.

Meeting the Lisbon objectives implies ensuring that Europe is made a more attractive place in which to invest and work; promoting knowledge and innovation; and shaping policies that allow European businesses to create more and better jobs.

In a Communication adopted in October 2005, the Commission highlighted how taxation and customs policies can contribute to the attainment of the Lisbon objectives. In particular, taxation policy can contribute to raising the efficiency of our economies by a better allocation of production factors as well as to improving the competitiveness of our companies. It can also generate more competition in the markets, boost trade and support knowledge and innovation.

All our initiatives in the taxation field pursue the objective of making the European Union more competitive, stimulating investment and growth, and creating more jobs in the present context of globalization, while respecting the principle of subsidiarity.

In the direct taxation field, however, the European Union is far from being regarded as a single market by corporations. At the time of writing, EU enterprises have to deal with 27 different tax systems with separate accounting.

Strategic choices of enterprises in the internal market are thus influenced by significant tax obstacles. Double taxation, high compliance costs, and tax costs involved in business restructuring induce firms to invest and operate domestically rather than in another EU member state.

Such barriers can be considered comparable to technical barriers whose relief can induce liberalization effects. Moreover, generally compliance costs constitute a pure deadweight loss, as they correspond to directly unproductive and recurrent activities.

The removal of such obstacles would allow businesses to make sounder economic choices that are based on the productivity of factors and are less distorted by the influence of certain extra costs. This would lead to an increase in the output of the economies of European member states and, depending on the conditions of the relevant markets and the actual behaviour of firms, downward pressures on costs and prices. This, in turn, would result in welfare gains.

It is my firm conviction that we need a real internal market in the EU, also in the taxation area. And it is no coincidence that, during the public consultation launched by the Commission services in 2006 on the future of the internal market, numerous stakeholders, including business federations, expressed concerns on tax obstacles and explicitly supported the Commission's proposals in the taxation field.

KEY ISSUES IN THE EUROPEAN AGENDA FOR TAXATION

The Commission's approach for the future as regards taxation policy is best illustrated by two examples: the Common Consolidated Corporate Tax Base (CCCTB) and tax policy co-ordination.

Common Consolidated Corporate Tax Base

The most ambitious measure in the field of corporate taxation is the Common Consolidated Corporate Tax Base. Our Communication in April 2006 on the 'Progress to date and the Next Steps' outlined how far we have got and what we plan to do in the next two years in order to present a Community legislative proposal in 2008.

Advantages of the CCCTB

A CCCTB would enable companies operating in the internal market to follow the same rules for calculating their tax bases in different member states of the EU.

There are overwhelming advantages associated with the introduction of a Common Consolidated Corporate Tax Base. If companies can apply a single EU-wide set of rules for company tax purposes, they will not encounter many of the tax obstacles that they currently face when they do business in more than one member state in the EU.

In fact, a Common Consolidated Tax Base would solve the current tax problems linked to cross-border activities and restructuring of groups of companies.

In this way, a CCCTB would significantly reduce compliance costs because groups would no longer need to comply with the tax reporting requirements of numerous national systems. Should the adoption take the form of a consolidated tax base, as the Commission strongly advocates, it would eliminate the huge costs and uncertainties of complying with transfer pricing rules within the EU.

Even more crucially, it would allow for automatic cross-border consolidation of profits and losses, thus preventing profits and losses from being stranded in different member states as at present.

The consolidated profit would be apportioned among the countries where the firm operates. Consequently a method for sharing the consolidated tax base between member states will be needed.

How do we operate?

Member states are fully involved with the preparatory works. All of them participate in a Commission Working Group, and five of them even chair sub-groups on specific issues.

We work in transparency. All the working documents are published on our website. We publish these to ensure transparency and encourage comment and participation from as wide a range of interested parties as possible.

We associate the key stakeholders. We have organized from time to time Working Group meetings in extended form so that business representatives and academics can express their opinions in our technical discussions.

We have a clear time-frame in mind. The Commission's intention is to publish a Communication on the CCCTB during the first semester of 2007, under the German Presidency, outlining the Commission's thinking on the progress achieved and the work to be done.

Broad outlines of the CCCTB

So what are the broad outlines of the Commission's plans?

First, we are looking to propose a broad base which is as simple to operate as possible, without of course opening up opportunities for companies to escape the fair taxation of their profits. We want it to be significantly more straightforward to operate under one common base than under the current 25 different bases.

Second, we want it to be consolidated. Consolidation is particularly important for two main reasons – (1) it helps to resolve the problems created by the absence of cross-border loss relief and (2) it will help us simplify the current problems caused by the complexities of applying the arm's-length pricing method to transactions between group companies within the internal market. I know this means we have to design a method of 'sharing out' the consolidated base between member states for them to tax at their chosen rates but I firmly believe we will be able to design a method.

Third, we believe it should be optional. It is not for the Commission to propose a compulsory new tax base for all companies in the EU. We will be proposing a tax base which member states should make available to those companies who wish to choose it. However, I should add that we will not be suggesting a choice every year for every company – the choice will be for a whole group to decide, for a number of years.

To summarize – three important features – broad and simple, consolidated with a sharing mechanism, and optional rather than compulsory.

Enhanced cooperation

Now, I want to address the question of what happens if not all member states support our legislative proposal.

In accordance with the Treaty, we will propose legislation for all member states. Only if the Council decides that it cannot reach unanimous agreement and asks the Commission to consider a proposal for a group of member states will we consider moving forwards under 'enhanced cooperation'. I know you can read that there are a few states who already say they are opposed, but this always surprises me. Why be opposed to a proposal that has not yet been made? Wait and see what the final proposal is like and then decide. Of course, if the Council does not believe unanimous agreement is possible, the Commission will consider 'enhanced cooperation' – we cannot afford to miss out on the opportunity to improve the internal market when the Treaty has set out how to proceed with a group of member states. But this is some way ahead – let us finalize the proposal before we address these issues.

No harmonized corporate tax rate

At this stage, let us be clear on one essential point: it is not my intention to propose a harmonized corporate tax rate.

The analysis of empirical data permits us to state that up until now the divergence in taxation rates has had a limited role in influencing the localization of investment in the EU. The polarization of the debate on this topic seems to be disproportionate with respect to the reality. Nevertheless, the Commission services are carefully monitoring the developments in the capital and corporate taxation area in view of the general concerns expressed by member states and different stakeholders.

There are several factors determining the choice of localization of firms. According to recent surveys conducted among businesses, the taxation level is considered as being only the seventh factor influencing the choice of firms, well below other elements characterizing the structure of the economy, such as access to the market, investment climate, labour cost, presence of an educated labour force, quality of infrastructure and public services.

According to an OECD study, differences in taxation rates can explain no more than 3 per cent of differences in investment flows. In general, the taxation level does not seem to be among the main concerns when deciding to invest abroad.

Several studies point out that the logic of localization in the new member states has been mainly market-seeking and has been driven by productivity and the low cost of labour. According to a report of the French Council of Taxes, the taxation advantage (differences of corporate rate with the high-rate EU countries) for a firm deciding to invest in Poland can represent no more than 2 per cent of its value added, whereas the value of the benefit realized in terms of labour costs can attain as much as 50 per cent of the firm's value added. The access to consumers is certainly another main force driving investments in these countries.

The initiative the Commission will take in 2008 aims at harmonizing the corporate tax base while member states will keep their full sovereignty in determining their corporate taxation rate. Each state will apply its own tax rate to its share of the consolidated base.

As a result, companies will benefit from a simpler and more transparent corporate tax system in the EU, and fair tax competition will be enhanced.

A More General Strategy Ensuring Better Co-ordination of Member State Tax Systems

The objective of improving European competitiveness, growth and employment should be pursued not only via harmonization measures. Within the institutional framework, where decisions are taken by unanimity on taxation matters, soft law instruments, such as co-ordination, can also be very fruitful.

In its contribution to the 2005 Hampton Court Summit, the Commission underlined the need for a co-ordinated approach at the EU level and effective administrative co-operation between member states as it could significantly improve the performance of tax systems. Co-ordination does not mean harmonization. Often harmonization is neither necessary, nor desirable.

We still have a situation where individual or corporate taxpayers, in cross-border situations, are liable to be the subject of discrimination or suffer double taxation. Conversely, from a member state perspective, there is greater potential in cross-border situations for inadvertent non-taxation or abuse and hence erosion of tax revenues. These problems have only been partly addressed through the OECD process and member states' bilateral tax treaties, which fail to take into account the EU dimension.

I believe that the problems posed by the interaction of multiple tax systems can often best be resolved through collective efforts by member states. It is often difficult or insufficient to achieve fully coherent tax systems through unilateral measures only. Proper co-ordination and co-operation between member states can best enable them to attain their tax policy goals more effectively and protect their tax base while eliminating discrimination and double taxation.

The aim will thus be to help member states ensure that their tax systems are compatible with the Treaty and also with each other.

My intention is to come forward in the near future with a series of initiatives designed to promote better compliance with Community law and more coherent treatment of taxpayers subject to more than one tax system.

Initiatives will relate both to individuals and to companies and will focus on a number of areas where there are pressing problems, for instance cross-border loss relief, exit taxes and taxes on transfer of assets, withholding taxes on cross-border income, anti-abuse rules and inheritance taxes.

Within the framework of this strategy, I will present to the College a package of three communications on tax co-ordination. The first one will deal with the general objectives of co-ordinating member states' direct tax systems in the internal market. The second one will deal with exit taxation in the corporate sector and the third one with the tax treatment of losses in cross-border situations. In doing so, we will take into account the findings of the European Court of Justice, in particular in the Marks & Spencer case, in seeking to find a proper balance between the interests of the internal market and the need to prevent abuse and erosion of the tax base.

I would emphasize that ultimately it is only through the CCCTB that fully satisfactory solutions can be found to the problems of cross-border loss consolidation. There are limits to what can be achieved through co-ordination. But it is still possible to improve the situation through better co-ordinating existing systems.

In addition to initiatives in specific areas we are currently exploring the scope for a general mechanism for resolving instances of double taxation. At present we have machinery in place for binding arbitration in the transfer pricing field.

It seems to me that there is a need for a mechanism dealing more generally with the instance of double taxation for individuals and companies.

CONCLUSIONS

Having in mind the concerns mentioned above, today's debate on the contribution of taxation to European competitiveness, growth and employment is particularly welcome. However, I am aware of the fact that the unanimity principle applied to tax matters makes it extremely difficult to reach overall political agreements. But in cases where broad (that is, majority) agreement emerges, we must not forget that existing treaties offer us instruments – like enhanced co-operation – that have not yet been fully exploited.

NOTE

1.   European Commissioner for Taxation and Customs Union, Member of the European Commission.

Who bears the risks of FDI financing? Selected views of the EIB

Ivan Pilip

The underlying patterns of FDI flows and its financing imply that the related risks are borne by a cascade of players. First in line are the investors themselves, simply because equity investments tend to be more risky than others. Second in line are the home and host countries of FDI flows, because these will have an impact on the general macroeconomic stability of the countries involved. And third, of course, are financial institutions financing FDI, including the European Investment Bank (EIB), whose views I will try to express in this chapter.

Since the EIB started its operations in Central and Eastern Europe in 1991, it has become one of the major players for the financing, or generally co-financing, of big projects such as infrastructure investments or FDI deals in these countries (see Figure 1).

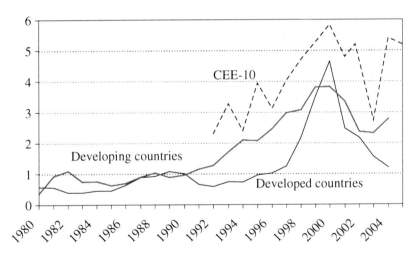

Source: UNCTAD.

Figure 1   Gross FDI inflows to CEE-10 countries (as % of GDP)

Put differently, from the approximate EUR 40 billion to EUR 45 billion that the EIB has lent per year in the early years of the new millennium, 10 per cent, or about EUR 4 billion, have gone to what are now the new member states – and part of that money has supported FDI in these countries.

While FDI is not a new phenomenon, it has rapidly increased in our times of globalization – in other words, the question 'Who bears the risk?' is more topical than ever also for us at the EIB. As a case in point, the countries that bear the risk of FDI are not just the countries on the receiving end of the investment, but also the countries on the giving end, as they may stand to lose investments, production and jobs in the process. With regard to the support of FDI, above all with regard to FDI flows to the new member states of the European Union and EU candidate countries, the EIB is in the special position that it is owned by all 27 member states of the European Union. Against this background, we have had tough discussions on whether we really should support investment projects in given new member states if such an investment would be tantamount to reducing production in some old member states of the European Union. Discussions of this kind have not happened very frequently but they were not exceptional either. In the face of globalization trends, we have repeatedly had to inform our supervisory board: if you don't accept our support to move a given investment to Slovenia, Bulgaria or Hungary, it might go even further east; and, more importantly, by limiting our possibilities to co-finance these investments you will hardly interrupt or disturb the process that is in motion and that will probably continue to grow.

From this point of view, the role of Central and Eastern European countries is really very important in Europe, as evidenced by the EIB's estimates about inflows to the EU's new member states from 1998 to 2005. With the exception of 2001 and 2003, these inflows have been on an impressive growth path (see Figure 2).

Of course, above all when the EIB first started to fund major cross-border investment projects, we tried to analyse the specifics of FDI in greater depth, because by definition it involves investment in less familiar territory. In addition to normal commercial risks, there are some real or at least less known or perceived political risks, as for example currency risks (and opportunities) including transferability and convertibility; war, civil unrest or expropriation; breach of contract; denial of justice; and the like.

From this point of view, the enlargement of the European Union was a crucial development. After all, investors have felt much more confident with a given country once it has become a member of the European Union, because EU membership made the general legal system and the rules of the game much more understandable and much more reliable.

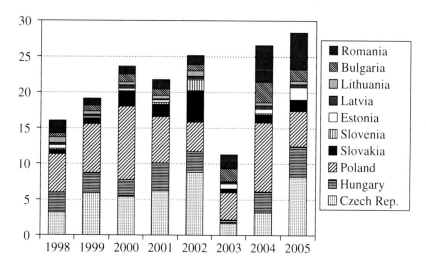

Source: wiiw.

Figure 2   Net FDI inflows to CEE-10 (in EUR billion)

Anyhow, certain risks still remain. As usual, and as mentioned above, the highest risk is on the equity part. By definition, equity investors bear the full range of risks. Next in line are local lenders. They bear the usual credit risks and might, indirectly, also bear some of the political risks to the extent that they impair the creditworthiness of the borrower. Finally, offshore lenders, including the EIB, face the usual credit risks plus certain currency-related risks, for example, transferability, convertibility. However, the EIB is not allowed to be exposed to exchange rate risk, and whenever possible, tries to provide its borrowers with an opportunity to do likewise by providing loans in local currency. Indirectly, the EIB is, however, also exposed to political risks to the extent that they impair the creditworthiness of the borrower as well.

How have we tried to assist investors in this process? Principally we tried to somehow reduce the political risk, which we perceived to be the most important risk, above all when we first started to support FDI flows to Central and Eastern Europe at the beginning of the 1990s. To this effect, we assumed a dual role: first, the EIB provided long- and medium-term loan finance on similar terms and conditions as within the EU. Second, we attempted to contain political risks to the EIB and to its borrowers by concluding 'framework agreements' with the host countries.

These provide for equal treatment for all borrowers and loan operations. They also ensure currency convertibility and transferability. And they make sure that no withholding tax would be levied on interest payments. Obviously, these framework agreements were no panacea, but so far they have worked in all countries in which the EIB operates (except one country, which is not located in Central and Eastern Europe).

Incidentally, we also try to use this model for extending our operations further east and towards the Balkan states; all in all our operations outside the European Union account for about 10 per cent of our investments, or for 8 to 9 per cent of our investment loans. In the same vein, we have also recently tried to concentrate on supporting the EU's so-called neighbourhood policy, which also means extending our operations to Balkan countries and to countries to the east of the European Union's new borders.

In this respect, let me point to the so-called 'mandates' that the European Union gives to the EIB for operations in different neighbouring countries along with its guarantee of last resort. The mandates for the years 2007–2013 were decided at the end of 2006 and their size significantly increased to EUR 27.8 billion. From 2004 to 2007, for example, the EIB's mandate for the EU's Eastern neighbours – meaning Belarus, where we have currently no operations, because of the political situation, Ukraine and Moldova – covers operations of up to EUR 500 million, which is a relatively high volume.

We also used this mandate to cover the political risk for our lending, alongside the individual framework agreements that are meant to provide a stable context and thus some form of security for individual operations. In this respect, the EIB signed framework agreements with Ukraine in 2004 and another with Moldova in 2006. In the case of Belarus, we have not yet made such a move, because the political system of Belarus does not yet appear to be ready for support by the main European institutions.

To give some examples about major concrete investments that the EIB has supported in the EU's new member states in the past, we provided financing for the Volkswagen/Skoda project, and we still continue to cooperate with the Volkswagen group, not just in the Czech Republic, but also in Slovakia and several other countries; for instance in 2006 we provided Volkswagen with a new loan in support of R&D investments in the Czech Republic and Slovakia. Other examples for the Czech Republic include the Benteler group, Deutsche Post and the joint venture of Toyota and Peugeot. For Slovakia, I might add Mondi (part of the Anglo-American group). In Poland, the EIB has financed projects by Thomson (Polkolor), MAN, Voest-Alpine and Brembo; and in Hungary we have supported projects by EON, Denso, Sanyo and Voest-Alpine.

To briefly discuss the impact of FDI for the host countries, there is definitely, at least in the short term, a positive effect on the balance of payments. On the plus side, I can also add the transfer of know-how and

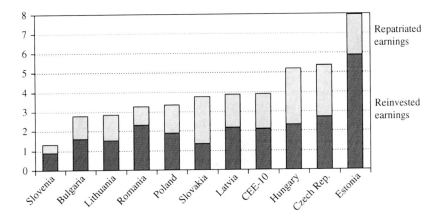

Source: wiiw.

Figure 3   *FDI – re-investment of earnings (in % of GDP; average 2004–2005)*

technology, as well as positive direct and indirect employment effects. The studies that we have undertaken have also found a relatively high level of re-investment of earnings in these countries (see Figure 3), which means that this decreases the macroeconomic risk to the balance of payments for the long term. Such risks need to be borne in mind; after all, while equity invest-ments are by definition made for longer time horizons, high-level policy makers may decide to repatriate funds, which could endanger the macroeco-nomic stability of the countries involved.

Still, this is just an academic thought. At EIB, we have not had any such signals; on the contrary, many companies are seeking our assistance and financing for additional projects in the EU's new member states.

This notwithstanding, the new situation and development of the coun-tries also leads to changes in the attractiveness of FDI financing, because the positive changes in the new member states have broadened financing opportunities for these states and have allowed the financial markets to play a much bigger role than they used to.

We at EIB work on the principle of not-for-profit financing. Our model of financing is that we use our shareholder structure and our AAA rating. We borrow on the market at AAA prices and, as we lend on these funds to different countries and different projects, the sovereign or sub-sovereign loans of our benchmark are more or less the bond issue or the curve of bonds of the individual states involved. This notwithstanding, our invest-ments or loans to companies are still influenced by the risk pricing of the

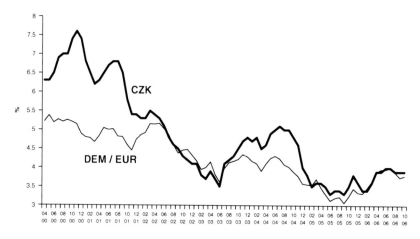

Source: Bloomberg.

Figure 4   *Convergence of Czech and German 10-year government*
           bond yields

individual projects – very much like the risk pricing of normal commercial banks.

To put it differently, for us at EIB, the situation has become more difficult, but this is at the same time a very good signal about the development in the countries of Central and Eastern Europe – as evidenced for instance by the convergence of Czech bond yields with German bond yields (Figure 4). Some years ago, using the EIB's foreign currency loans to finance projects in Central European states would not have been a viable option. But the situation started to change more or less when those countries joined the European Union. Since then, the Czech and German spreads have been almost the same, and there were even short periods when the Czech currency performed better.

A comparison of Euribor with Pribor, the Czech central bank's fixing of interest rates on interbank deposits, tells a similar story. In 1997, when the EIB started to borrow in Czech crowns, the spread was 50 basis points; in subsequent times of crisis it jumped to as much as 200 basis points. At the time of writing, however, the difference between the two was just a few basis points, and sometimes the Pribor rate is even below the Euribor rate (Figure 5).

Of course, the situation of the Czech currency is still a bit special given its macroeconomic situation. In comparison, the EIB can provide much greater support and higher 'financial value added' to projects in other countries, such as Romania, Poland and Hungary. This notwithstanding, even

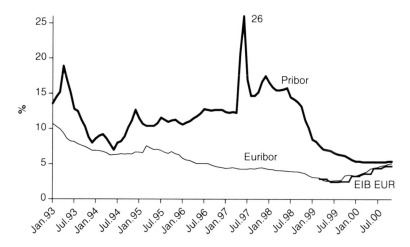

Source: Bloomberg.

Figure 5   *3M PRIBOR, 3M EURIBOR and EIB EUR pool rate*
            1993–2000

the figures for the Czech Republic show that the Central European countries, also thanks to foreign-bank investments and EU enlargement, have
become a very stable part of Europe and a very attractive target for foreign
investments and for further development.

Finance in transition: banks at the vanguard of foreign direct investors

Erik Berglöf[1] and Samuel Fankhauser[2]

The financial sectors in the former communist East have changed beyond recognition. They now offer attractive opportunities. In little over a decade, the financial sectors in Central and Eastern Europe and the former Soviet Union have undergone an extraordinary transformation. In place of the communist system of state-controlled credit allocation, vibrant financial markets have emerged in which a diverse range of institutions increasingly provide finance to aspiring entrepreneurs, firms seeking to expand and households wishing to improve their living conditions. The key driving forces behind this transformation have been broad improvements in the regulatory environment, privatization and market entry by foreign banks – which have thus been at the forefront of foreign direct investors in the region.

The 2006 *Transition Report* of the European Bank for Reconstruction and Development (EBRD) reviews these remarkable developments. It reveals how financial systems in the former communist East have grown not only in size, but also in stability, complexity and sophistication. Progress has been particularly striking in the new EU member countries of Central Europe and the Baltics. In many parts of South-Eastern Europe and the former Soviet Union, the financial sector continues to be underdeveloped.

The availability of finance has increased rapidly over the last few years as basic regulatory and supervisory frameworks were put in place. Between 2000 and 2005 the amount of domestic credit to the private sector – a widely-used measure of financial depth – has increased by almost two thirds, from 17 per cent of GDP to 28 per cent of GDP. Lending to households, particularly through mortgage loans, has grown especially strongly. It now accounts for over 40 per cent of total credit to the private sector, compared with less than 20 per cent in 2000 when the credit market was much smaller.

In addition to developments in the banking sector we can observe a strong, parallel growth in other areas of finance, such as stock and bond markets, insurance, leasing, pension funds and private equity. These developments are highly inter-connected. For example, the improved functioning of stock markets brings transparency and better valuation to financing activities, and bond markets help to develop inter-bank markets which are critical to the liquidity of the financial system. Corporate bond markets are much harder to develop and have generally only emerged in response to failures in the banking system. In the long term, they serve as an important check on the dangers of excessive lending by banks to client companies. However, despite strong developments in the non-bank segment of the market, financial sectors in Eastern Europe remain dominated by banks.

Foreign banks at the vanguard of other foreign direct investors have played a crucial role in these developments. Attracted by better growth prospects and higher margins than in their home market, many Western banks have expanded into Central Europe and South-Eastern Europe, either through the acquisition of existing banking assets or as new entrants. Increasingly, they are also looking at the former Soviet Union, in particular Ukraine.

The entry of foreign banks in this region is unique in both its scale and coverage. Slovenia is now the only country in Central and South-Eastern Europe where the market share of foreign-owned banks is less than 50 per cent. In Albania, Bosnia and Herzegovina, Croatia, Estonia, Lithuania and Slovakia foreign banks control over 90 per cent of the sector. Historical and cultural ties have played an important part in shaping this expansion: Austrian banks, for example, feature especially prominently in Central Europe, while Nordic banks dominate in the Baltic States. Italian banks have been particularly active in South-Eastern Europe.

The foreign entrants have been rewarded for their risks with attractive returns. Since the Russian financial crisis in 1998, bank profitability in Eastern Europe has been consistently and significantly higher than it is, for example, in the euro area. In 2005 the average return on assets for banks in central Europe, the Baltic States and South-Eastern Europe was around 1.5 per cent, compared with 0.9 per cent in Greece, Portugal and Spain. For banks in the former Soviet Union the return on assets was over 2.5 per cent.

The presence of foreign banks has also been beneficial for the host countries. Their market entry has been associated with improvements in bank performance, a widening access to banking services and greater diversity in the types of services on offer. An EBRD survey of 220 banks in the region found that newly-created foreign banks (although not existing banks acquired by foreign institutions) have lower cost-to-asset ratios and tend to grow faster than domestic banks. Foreign banks – both acquired and newly created – generally have stronger loan portfolios, as evidenced by a lower ratio of loan loss provisions to interest income.

A look at the loan portfolios reveals that foreign banks are more actively involved in household lending, in particular mortgages, than domestic banks. As such they are an important driver of the rapid growth in consumer lending witnessed in recent years. However, as their knowledge of local markets improves, they are also increasingly willing to serve corporate clients, including small and medium sized enterprises. Of some concern may be the fact that almost 50 per cent of their household loans are extended in hard currency. While this reflects the international funding base of foreign banks, it exposes their clients to exchange rate risks that they may be ill-equipped to understand and absorb.

The fast growth in credit and the diversification of financial products would not have been possible without significant improvements in the legal and regulatory framework. The *Transition Report* demonstrates that a better institutional quality is associated with greater financial depth, increased lending to small business and households and a broader range of services provided by banks. The striking increase in mortgage lending for instance reflects not only the emergence of private housing markets, but also the increasing ability of the financial sector to take collateral and to rely on legal systems for effective enforcement. Nevertheless, the legal and regulatory environment remains difficult, particularly in the former Soviet Union and in parts of South-Eastern Europe. Further institutional reforms, particularly towards the consistent application of rules and regulations, will be needed to support continued growth and development in the financial sector.

The rapid expansion of bank lending has caused some central banks to impose regulatory measures to slow down credit growth. It is easy to share their concern about the impact of unchecked growth on financial sector and macroeconomic stability, particularly in weaker regulatory environments.

Nevertheless, the prospects for the financial sectors in Eastern Europe remain positive. Even after years of double digit growth, there remains substantial pent-up demand, and financial sectors remain comparatively shallow. In the new EU member countries, domestic credit to the private sector, relative to GDP, is still only about half the level of the old European Union. In South-Eastern Europe and the former Soviet Union it is less than a quarter. Further growth is needed, and can be expected, before the financial sectors in these countries converge to the standards of mature market economies.

NOTES

1. Chief Economist, EBRD, London, berglofe@ebrd.com.
2. Deputy Chief Economist and Director, Strategy and Analysis, EBRD, London, FankhauS@ebrd.com.

Economic and monetary challenges of euro area enlargement

Jürgen Stark

INTRODUCTION

On 1 May 2004 the European Union witnessed its biggest enlargement so far: ten central European and Mediterranean countries joined the Union. In January 2007 two other countries – Bulgaria and Romania – followed suit and the European Union now comprises no less than 27 members. These events mark real milestones in the history of Europe. After more than half a century of political and economic division, the enlargement of the European Union has finally brought economic stability and a hitherto unthinkable degree of political cooperation, based on democracy and the rule of law, to large parts of Europe. The enlargement process has been long and involved much effort from both the then accession countries as well as from the old EU members.

The new member states had to undertake far-reaching legal and economic reforms in order to comply with the EU *acquis communautaire* and to cope with the market pressures of the single market. Although further work still needs to be done, they have significantly liberalized and modernized their economies, which are now expanding dynamically. For the old member states the enlargement meant tougher competition and additional pressure to pursue structural adjustments and intensify innovation. Moreover, in the spirit of solidarity, they supported the enlargement process financially through the EU budget.

Enlargement has greatly contributed to growth and employment in the new member states, which is mainly attributable to strengthened trade and financial integration, including significant foreign direct investment flows and the availability of EU funds. But the old member states benefit from this process as well. Fears in the old member states about job losses and downward pressure on wages due to massive migration and the relocation of activity have proved to be exaggerated. At the same time, enlargement has created new opportunities for firms based in the old EU countries. They have gained better access to new member states' markets, thus enabling

them to sell their products there and to obtain cheaper inputs for their production, which in turn enhances their productivity vis-à-vis third countries.
Similarly, European Union consumers – in the old and new member states
alike – have benefited from a greater choice of products that are available
at lower prices. In addition, the enlarged single market has been conducive
to enhancing the dynamism and strength of the EU economy, thus placing
it in a better position to weather global competition.

Despite this very positive picture and the fact that the functioning of the
enlarged European Union has been smooth so far, it has to be stressed that
many of the old and new member states are still facing considerable economic challenges. Although the catching-up process in the new member
states has been rapid in recent years, it is not over yet. Most of the new
member states still have a significantly lower level of income per capita than
most old member states. Consequently, the European Union has become a
more heterogeneous region in terms of economic development after the
recent enlargement.

Full membership of Economic and Monetary Union (EMU) is yet to
come for the new member states, thus posing another important challenge
for them. Seven of them have already advanced in the process of monetary
integration by joining the Exchange Rate Mechanism II. Among this
group, Slovenia managed to complete the process and as of 1 January 2007
it became the 13th member of the euro area – a development that is warmly
welcomed by the Executive Board and the Governing Council of the
European Central Bank.

Against this background, I would like to share my views on the challenges of further euro area enlargement. First, I will briefly describe the
formal stages of the euro adoption process and elaborate on the main challenges for the new member states stemming from this process. I will stress
the need for achieving a high degree of nominal, real and legal convergence,
as well as for strictly assessing the convergence criteria. Then, I will delve
into challenges for current and prospective members of the euro area,
dealing particularly with the need for responsible structural and fiscal policies. Such policies are a matter of common concern in a monetary union,
and they are essential for effective conduct of a common monetary policy
as well as for sustained growth in a highly competitive global environment.

CHALLENGES ON THE ROAD FROM EU TO EURO AREA MEMBERSHIP

Let me briefly recapitulate the formal stages of euro adoption as given by
the Treaty establishing the European Community. Unlike Denmark and the

United Kingdom, the new member states do not have an opt-out clause and are currently members of Economic and Monetary Union with a derogation, which means that they are expected to adopt the euro once they have fulfilled the convergence criteria. The first step on this 'road to the euro' is to join the Exchange Rate Mechanism II (ERM II). Participation in this mechanism is meant to be a test period, during which countries have time to prepare their economies for euro adoption and to ensure the sustainability of the convergence process. After having participated in the ERM II for at least two years, a country may qualify to adopt the euro, subject to a formal assessment of the fulfilment of the convergence criteria relating to price, fiscal, exchange rate and long-term interest rate developments.

Without going into too much detail on the convergence criteria, I would like to stress just two points. First, the sustainability of the convergence process is examined on the basis of a coherent analytical framework specified in our Convergence Reports. Over the years this framework has consistently been used across time for all examined countries and we will continue to use it for future analysis. Another Convergence Report is prepared by the European Commission.

Second, in our examinations we have always emphasized that the compliance with the convergence criteria must be achieved on a sustainable basis and not only at a specific point in time. Both considerations are of utmost importance for the credibility of EMU.

Let me also emphasize legal convergence, which is sometimes somewhat overlooked due to discussions focusing primarily on progress in economic convergence or the lack thereof. Yet, as achieving convergence in both dimensions is required by the Treaty, both are equally important. In general, legal convergence requires the compatibility of national legislation – including the statutes of the central bank – with the Treaty and the Statute of the European System of Central Banks. In this context the legal assessment considers four types of central bank independence, namely functional, institutional, personal and financial independence. Against this background I would like to emphasize again that the independence of a central bank from political institutions is absolutely crucial. Not only must it be safeguarded by legal acts in all its dimensions, but it must also be observed in practice.

Given the formal procedures for adopting the euro, the main challenge for the new member states is to achieve a high level of sustainable convergence. Let me stress that serious consideration of this goal is in the new member states' own interest. Premature entry to the euro area might have negative consequences for that particular country, and an insufficiently prepared newcomer may have problems maintaining economic and financial stability as well as low inflation.

The current monetary policy framework of the European Central Bank has been very successful and so there will be no changes in the monetary policy objectives and strategy. This implies that the new member states joining the euro area will have to adjust to the current regime, making careful preparation essential to achieve a high degree of real convergence prior to the adoption of the euro. At the same time it becomes clear that such careful preparation is equally important for the credibility of the entire EMU project as well as for confidence in the ECB and the euro.

Against this background let me note that many new member states have recently postponed their euro adoption plans. In some cases these decisions resulted from the inability to fulfil the convergence criteria due to rising inflationary pressures, in other cases from unsound government budgetary positions. It is obviously up to the individual countries to decide whether or not to fix euro adoption dates. But if dates are fixed, this should be done in a credible and realistic manner, taking into account the need to fulfil the criteria for economic convergence on a lasting basis. Setting a realistic timetable for euro adoption will help to anchor domestic economic policies and to avoid unwanted market tensions. By contrast, setting unrealistic timetables can result in challenging situations when it comes to communicating with markets and the general public.

CHALLENGES FOR CURRENT AND PROSPECTIVE EURO AREA MEMBERS

As already indicated, participation in a monetary union has important implications on domestic economic policies. Given that the key objective of the ECB is to maintain price stability in the euro area, the successful implementation of this objective is the key channel via which monetary policy contributes to economic growth and job creation. Yet the creation of other conditions equally necessary for economic expansion, prosperity and a smooth functioning of EMU lies beyond the scope of monetary policy. Such conditions are in particular a sound fiscal policy and sufficiently flexible labour as well as product and capital markets, which in turn often require the implementation of comprehensive structural reforms. Therefore the challenge is to implement a set of structural reforms in those areas where major deficiencies have been identified. Although specific priorities may differ from country to country, the general directions are common.

As regards fiscal policy, a few EMU member states have exhibited considerable fiscal imbalances and have been subject to the excessive deficit procedure in recent years. Similar situations have also been observed in several non-euro area EU member states. Although some progress regarding fiscal deficits has been made recently, much of it was due to the improving economic environment and revenue windfalls. Structural consolidation has often not been sufficient. Hence there is no reason for complacency and the current 'good times' must be used determinedly to eliminate the remaining fiscal imbalances on a sustainable basis.

One should remember that sound fiscal policies are not only important for the credibility of EMU but also for long-term growth. In accordance with the EU Stability and Growth Pact, sound fiscal policies also support macroeconomic stability and ensure a predictable economic environment. The resulting reduction in uncertainty promotes longer-term decision-making, notably with regard to investment, and fosters economic growth. Thus adhering to the rules of the Stability and Growth Pact is very important. We must be aware that sound fiscal positions are also crucial in order to meet the increasing fiscal costs caused by population ageing. In this regard an important challenge for fiscal policy is to design the expenditure and revenue structure in a way that reduces inefficient public spending and supports productivity-enhancing physical and human capital accumulation.

Regarding the labour markets, a major challenge for structural reforms is to find the right balance between social considerations and individual incentives maximizing economic welfare. Areas of particular interest are social transfer systems, employment protection laws and wage-setting mechanisms, including wage indexation, as well as policies supporting the creation of new businesses. From the point of view of monetary policy it is also vital that labour market reforms contribute to wage adjustments that reflect more closely regional and sectoral productivity differences.

Turning to product market reforms, they play a key role in enhancing innovation, ensuring an efficient allocation of resources and creating a business-friendly environment. In recent years much headway has been made in the EU regarding the integration and level of competition in product markets. Nevertheless, substantial barriers to free competition continue to exist in some areas, preventing for example the integration of services markets and the effective competition in a number of network industries.

Regarding financial markets, structural reforms should aim at facilitating a more effective allocation of savings towards the most rewarding investment opportunities as well as at securing financial stability. Greater financial integration fosters financial development, the modernization of the financial system and ultimately economic growth. A part of this integration is evident in large foreign direct investment flows within Europe.

It must be stressed that although non-monetary economic policies are at the discretion of individual member states, they must be treated as a matter of common concern. Neglecting reforms in one country can have negative implications not only for this particular country, but also for other members of the EMU. Therefore all euro area countries should do their best to advance with their reform agendas. Sharing a common currency means sharing a common destiny. In addition, the need for structural reforms and sound fiscal policies is not limited to members of a monetary union. Flexible and well-functioning markets are a universal need in a highly competitive and rapidly changing global economic environment. From this point of view, the general call for structural reforms and sound fiscal policies applies equally to current as well as future euro area countries. Let me also stress that in the case of the new member states, such reforms will not only allow them to cope with the challenges of a monetary union, but it will also enhance the current catching-up process and alleviate any transition costs related to the still ongoing restructuring of their economies.

CONCLUSIONS

Given that the new member states are sooner or later expected to join the euro area, the key challenge for this enlargement process is to ensure a high degree of durable convergence in these countries. This should be reflected in nominal, real as well as legal convergence. The fulfilment of this goal will be important, not only for the successful macroeconomic performance of the new EMU members, but also for the credibility of the entire EMU. Therefore the examination of the convergence criteria must be undertaken and will be undertaken in a strict manner according to the principles stipulated by the Treaty. The success of the enlarged EMU also hinges on how well labour, capital and product markets in the current and prospective members are functioning. Within the framework of the euro area's single monetary policy, it is of key importance for all member countries to identify and effectively implement the appropriate structural and fiscal policies.

A special academic perspective on FDI

Measuring the impacts of FDI in Central and Eastern Europe

Robert E. Lipsey[1]

1. INTRODUCTION

In one sense the issue of the desirability of inward FDI for host countries seems to have been decided. Policy making has come to ignore the ambiguous and inconclusive academic literature and, in most countries, has shifted away from measures restricting and discouraging inward FDI. Many countries have not only reduced such restrictions, but have also moved toward encouraging FDI with tax and other incentives. UNCTAD's compilations of regulatory changes by host countries since 1991 show that they have been overwhelmingly favourable to inward FDI, although recent years have seen more unfavourable changes – the highest share in the compilation amounting to 20 per cent in 2005. The unfavourable changes were concentrated in extractive industries and in Latin America (UNCTAD, 2006, pp. 24–5).

Something must have happened to influence so many countries' policies. I suppose it is the success that a few countries have apparently had in achieving rapid economic growth after moving from virtual prohibition of direct investment to active encouragement of it. Ireland and China are two notable and conspicuous examples of countries that reversed a long-standing antipathy toward foreign investors and that have achieved rapid growth in which foreign-owned firms have played a very large part.

An aspect of the role of FDI that I think is almost beyond dispute is that much of the world's stock of technological knowledge is possessed by multinational firms. That can be seen partly in the fact that labour is so much more productive in these firms than outside them; multinationals probably produce more than 10 per cent of the world's output, but employ only 1 or, at most, 2 per cent of the world's labour. Whenever comparisons are made within countries, it appears that not only are foreign multinationals more productive than domestic firms in general, as measured by labour productivity or total factor productivity (TFP), but among domestically-owned firms, those that are multinational are more efficient than non-multinational firms, even within the same industries and taking account of other factors affecting efficiency.

What is it that we want to know about the impacts of FDI? Quite often the issue is put in the context of the use of subsidies or other incentives specific to foreign-owned firms, and the question posed is whether these subsidies are worthwhile. I think that that is the wrong context and distorts the issue. The most important measures favourable to inward FDI, in my view, are to remove prohibitions against it, to remove other measures that discriminate against foreign firms, to reduce or remove impediments to trade and open markets, and to improve governance.

One of the main technological advantages of foreign-owned firms is their knowledge of international markets and the ability to judge and compare the costs of different locations for production, particularly locations for fragments in long lines of production that extend across several countries. Subsidies and other preferential arrangements can distort the choices of locations, leaving uneconomic white elephants after the preferential arrangements end. In some of the most successful cases of growth through exploiting foreign investment, foreign firms have been able to look past host countries' current comparative advantages in exporting and to see potential comparative advantages that exploit the combination of the host country's resources with the technology and other knowledge of the foreign firms.

Many studies have asked whether attracting foreign firms will make a recipient country grow faster than it would without foreign investment or with only portfolio investment. There is little reason to expect that the effects of inward investment should be the same for all host countries. A country with a long history of forbidding or discouraging inward investment, that then opens up to it, may have an industrial structure with large gaps in newer or more technologically advanced industries that investors can fill, while a country that has been open to investment may present a much more competitive milieu. A country that is open to trade may attract elements of firms' worldwide production that are combined with those in other countries before becoming final products, while a country that restricts trade or hinders it by inefficiency or corruption may not attract such investment. More generally, countries that provide reliable and predictable legal systems and efficient public administration may receive more investment and profit more from it than countries with poor governance.

FDI flows very unevenly to the various sectors of an economy. As more disaggregated data become available, one could ask about the effects of FDI inflows on particular industrial sectors or regions, particularly the industries or regions receiving the investment, but also others that buy from or sell to those sectors. These questions have not usually been studied with balance of payments data, because their sectoral detail is poor in most countries and often is not closely related to the sectoral breakdown of employment, sales, physical capital stock or production. Instead, these questions have been studied using data from production censuses in recipient countries, often confined to the manufacturing sector or manufacturing and mining.

Not only are sectors affected differently, but not every firm within a sector is likely to be affected in the same way by the entrance or expansion of foreign-owned firms. The firms with the most up-to-date technologies may respond differently from those that were laggards. Large firms may fare differently from small firms. Exporting firms may respond differently from completely domestic firms. All these questions require a different kind of data for research. The questions can be reliably answered only with the use of firm or establishment microdata, in which individual firms' attributes can be related to their subsequent performance. With these individual firm data, one can ask what happens to a particular domestically-owned firm that becomes foreign-owned or to a foreign-owned firm that becomes domestically-owned, and to other firms in the same industry or location.

The latest development, still at an early stage, is that we are beginning to get data on individual workers within the individual firms. With such data we can begin to see what happens to workers of different types, skills, experience and education when their employers become foreign-owned or cease to be so.

2. IMPACTS OF INWARD FDI ON HOST COUNTRY GROWTH

Over the years there have been many attempts to test whether any general relationship could be found between inflows of FDI to a host country and host country economic growth. The only data on such inflows, or the resulting stocks of direct investment capital, covering many countries and long periods, are those based on financial flows, as recorded in balances of payments and national accounts.

In contrast, most theories about how FDI might accelerate growth in a host country rely on the effects of foreign-owned production taking place there. Production by foreign multinationals might raise the level of competition in the host economy, bring superior technology that could be used by the foreign-owned producer or imitated by domestic firms, train host country workers in more efficient production methods, which they would use in working for the foreign firm or carry with them to other firms, and so on. I do not want to try to catalogue all the possible channels of transmission, but to emphasize that they depend on a foreign presence that involves production in the host country.

Data on such FDI exist for only a few countries, mostly for short periods. Where they do exist, as for the United States, we can compare them with the FDI flow and stock data. Are the balance of payments and national accounts data good indicators of the extent of FDI production, capital stock or employment in a country? The short answer is that they are very rough, but not wholly inaccurate, measures of the country distribution of FDI production, employment and fixed capital at any one time, but very poor measures of changes over time. Thus, when we use the balance of payments measures to proxy for FDI production or employment changes, we are observing the latter through a thick fog. A couple of examples make the point. Hong Kong is the largest outward investor among developing countries, but half of Hong Kong's stock of outward FDI was – according to UNCTAD (2004, p. 26) – in four tax havens: the British Virgin Islands, Bermuda, Panama and the Cayman Islands. I think we can be sure that the productive activity involved, if there was any, was not in those locations. Luxembourg was reported to be the world's largest recipient of FDI in 2002, accounting for 19 per cent of all the world's inflows 'because it offers favourable conditions for holding companies and for corporate HQ, such as certain tax exemptions' (UNCTAD, 2003, p. 69). We can be sure that if any production was being financed, it did not take place in Luxembourg. The Bureau of Economic Analysis (BEA) reported (Koncz and Yorgason, 2005, p. 45) that the share of holding companies in the US investment position abroad reached more than a third in 2004, concealing both the location and the industry composition of any associated production.

A recent and sophisticated analysis of this type of data by Carkovic and Levine (2005) concluded that 'the exogenous component of FDI does not exert a robust, positive influence on economic growth' and that 'there is no reliable cross-country empirical evidence supporting the claim that FDI per se accelerates economic growth' (p. 197). The negative conclusion was expressed cautiously: 'after controlling for the joint determination of growth and foreign capital flows, country-specific factors and other growth determinants, the data do not suggest a strong, independent impact of FDI on economic growth' (p. 198). Finally, 'the results are inconsistent with the view that FDI exerts a positive impact on growth that is independent of other growth determinants' (p. 219).

In his comments on these results, Melitz (2005) challenged part of the interpretation, pointing out that the results that do not include controls for trade openness, but do control for many other country characteristics, show a positive relation of FDI to growth. Melitz noted that vertical FDI implies trade and that both are determined by country policy toward trade and investment. In that case, controlling for trade openness wipes out the relationship between economic growth and the combination of trade and investment.

Another possible interpretation of the role of trade openness is that the combination of FDI with trade tends to distinguish what I am tempted to call 'genuine' FDI stocks, that is, FDI stocks associated with production, from financial FDI stocks that have no production attached to them. The connection between the benefits from inward FDI and the trade policy of the host country echoes an earlier suggestion by Bhagwati (1978) that growth effects of FDI could be positive or negative, with negative effects associated with import-substitution policies.

One lesson that Carkovic and Levine drew from their study is that the results 'do not support special tax breaks and subsidies to attract foreign capital' (p. 198). In one sense this conclusion does not clash with the comment by Melitz. Inward FDI attracted by an open trade regime may conform to existing or potential comparative advantages in trade, but FDI attracted by tax breaks or subsidies, especially if protection is part of the incentives, may be more likely to fit badly with the host country's comparative advantages and may be less likely to be associated with enlarged trade. Moran's (2005) paper in the same volume gave many examples of such ill-fitting foreign investments.

All these analyses assume that the balance of payments data on FDI really do measure the amount of foreign-owned production in a host country. In fact, they do not for many reasons. Even if they are correctly measured by the principles laid down by the IMF (1993), the data do not measure either FDI output or FDI input in the host country. For one thing, the reported country of location of FDI represents only the first stop on what may be a long trek from the originating country to the location where production takes place – a stop determined by tax or other financial considerations rather than suitability as a production location. Furthermore, since a large part of the exported FDI capital may be intangible or intellectual capital, it has no discernable geographical location. Its only real location is its ownership within the multinational firm. The parent firm can choose a nominal geographical location, usually for tax minimization, but use the asset in production anywhere in the world.

In view of the ambiguity in the meaning of the location of financial flows and stocks of FDI, a better summary of the results of analysing these data might be that the conventional measures of flows and stocks of FDI do not appear to unambiguously determine or affect host country economic growth, but that the combination of FDI and open trade policy may serve to distinguish those flows or stocks of FDI that are associated with production in a country from those that are just passing through or represent an internal allocation of intangible property to that country without any link to local production. These flows or stocks or these combined with open trade policy do seem to promote host country growth. I also might note that even the studies that take a sceptical view of this relationship rarely find a negative effect of FDI.

One study of FDI inflows and aggregate economic growth based on balance-of-payments FDI data was confined to the Central and Eastern European countries and those of the former Soviet Union. That scope was justified by the argument that the backwardness of these countries meant that the FDI there represented more of a pure case of technology transfer than elsewhere (Campos and Kinoshita, 2002). The conclusion in that case was that for these countries, the relationship was 'positive, significant, and robust' (p. 417).

Given the defects of the balance of payments data and the lack of a clear connection with FDI production, my conclusion is that, for large groups of countries, they are a dead end for research on the effects of FDI and are not worth further pursuit or efforts at refinement. Aside from the deficiencies of the data I have described, my suspicion is that, despite the efforts of the IMF to push for uniform standards of reporting, the FDI data are deteriorating rather than improving, because they are dependent on firms' bookkeeping, and firms are becoming more adept at manipulating the bookkeeping for tax minimization purposes.

If we accept the idea that little can be learned from studies in which FDI is represented by balance of payments flows and stocks, we are led to studies that measure FDI by production, sales, labour input or capital input. These variables are available only for much smaller groups of countries, but they have the advantage that they can be subdivided by industry. In some cases, they can also be subdivided into individual firms or establishments or into groupings of firms based on their individual characteristics. I review here a few of these industry and firm studies concentrating on CEECs in the EU or those about to enter. These are all cases where the individual countries have had the common experience of moving from economies based on central planning, with little foreign involvement and little trade, to various degrees of private enterprise, encouragement of inward investment and more open trade.

3. THE COUNTRIES OF CENTRAL AND EASTERN EUROPE AS LOCATIONS FOR FDI

The CEECs are very recent arrivals in the FDI landscape. They are, along with China and Ireland, interesting laboratories in which to observe the impact of inward FDI. For the most part, they had not been recipients of FDI to any important degree before 1990 (the conversion of Ireland to welcoming FDI had come much earlier). In 1990, the CEECs were far below the average country with respect to inward FDI stocks, considering their size. That is clear if we fit a log equation explaining the reported inward FDI stock across about 150 countries in 1990 by real (purchasing power adjusted) gross output. The equation explains about 60 per cent of the variance across countries. Most of the CEECs did not report any inward FDI at all at that time and the ones that did, Czechoslovakia, Hungary and Poland, reported stocks that were 40 per cent of the predicted value (Czechoslovakia) or much less.

After 1990, the CEECs lowered the barriers to FDI to varying degrees. By 2003, the last year for which we have a full set of countries reporting inward FDI stocks, a similar log equation explained about two thirds of the variance in inward FDI stocks, and all of the CEECs reported some amounts. The equation predicted inward FDI levels far higher than those predicted for 1990, four to six times as high, but by that time the inward stocks in the Czech Republic, Estonia, Hungary, Poland and the Slovak Republic far surpassed the predicted levels. FDI in Latvia, Lithuania, Romania and Slovenia was close to the predicted values and only Bulgaria was well below, as was China, despite the huge flows to that country.

Many studies of the location of FDI now include measures of governance or other institutional quality that are not readily quantifiable but seem to influence corporate decisions. The World Bank has been issuing governance indicators covering almost a decade now and these provide some picture of the changes taking place in the CEECs in this respect.

A striking change for the CEECs has been the improvement in all their measures of governance since the first ones in 1996. For the six governance measures calculated by the World Bank (Kaufmann et al., 2006) the average score for the CEECs in 1996 was only 22 per cent of the average for the 15 pre-1995 EU members. By 2005, the ratio had reached 48 per cent. Some of the CEECs scored higher than Italy or Greece in 2005, but only the Czech Republic had scored higher than both of them in 1996. The improvement in governance may have helped to attract inflows of FDI, but it could also be that the hope of attracting FDI led to the improvements in governance.

Most of the progress in the governance ratings for CEECs since 1996 took place between 1996 and 2003. Since then, the average has been roughly constant, even slipping back a little. It may be no coincidence that they applied for EU membership between 1994 and 1996, and most of them entered the EU in 2004. The improvement in governance, intended to facilitate or permit EU entry, may have had the secondary effect of encouraging inward FDI. That reflects a persistent problem of analysis; the effects of joining the EU or of receiving inward FDI are mixed with the effects of actions aimed at achieving EU membership or encouraging inward investment.

If we add the World Bank governance scores (in arithmetic form, since they can be negative) to the prediction of the level of inward FDI, the per cent of variance in FDI levels explained rises from 67 to 77 per cent and the predicted values for most countries listed are higher, a little closer to the actual values but still below them, except in Estonia, Latvia, Lithuania and Slovenia – four of the smallest countries.

Outward FDI data from US surveys provide the fullest information on what foreign affiliates actually do, but the CEECs have never been a major destination for US investment. In 2003, they accounted for about 2.7 per cent of the employment in US affiliates, 0.4 per cent of assets and 1.5 per cent of net property, plant and equipment (US BEA website). What we can see from the data that do exist, dominated by the Czech Republic, Hungary and Poland, is that for US multinationals, the attraction of these countries is for labour-intensive activities. The average assets per worker of US affiliates in the CEECs in 2003 was around USD 150 000, lower than the ratio in Latin America, at a little over USD 200 000, and much lower than that in developing Asia, at about USD 430 000. The average for affiliates in the pre-1995 EU was around USD 1.3 million. The US investments were concentrated in manufacturing and, within manufacturing, in transport equipment, plus electrical machinery in Hungary and foods in Poland (Mataloni, 2005).

For Germany, in contrast to the United States, the CEECs were a major location for FDI. In 2004, they accounted for over 16 per cent of the employment in German firms' affiliates, but for only 3 per cent of assets (Deutsche Bundesbank, 2006). That large difference reflects the low capital intensity of these investments. The average assets per employee in 2003 – EUR 1.2 million worldwide, EUR 1.5 million in the United States, and EUR 1.8 million in the 15 pre-1995 EU area – were only about EUR 200 000 in the CEECs as a group. That was above the 170 000 levels in Latin American affiliates and the 160 000 in China, but far below that in other developing countries in Asia, at over EUR 600 000.

German manufacturing investment in the CEECs was remarkably con- centrated in motor vehicles, even in 1992–94, in the two countries for which we have data by industry (Deutsche Bundesbank, 1997). By 2002–2004, the concentration in that industry had increased and was quite general across the CEECs (Deutsche Bundesbank, 2006). By then, two thirds of the German investment was in motor vehicles and it was the leading FDI industry group in the Czech Republic, Hungary, Poland and Slovakia. Romania was the exception, with electrical machinery the leading sector, followed by motor vehicles, chemicals and non-electrical machinery.

One probable result of the industry concentration of German FDI in these countries can be seen in the changes that took place in the revealed export comparative advantages of the countries. During the 1990s, the comparative advantage in machinery and transport equipment increased or the comparative disadvantage decreased in nine of the 11 countries.

A few observations are suggested by the aggregate inflows from balance of payments data. One is that there was a clear positive relationship between countries' average governance scores and per capita FDI inflows over the 1990s. Bulgaria and Romania had the lowest governance scores and the lowest inflows of FDI per capita. The Czech Republic, Hungary and Estonia had the highest governance scores and the highest inflows per capita. The main outlier was Slovenia, with the highest average governance score but only average FDI inflows per capita. Governance scores did not have as clear a relation to the ratio of inflows to nominal GDP, although the relationship was mostly positive, except again for the Slovenia outlier.

4.   STUDIES BASED ON FIRM AND INDUSTRY DATA

There have been quite a few studies based on firm microdata of FDI in the CEECs. The periods covered are usually short for observing the effects of foreign ownership, some of which may require a long-term perspective.

All the CEECs have received some attention but the more important FDI destinations have received more attention than the smaller ones. An impressive degree of care has been given to problems of dealing with short panels, unbalanced panels, endogeneity, the clustering of observations and its effect on measures of standard errors, and different ways of dealing with panel data. Studies have examined effects of foreign investment on the recipient firm, spillovers of productivity and wages to indigenous firms, and the entry and exit of indigenous firms.

These studies find most definitively that foreign participation increases the productivity of the affiliate itself (Evenett and Voicu, 2001, for the Czech Republic, and Damijan et al., 2003, for ten countries). In a study of the effects of privatization in two CEECs (Hungary and Romania) and Russia and Ukraine, Brown et al. (2006) found that privatizations to foreigners led to growth in the privatized firms' total wage bills. In the two CEECs, the growth consisted of both increases in employment and increases in average wage levels. The wage gains reflected gains in productivity in these privatizations.

There is weaker and more complex evidence from the same studies for intra-industry productivity spillovers from foreign-owned to domestically-owned firms. As usual, characteristics of the foreign and host-country firms and industries are significant determinants of spillovers. Javorcik and Spatareanu (2003) found evidence for intra-industry spillovers from wholly-owned foreign firms but not from joint ventures in Romania. In another study of Romania, Altomonte and Pennings (2005) found positive intra-industry effects on domestic firms' productivity from initial foreign investments in an industry and region, but weaker and eventually negative effects as the foreign share grew. In a study mainly devoted to the question of 'crowding out' of domestically-owned firms by foreign-owned ones, Kosová (2005) found evidence of intra-industry technology spillovers in the Czech Republic. The entry of foreign-owned firms initially increased the exit rate of domestically-owned firms in the same industry, but after the initial setback, higher growth of foreign-owned firms represented domestic demand creation that increased both the growth rates and the survival of domestically-owned firms. As in other host countries, indigenous firms that exported, performed R&D and led their industries in productivity were more likely to gain spillovers from FDI.

Javorcik and Spatareanu (2003) found that joint ventures produced positive upstream spillovers to suppliers, while wholly-owned foreign firms produced negative upstream spillovers; probably because joint ventures tended to continue long-standing relationships with suppliers while wholly-owned foreign firms, using more advanced technology, required more sophisticated suppliers from abroad. It might also be – although not suggested by the authors – that wholly-owned firms are more likely to be part of multinationals' internal supply chains and therefore more likely to depend on associated firms in other countries for intermediate products; this may not be an important aspect of supplier choices for affiliates in the CEECs though. An earlier paper by Javorcik (2004) on Lithuania had also found evidence of spillovers to upstream industries but not intra-industry, and also – as in the Romanian study – for joint ventures but not for firms that were wholly foreign-owned.

Quite a few recent studies have attempted to explain what attracts FDI, or particularly German FDI, to the CEECs. One by Bellak and Leibrecht (2005) studied FDI inflows into eight CEECs from seven home countries, arguing that, for those countries, FDI flows are 'a reasonable proxy of the annual change in property, plant and equipment' (p. 8). As expected, host country size was positively related to the inflow, and the actual, rather than the statutory, bilateral tax rate was negatively related. In another paper using balance of payments measures – in this case the inward FDI stock – but including also the countries of the former Soviet Union, Kinoshita and Campos (2003) referred to these as forming 'a unique situation akin to a natural experiment' (p. 1). The results pointed to institutions, specifically rule of law and quality of bureaucracy, low labour costs, trade openness, progress towards economic reform and past FDI, interpreted as agglomeration advantages; no tax variable was included.

A gravity model paper by Borrmann et al. (2005) explained German FDI production, rather than bilateral financial flows, again with no tax variable. It found that German FDI production in 'core' CEECs already exceeded 'normal' levels in 2001, but the authors were reluctant to describe this high level as 'overshooting' that would imply future reductions or even a slowing of growth.

Although German affiliates in the CEECs are clearly more labour intensive than those in the rest of Europe, Buch and Kleinert (2006) find that market access, and not only low production cost, is a major incentive to invest in the CEECs. What determines the choice of locations among the CEECs is less important for political and policy discussions in home countries than the choice between home production in Germany and production in the CEECs. Becker and Mündler (2006) calculate the effects of changes in wages in Germany and in the CEECs on the allocation of employment by German multinational firms. The effects are twofold: on the establishment of new foreign locations, the locations of which then tend to be stable, and on the allocation of jobs between home and existing foreign locations. They find significant effects on a firm's location of employment from wage changes both at home and abroad, which they describe as 'a salient impact on multinational labour substitution' (p. 44).

The omission of tax rates from many studies was something of a surprise. However, in response to a call for papers for a workshop on studies of FDI based on microdata, we received many proposals for papers dealing with the influence of tax rates, including proposals dealing with European FDI. That seems to suggest that the issue is becoming more important for European countries.

Despite my belief that microdata are the road to progress in understanding FDI, there are some limitations that I think should be kept in mind.

One issue in studies comparing domestically-owned and foreign-owned plants or firms is whether the observed differences are the consequence of foreign ownership, with its accompanying superior technology and efficiency, or are only the result of differences in the size of plants, their use of intermediate inputs, their dependence on imported intermediate inputs, their capital intensity or other measurable differences in their structure. If all these differences are taken into account, it is presumably possible to know – provided that there is substantial overlap between domestic and foreign plants in their characteristics, that they are producing the same goods or services and of the same quality – whether foreign-owned and domestically-owned plants produce on different production functions.

Usually these conditions are not met. Industrial data are rarely detailed enough to permit comparisons of quality, domestically-owned plants are usually much smaller on average than foreign-owned plants (that is true in the United States as it is in developing countries), intermediate product inputs are often proprietary and not available to domestically-owned firms, and the technology needed to operate a large plant may be unavailable to a domestic producer. My conclusion is that we should not confine our interest to differences between foreign-owned and domestically-owned plants that can be unequivocally attributed to foreignness. We should also study differences that are associated with foreign ownership but cannot be attributed unequivocally to that foreign origin.

Another general problem is how to draw conclusions about the economy as a whole from microdata. For example, a finding that a rise in wages at home leads multinationals to substitute X jobs in its foreign affiliates for jobs at home tells us what will happen to that firm's employment at home but does not tell us what the effect on aggregate home employment will be, if any, or whether the effect will be on home wages or the distribution of employment among firms, or the composition of home production. It is difficult to go from the effects on the firm, which are in the microdata set, to broader impacts that may be outside the data. When a state or locality in the United States offers incentives to a large new foreign manufacturing operation, it may be hoping for, and/or fearing, impacts on agriculture and retail trade, as farm and retail workers shift to better paid manufacturing jobs, and on wages in these industries as well as in manufacturing. There may also be impacts on local and state government budgets, as subsidy costs compete with traditional government activities, and changes in the population and labour force in response to the industrial changes. It is a challenge to keep in mind, and even more a challenge to explore, these broader consequences of industrial change.

NOTE

1. I am indebted to Jing Sun for excellent research assistance.

REFERENCES

Altomonte, Carlo and Enrico Pennings (2005), 'Testing for marginal spillovers from foreign direct investment', Amsterdam and Rotterdam, *Tinbergen Institute Discussion Paper* TI 2005-101/4.
Becker, Sascha O. and Marc-Andreas Mündler (2006), 'Margins of multinational labor substitution', Frankfurt-am-Main, *Deutsche Bundesbank Discussion Paper*, Series 1: Economic Studies No. 24/2006.

Bellak, Christian and Markus Leibrecht (2005), 'Do low corporate tax rates attract FDI? Evidence from eight Central and East European countries', Nottingham, *Leverhulme Centre Research Paper* 2005/43.

Bhagwati, Jagdish N. (1978), *Anatomy and Consequences of Exchange Control Regimes*, Special Conference Series on Foreign Trade Regimes and Economic Development, **11**, Cambridge, MA: Ballinger.

Borrmann, Christine, Rolf Jungnickel and Dietmar Keller (2005), 'What gravity models can tell us about the position of German FDI in Central and Eastern Europe', Hamburg, *HHWA Discussion Paper* 328.

Brown, J. David, John S. Earle and Ámos Telegdy (2006), 'Does privatization hurt workers? Lessons from comprehensive manufacturing panel data in Hungary, Romania, Russia, and Ukraine', Kalamazoo, MI, *Upjohn Institute Staff Working Paper* 05-125, February.

Buch, Claudia M. and Jörn Kleinert (2006), 'Who goes East? The impact of enlargement on the patterns of German FDI', Tübingen, Institut für Angewandte Wirtschaftsforschung, *IAW-Diskussionspapiere* 24.

Campos, Nauro F. and Yuko Kinoshita (2002), 'Foreign direct investment as technology transferred: Some panel evidence from the transition economies', *The Manchester School*, **70** (3) June, 398–419.

Carkovic, Maria and Ross Levine (2005), 'Does foreign direct investment accelerate economic growth?', in Th. H. Moran, E.M. Graham and M. Blomström (eds), *Does Direct Investment Promote Development?*, Washington, DC: Institute for International Economics, pp. 195–220.

Damijan, Jože P., Mark Knell, Boris Majcen and Matija Rojec (2003), 'Technology transfer through FDI in top-10 transition countries: How important are direct effects, horizontal and vertical spillovers?', *William Davidson Working Paper* No. 549, Ann Arbor, MI, February.

Deutsche Bundesbank (1997), *Kapitalverflechtung mit dem Ausland*, Statistische Sonderveröffentlichung 10, May.

Deutsche Bundesbank (2006), *Kapitalverflechtung mit dem Ausland*, Statistische Sonderveröffentlichung 10, April.

Evenett, S. and A. Voicu (2001), 'Picking winners or creating them? Revisiting the benefits of FDI in the Czech Republic', Switzerland: University of St. Gallen.

International Monetary Fund (IMF) (1993), *Balance of Payments Manual, Fifth Edition, 1993*, Washington, DC: International Monetary Fund.

Javorcik, Beata Smarzynska (2004), 'Does foreign direct investment increase the productivity of domestic firms? In search of spillovers through backward linkages', *American Economic Review*, **94** (3), June, 605–27.

Javorcik, Beata Smarzynska and Mariana Spatareanu (2003), 'To share or not to share: does local participation matter or spillovers from foreign direct investment?', Development Economics Research Group Research, *Policy Research Working Paper* Series No. 3118, The World Bank.

Kaufmann, Daniel, Aart Kraay and Massimo Mastruzzi (2006), *Governance Matters V: Aggregate and Individual Governance Indicators for 1996–2005*, Washington, DC: The World Bank, September.

Kinoshita, Yuko and Nauro F. Campos (2003), 'Why does FDI go where IT goes? New evidence from the transition economies', Ann Arbor, MI, *William Davidson Institute Working Paper* No. 573, June.

Koncz, Jennifer L. and Daniel R. Yorgason (2005), 'Direct investment positions for 2004: Country and industry detail', *Survey of Current Business*, **85** (7), July.

Kosová, Renáta (2005), *Do Foreign Firms Crowd Out Domestic Firms? Evidence from the Czech Republic*, Washington, DC: The George Washington University.

Mataloni, Raymond J., Jr. (2005), 'US multinational companies: Operations in 2003', *Survey of Current Business*, **85** (7), July, 9–29.

Melitz, Marc J. (2005), 'Comment', in Th.H. Moran, E.M. Graham and M. Blomström (eds), *Does Direct Investment Promote Development?*, Washington, DC: Institute for International Economics, pp. 273–7.

Moran, Theodore H. (2005), 'How does FDI affect host country development? Using industry case studies to make reliable generalizations', in Th.H. Moran, E.M. Graham and M. Blomström (eds), *Does Direct Investment Promote Development?*, Washington, DC: Institute for International Economics, pp. 281–313.

Moran, Theodore H., Edward M. Graham and Magnus Blomström (eds) (2005), *Does Direct Investment Promote Development?*, Washington, DC: Institute for International Economics.

UNCTAD (2003), *World Investment Report, 2003*, United Nations, New York and Geneva.

UNCTAD (2004), *World Investment Report, 2004*, United Nations, New York and Geneva.

UNCTAD (2006), *World Investment Report, 2006*, United Nations, New York and Geneva.

PART I

Home and host country effects of FDI

1. The role of FDI in transition

Josef Christl[1]

In this contribution, I would like to briefly review the relevance of foreign direct investment (FDI) for Central and Eastern European host countries in transition. In general, there are three ways a host country is affected by the inflow of FDI:

- Increase in the capital stock: most fundamentally, an inflow of capital will benefit any country in which this factor of production is scarce. FDI can compensate for the lack of sufficient investment by residents and, according to the basic neoclassical growth model, the resulting higher capital/labour ratio raises national welfare measured as GDP per capita. For this kind of positive effect to arise, it is sufficient to assume foreign and domestic capital to be homogeneous.
- Higher productivity: moreover, foreign-owned firms tend to operate more productively than domestic firms; therefore an increase of FDI causes overall productivity in the host country to increase. The empirically well documented higher productivity of foreign firms is typically ascribed to the superiority of foreign technology imported by host countries through FDI; hence, foreign and domestic capital are heterogeneous.
- Positive spillovers: finally, the higher productivity of foreign-controlled firms might spill over to the rest of the economy. While the notion of 'spillover' might imply that these effects occur more or less automatically, specific channels of transmission need to be in place for spillovers to materialize. Among the channels identified by economists are the knowledge transfer via employees who change from foreign firms to domestic ones, the spreading of production standards imposed on foreign firms' domestic subcontractors, or simply the increase of competition resulting from the entry of foreign firms into previously sheltered markets. The amount of spillovers depends on both the policies that the host country applies and the business strategies that foreign investors pursue.

INCREASING THE CAPITAL STOCK IN TRANSITION

At the beginning of the transition process in Central and Eastern European countries (CEECs), *capital scarcity* was indeed predominant in the area. Although saving rates tend to be rather high in centrally planned countries, it is fair to say that the accumulated funds were not invested in the most efficient way. After the regime change, a good portion of the existing capital stocks depreciated, and as involuntary saving ceased and consumption opportunities increased, domestic investment became too low to keep up with the emerging need for capital formation. One way to finance the gap between households' willingness to save and firms' need to invest was the inflow of FDI. To give a few figures, the decade after 1992 saw an annual net inflow of FDI funds to the Czech Republic of approximately 5 per cent of GDP on average, a figure even topped by the equivalent of 6 per cent of GDP in the case of Hungary. Since 1998, the CEECs have been able to fund their current account deficits almost entirely through FDI. For 2006, the EBRD (2006) projects net FDI inflows to even exceed the current account deficit in the Czech Republic, Poland or Slovenia. While some of these additional funds were used to finance mergers and acquisitions (M&A), we can assume that FDI also contributed to capital formation. I should add, perhaps, that Calderon et al. (2004) provides evidence that an increase in M&A also leads to an increase in greenfield investment.

The rather constant inflow of FDI into CEECs during their transition process in the 1990s helped to integrate them into the framework of the international division of labour. The UNCTAD's Transnationality index, which takes into account FDI inflows, FDI inward stocks, value added and employment of foreign affiliates, ranks five new EU member states among the top ten developed countries identified for 2006 (UNCTAD, 2006).

HIGHER PRODUCTIVITY

The *productivity increasing effect of FDI* is not limited to transition economies. We can even observe some degree of productivity gap between foreign-owned and domestically-owned firms within countries with a similar capital endowment. For example Griffith and Simpson (2001) find for the UK that foreign-owned firms have always significantly higher labour productivity than those under domestic ownership. Given that most FDI projects are launched by large firms that might be able to reap economies of scale and by firms in capital-intensive manufacturing sectors which typically exhibit above-average productivity rates, the stimulation of productivity

Table 1.1   *FDI stocks and GDP growth in the Central and Eastern European member states of the EU (2005)*

	FDI Stocks 2005, EUR million	FDI Stock 2005, as % of GDP	GDP growth Ø 2000–2005
Czech Republic	50 404	51.2	3.4
Estonia	10 371	98.4	8.6
Hungary	51 737	58.9	4.8
Latvia	4035	31.9	7.8
Lithuania	5446	26.5	6.9
Poland	70 000	29.1	2.7
Slovakia	13 000	34.8	3.3
Slovenia	6000	21.9	3.5
Bulgaria	8531	39.8	5.0
Romania	20 130	25.4	4.7

Note: Ø = average value.

Source: Eurostat, wiiw.

rates by FDI inflows is not surprising. Djankov and Hoekman (2000) confirm this effect for the Czech Republic, and Konings (2001) does the same for Bulgaria, Romania and Poland. For an overview of the relationship between FDI stocks and GDP growth rates in the new EU members from Central and Eastern Europe, see Table 1.1.

The most acknowledged source for the productive advantage of firms established or controlled by FDI is their improved access to more efficient technologies. In this context the term technology refers to a broad range of items from the most recent machinery to more efficient management techniques. The decision of a foreign firm to transfer new technologies to a host country hinges crucially on a set of factors, including the decisive discrimination between import substitution and export-oriented FDI and their different effects on the growth potential of the host country. I would like to single out and briefly discuss the absorptive capacity of the host country.

Absorptive Capacity

The term absorptive capacity refers to the ability of an economy to gather new technologies and successfully implement them into the production process. In this sense, emphasis is placed not on the capacity to generate innovations, but on the capacity to absorb processes that have been innovated elsewhere. The most important factor for the absorptive capacity is the quality of domestic human capital, whose importance for the growth effects of FDI was already stressed by Borensztein et al. (1998). In this respect the new member states of the EU had a great advantage in their transition process, namely the high skills of the human capital available in these countries, notwithstanding the fact that some observers deplored that there were 'too many rocket scientists and too few marketing clerks'[2] around. But the stock of human capital was obviously sufficient for many foreign firms to smoothly transfer their latest technologies downstream. Actually, some empirical studies (for an overview, see Riess and Uppenberg, 2004) conclude that a smaller technology gap between two countries involved makes for stronger productivity-enhancing effects of FDI. Therefore, the new EU member states can expect to continue to profit from FDI inflows even when their transition processes have been more or less completed.

At the same time, when trying to measure the productivity effects of FDI, we might be confronted with an endogeneity problem. Firms investing in foreign countries might try to 'skim the cream', which means they probably choose to take over the most productive companies, leaving less efficient plants to domestic owners. So, for example, the 2005 Transition report by the EBRD stated that foreign-owned firms exhibit higher levels of efficiency, and related that fact *inter alia* to their acquisition of better-performing domestic firms in transition countries. Campos and Kinoshita (2002) especially account for endogeneity and causality problems in their panel regressions on 25 CEECs and members of the Commonwealth of Independent States (CIS) and find robust positive effects of FDI.

POSITIVE SPILLOVERS

Finally, transition economies might benefit from FDI when innovative *technologies* or, in general, *knowledge* introduced by a foreign investor *spills over* to the domestic firms. I have outlined some of the transmission channels of these spillovers above. Empirically, it is not easy to track down spillover effects of FDI in Central and Eastern Europe. Regarding the fact that all new EU member states are small, open economies and therefore should employ an export-led growth strategy, we also might expect foreign-owned firms to dedicate substantial parts of their production for exports. As they have to compete on world markets, one might expect the foreign investors to transfer their latest technologies to the host countries. Hence, the FDI inflows should induce positive spillovers of a reasonable magnitude.

To conclude from an Austrian perspective, Austrian firms have been major players in the Central and Eastern European countries and have been among the most active investors during the transition process in the CEECs. In 2004 the CEECs accounted for 38 per cent of Austrian FDI outflows, thus exceeding the share of FDI targeting the old EU member states. Currently, Austria is the third-biggest investor in the CEECs behind Germany and the Netherlands; if the accumulated FDI flows are measured in per cent of GDP, Austria is actually the biggest investor in that region.

NOTES

1. Wolfgang Pointner, of the OeNB's staff, contributed to these remarks.
2. Campos and Dabusinskas (2002).

REFERENCES

Borensztein, E., J. De Gregorio and Jong-Wha Lee (1998), 'How does foreign direct investment affect economic growth?', *Journal of International Economics*, **45** (1), June, pp. 115–35.

Calderon, C., N. Loayza and L. Serven (2004), 'Greenfield foreign direct investment and mergers and acquisitions – feedback and macroeconomic effects', *World Bank Research Working Paper* 3192.

Campos, N. and A. Dabusinskas (2002), 'So many rocket scientists, so few marketing clerks: occupational mobility in times of rapid technological change', *CEPR Discussion Paper* 3531.

Campos, N. and Y. Kinoshita (2002), 'Foreign direct investment as technology transferred: some panel evidence from the transition economies', *CEPR Discussion Paper* 3417.

Djankov, S. and B. Hoekman (2000), 'Foreign investment and productivity growth in Czech enterprises', *World Bank Economic Review*, **14** (1), 49–64.

EBRD (2005), *Transition Report 2005: Business in Transition*, London.

EBRD (2006), *Transition Report 2006: Finance in Transition*, London.

Griffith, R. and H. Simpson (2001), 'Characteristics of foreign-owned firms in British manufacturing', *IFS Working Papers* 01/10.

Konings, J. (2001), 'The effects of foreign direct investment on domestic firms: evidence from firm level panel data in emerging economies', *CEPR Discussion Paper* 2586.

Riess, A. and K. Uppenberg (2004), 'The internationalisation of production: moving plants, products, and people', *EIB Papers*, **9** (1).

UNCTAD (2006), *World Investment Report 2006 – FDI from Developing and Transition Economies: Implications for Development*, New York.

2. Foreign direct investment spillovers in emerging market economies

Yuriy Gorodnichenko, Jan Svejnar and Katherine Terrell[1]

1. INTRODUCTION AND LITERATURE REVIEW

For most of the post-World War II period, official foreign assistance exceeded private capital flows to developing countries. However, the capital account liberalization that has taken place around the world in the last two decades has brought about a reversal: in each year since the early 1990s, private capital flows have exceeded official foreign assistance. Moreover, since the financial crises of the late 1990s, most private capital flows have taken the form of foreign direct investment (FDI). At the same time, governments in emerging market economies have tended to make numerous concessions to attract FDI in order to spur economic development with the expectation that FDI increases productivity both directly and indirectly through positive spillovers on domestic firms. Whereas there is growing evidence that foreign owned firms are more productive than domestic firms,[2] the evidence on the productivity enhancing spillover effects is mixed. In this chapter we report on results that we and others obtained to increase our understanding as to when, where and under what conditions FDI has positive spillover effects on domestic firms.

Foreign firms can have productivity 'spillover' effects on domestic competitors (horizontal spillovers) as well as on domestic firms that operate in upstream and downstream industries from the foreign firms (vertical spillovers).[3] The spillovers come about through a transfer of managerial practices, production methods, marketing techniques or any other knowledge embodied in a product or service, and they may be brought about through a number of channels. Local firms may learn to imitate new processes or improve the quality of their products through observation, interaction with foreign managers in business associations and chambers of commerce, and by hiring current or former employees of foreign multinational enterprises (MNEs).[4] Local firms may also benefit from the entry of new professional service providers (for example, consulting and accounting firms) or suppliers as a result of the MNE entry. Foreign firms may act as catalysts for domestic suppliers to improve the quality of their products or time efficiency by demanding higher standards.[5] On the other hand, foreign firms may have negative effects on domestic firms' output and productivity if they 'steal' the domestic firms' market or valuable workers and managers. If domestic firms are forced to cut back on production, they may experience a higher average cost as fixed costs are spread over a smaller scale of production (Aitken and Harrison, 1999).

Existing studies primarily examine 'horizontal spillovers' and do so within a production function framework, estimating the efficiency with which different firms use inputs to generate output. The effect of foreign presence on the productivity of domestic firms in a given industry is captured by the coefficient on the share of foreign firms' output or employment in that industry. The evidence from this research is mixed rather than being as positive as has been generally expected. Most studies suggest that the horizontal spillover effect of MNEs in developing countries is insignificant or negative (for example, studies of Morocco by Haddad and Harrison, 1993; Venezuela by Aitken and Harrison, 1999; Bulgaria and Romania by Konings, 2000; Russia by Yudaeva et al., 2003, and the Czech Republic by Kosova, 2004). On the other hand, several studies find positive horizontal spillovers in the more developed economies such as the United Kingdom (for example, Haskel et al., 2002) and the United States (for example, Keller and Yeaple, 2003).

The negative horizontal spillover effect is usually interpreted as being brought about by a low 'absorptive capacity' of domestic firms in the less developed countries. It is assumed that the larger the technology and human capital gaps between the domestic and foreign firms, the less likely the domestic firms are to gain from the presence of foreign firms. The implication is that positive spillovers should be found in more technologically advanced sectors or in the more industrialized countries.[6] There is some evidence supporting the human capital gap hypothesis, but the evidence with respect to the technology gap is mixed.

Using data on FDI flows from industrial countries to 69 developing countries, Borensztein et al. (1998) show that FDI is important for economic growth, but only in countries which have a minimum threshold stock of human capital (proxied by the share of the population with at least high school education). Blalock and Gertler (2002) find that plants in Indonesia that have more highly educated employees benefit more from the presence of MNEs.

With respect to the effects of technology gaps, Kokko (1994) and Takii (2001) find that the smaller the spillovers, the wider the technology gap between local and foreign-owned plants, whereas Sjoholm (1999) and

Blalock and Gertler (2002) find the larger the spillovers, the wider the gap, all using data for Indonesia. With US plant-level data for 1987–1996, Girma et al. (2001) find that local firms that are 'technologically comparable' to foreign firms enjoy greater spillovers. The findings may differ because of different measures of the technology: some studies use labour productivity and others total factor productivity. On the other hand, studies that proxy technology through the level of R&D tend to find positive horizontal spillovers in the R&D sector (see, for example, Kathuria, 2001, using Indian data and Kinoshita, 2000, using data from the Czech Republic).

Sabirianova et al. (2005b) differ from other studies in that they combine data on domestic and foreign owned firms and test whether foreign presence in a given industry affects productive efficiency of domestic and foreign firms differently. In particular, they examine whether foreign presence in emerging market economies affects positively the efficiency of foreign firms, which are more advanced and have a globally developed absorptive (learning) capacity, while having a smaller positive or a negative effect on the efficiency of domestic firms, which are less efficient and may not yet have developed their absorptive capacity. The authors find that in the manufacturing sector in both the Czech Republic and Russia greater presence of foreign firms in a given industry has a negative average effect on productive efficiency of domestic firms in that industry, but the effect is positive on the efficiency of other foreign owned firms. This result parallels the finding of Sabirianova et al. (2005a) that both in the Czech Republic and Russia, foreign firms that are closer to the technological frontier have a higher probability of improving their performance than foreign firms that lag further behind, but that domestic firms have about the same probability of moving closer or farther from the frontier irrespective of their initial position.

In addition to estimating the average effects over the 1993–2000 period, Sabirianova et al. (2005b) also examine how these effects change over time. Their dynamic estimates of the spillovers indicate that in the Czech Republic the negative spillover effect on domestic firms is alleviated over time, while in Russia the negative spillover effect becomes stronger over time. These findings suggest that in emerging market economies the hypothesized positive spillover (a) applies to foreign owned firms, which are relatively more efficient and prepared in terms of their absorptive capacity than local firms; (b) is negative but reversible among domestic firms in countries that open up and gradually adopt a market-oriented and enforceable institutional and legal framework; and (c) is increasingly more negative on domestic firms in countries that are more technologically backward, have opened up less to trade and foreign competition, and have not carried out fundamental legal and institutional reforms. The changing pattern in these two countries is intriguing, and raises questions as to whether they are driven by factors such as changing domestic policies with respect to competition, rule of law and openness to foreign investment and international trade.

The implication of Sabirianova et al.'s (2005b) findings may be extended further if one takes into account the findings of the aforementioned study of UK manufacturing by Griffith et al. (2002), whose estimates suggest that there is convergence to the frontier and that increased foreign presence within an industry raises the speed of convergence to the technological frontier. Taken together, these findings for the Czech Republic (CEE), Russia (CIS) and the UK (EU) are consistent with the notion that the spillovers from foreign presence are positive for all firms in relatively advanced economies, but that in the less developed economies they are positive only for foreign owned firms and may be (increasingly) negative for domestic firms. Overall, Sabirianova et al.'s (2005b) results suggest that future research needs to examine the differential effects that globalization may have on local and foreign owned firms in both the advanced and emerging market economies.

Another recent strand of the literature argues that FDI is more likely to have a positive effect on the host country's growth and development if the economy is open in terms of trade and FDI and is competitive (for example, Moran et al., 2005). Conversely, it is argued that in protected and distorted economies FDI is likely to cause the economic welfare of the host country to worsen:

> Foreign investors in countries with domestic content, joint venture and technology sharing requirements deploy production technique lagging far behind the frontier in international industry. Foreign affiliates with older technology and less efficient plants are not good candidates to develop from an infant industry to a robust world competitor. Local firms that sell to foreign affiliates in protected market are often subscale in size and inefficient in operation. (Moran et al., 2005, p. 376)

Supporting evidence on the positive impact of competition has been found by Blalock and Gertler (2004), who use Indonesian data to show that spillovers are higher in sectors with more competition. However, the relationship may not be uniform because Sembenelli and Siotis (2002) find, using Spanish data, that only firms in the R&D sector enjoy positive spillovers when there is more competition. Aghion et al. (2005) develop a model showing that firm responses to liberalization are likely to be heterogeneous, with technologically more advanced firms being more likely to respond by investing in new technologies and production processes, and find supporting evidence with Indian data. Hence, the impact of openness and competition may have different spillover effects depending on where the firm is relative to the technological frontier. In other words, foreign affiliates in better business environments tend to bring with them better technology and hence there is 'more to spill'. Javorcik and Saggi (2004) also argue that foreign affiliates that have higher level of technology tend to be wholly owned, rather than joint ventures. One might therefore see larger positive spillovers from wholly-owned foreign firms than from partially-owned foreign firms.

While there are numerous studies on horizontal (intra-industry) spillovers, there are relatively few empirical studies on vertical spillovers. This is surprising given that a relatively early analysis by Lall (1980) found positive backward linkage effects of foreign firms on the Indian trucking industry.[7] Moreover, vertical spillovers are more likely to be positive than horizontal spillovers since MNEs have an incentive to improve the productivity of their suppliers rather than that of their competitors.[8] The empirical papers that have appeared recently do indeed find evidence that is consistent with the view of technology transfer through backward linkages in the manufacturing sectors of Indonesia (Blalock and Gertler, 2005), Hungary (Schoors and van der Tol, 2001) and Lithuania (Javorcik, 2005). However, these studies rely only on a variable that is constructed from input–output tables at the industry level, rather than a direct firm-specific measure.

The study on which we are reporting in the rest of this chapter (Gorodnichenko et al., 2007) advances our understanding of the presence and magnitude of vertical and horizontal spillovers in seven key dimensions. First, using data on 15 transition economies, we provide much larger comparative evidence than has been possible to date.[9] Second, our analysis covers firms in both the service sector and manufacturing sectors. Most of the recent FDI is in services, and this important phenomenon has not been captured to date. Third, while much of the existing evidence is for medium and large firms, we are able to parse out the effects on small firms with less than 30 employees, which tend to be the new entrepreneurs and engines of growth in the transition economies. Fourth, our data is recent, covering the period 2002–2005, and our findings are hence especially relevant for public policy. Fifth, we provide a methodological advance by being able to analyse forward and backward linkages (vertical spillovers) of MNEs with a *direct firm-specific* variable and compare this with the results using the more indirect industry-specific variable based on input–output tables. We extend the analysis of forward and backward spillovers to include the concept of selling or buying from firms outside the country, that is, importing and exporting. There is no reason to believe that vertical spillovers are constrained to linkages with foreign firms within the host country alone (although the magnitude of effect may be stronger, given the geographic proximity). Sixth, our study advances the literature by shedding light on the impact of a country's institutions on the strength of vertical and horizontal spillovers. We explore whether spillovers vary with the country of origin (proxying for quality) of FDI and we estimate the effect on spillovers of three important aspects of the business environment: government corruption, bureaucratic red tape and the length of hold-up of goods at the customs. Finally, we address the question of whether the technology or human capital gap affects the strength of spillovers.

In the rest of this chapter we describe the data and discuss from a policy perspective the key results of Gorodnichenko et al. (2007). The interested reader is advised to go to the Gorodnichenko et al. (2007) paper for the formal derivation of the empirical methodology and the technical presentation of the estimated coefficients.

2. DATA[10]

We use data from the Business Environment and Enterprise Performance Survey (BEEPS), a joint initiative of the European Bank for Reconstruction and Development (EBRD) and the World Bank. The survey was first undertaken in 1999–2000, when it was administered to approximately 4000 enterprises in 26 countries of Central and Eastern Europe (CEE) (including Turkey) and the Commonwealth of Independent States (CIS) to assess the environment for private enterprise and business development. In the second round of the BEEPS, in 2002, the survey instrument was administered to approximately 6500 enterprises in 27 countries (including Turkey). In the third round, in 2005, the BEEPS instrument was administered to approximately 7900 enterprises in the same 27 countries covered by the second round of the BEEPS.[11]

The sampling frames of these 2002 and 2005 BEEPS are very similar. Both were designed to have the following general targeted distributional criteria:

- *Coverage of countries:* both were to be administered to 28 transition economies: 16 from CEE (Albania, Bosnia and Herzegovina, Bulgaria, Croatia, Czech Republic, Estonia, FR Yugoslavia, FYROM, Hungary, Latvia, Lithuania, Poland, Romania, Slovak Republic, Slovenia and Turkey) and 12 from the CIS (Armenia, Azerbaijan, Belarus, Georgia, Kazakhstan, Kyrgyzstan, Moldova, Russia, Tajikistan, Turkmenistan, Ukraine and Uzbekistan). In neither year could the survey be administered in Turkmenistan.

- *Sector:* in each country, the sectoral composition of the sample in terms of manufacturing[12] versus services[13] was to be determined by their relative contribution to GDP. Firms that operate in sectors subject to government price regulation and prudential supervision, such as banking, electric power, rail transport, and water and waste water, were to be excluded from the sample.
- *Size:* at least 10 per cent of the sample was to be in the small-size category and 10 per cent in the large-size category.[14] Firms with only one employee or more than 10 000 employees were to be excluded.
- *Ownership:* at least 10 per cent of the firms were to have foreign control and 10 per cent state control, based on more than 50 per cent shareholding.
- *Exporters:* at least 10 per cent of the firms were to be exporters, meaning that 20 per cent or more of total sales is exported.
- *Location:* at least 10 per cent of firms were to be in the category 'small city/countryside' (population under 50 000 inhabitants).

Table 2.1 summarizes the total number of interviews as well as the quotas achieved in each country for the main BEEPS III. The percentages given in the table are calculated on the basis of the completed (not the targeted) interviews.[15] As may be seen from the table, the data base is comprised of a total of 7942 firms, with 200–600 firms per country. The share of firms in services ranged from 50 per cent to 65 per cent across the 27 countries. Between two-thirds and three-quarters of the firms are small (less than 50 employees). Approximately 10 per cent of the firms are foreign owned and another 10 per cent are state owned. The share of firms that export more than 20 per cent of their output varies tremendously across these countries: from 5 per cent in Kazakhstan to 30 per cent in Slovenia.

The Gorodnichenko et al. (2007) study relies primarily on the 2005 BEEPS survey and to a lesser extent on the 2002 BEEPS, because for most of the variables of interest the 2005 BEEPS contain data on the rates of change from 2002 to 2005. In those cases when we cannot construct rates of change from the 2005 BEEPS, we construct them by combining information from the two, 2002 and 2005, BEEPS data sets.

In addition to the BEEPS data, we rely on data from input–output tables to construct some of the industry-wide spillover variables. We have only been able to obtain recent input–output tables for 15 of the 26 countries for which BEEPS were collected, which somewhat limits our analysis at this stage. The year and source of our input–output tables are presented in Table 2.2.

Table 2.1 Number of interviews and quotas achieved in BEEPS III (2005)

Country	No. of Interviews		City/Town			Sector		Main activity		Size of enterprise			Foreign owned	Export
	Target	Completed	Large	Medium	Small	Private	State	Industry	Services	Small	Medium	Large		
Albania	200	204	38.7%	40.2%	21.1%	91.2%	8.8%	49.5%	50.5%	74.0%	18.6%	7.4%	10.8%	20.1%
Armenia	200	201	51.2%	26.4%	22.4%	90.0%	10.0%	46.8%	53.2%	75.1%	13.9%	10.9%	11.4%	12.9%
Azerbaijan	200	200	64.5%	21.5%	14.0%	90.0%	10.0%	48.5%	51.5%	74.0%	18.0%	8.0%	11.0%	11.5%
Belarus	300	325	32.0%	52.0%	16.0%	88.6%	11.4%	42.2%	57.8%	71.4%	17.8%	10.8%	10.2%	16.3%
Bosnia	200	200	34.5%	49.0%	16.5%	90.0%	10.0%	45.5%	54.5%	61.0%	29.0%	10.0%	12.0%	18.0%
Bulgaria	300	300	23.7%	39.0%	37.3%	90.0%	10.0%	28.3%	71.7%	74.0%	16.0%	10.0%	10.3%	15.0%
Croatia	200	236	29.7%	31.8%	38.6%	89.0%	11.0%	44.9%	55.1%	64.8%	21.2%	14.0%	8.9%	19.1%
Czech Republic	300	343	21.9%	31.2%	46.9%	91.3%	8.7%	38.5%	61.5%	76.1%	16.0%	7.9%	9.0%	14.6%
Estonia	200	219	51.6%	21.0%	27.4%	90.9%	9.1%	32.4%	67.6%	74.4%	16.0%	9.6%	15.1%	14.2%
FR Yugoslavia	300	300	45.0%	35.3%	19.7%	86.3%	13.7%	37.3%	62.7%	65.7%	20.7%	13.7%	11.0%	16.3%
FYROM	200	200	60.5%	23.0%	16.5%	91.5%	8.5%	36.0%	64.0%	73.5%	16.5%	10.0%	10.5%	17.0%
Georgia	200	200	50.5%	32.5%	17.0%	88.0%	12.0%	30.0%	70.0%	74.5%	17.5%	8.0%	13.0%	13.5%
Hungary	300	312	34.6%	43.6%	21.8%	94.2%	5.8%	35.3%	64.7%	74.0%	16.3%	9.6%	13.8%	17.0%
Kazakhstan	300	300	40.3%	45.7%	14.0%	90.3%	9.7%	43.7%	56.3%	73.3%	16.0%	10.7%	11.0%	5.0%
Kyrgyzstan	200	202	32.3%	39.6%	28.2%	89.1%	10.9%	43.6%	56.4%	63.4%	26.2%	10.4%	14.4%	13.4%
Latvia	200	205	55.6%	10.7%	33.7%	88.8%	11.2%	22.9%	77.1%	74.1%	15.6%	10.2%	9.8%	12.2%
Lithuania	200	205	30.7%	37.6%	31.7%	87.8%	12.2%	36.1%	63.9%	68.3%	22.0%	9.8%	10.7%	19.0%
Moldova	200	200	44.0%	25.0%	31.0%	90.5%	9.5%	31.5%	68.5%	69.0%	21.5%	9.5%	10.5%	12.5%
Poland	550	580	14.1%	62.2%	23.6%	89.3%	10.7%	37.9%	62.1%	68.4%	21.9%	9.7%	9.5%	15.3%
Romania	300	315	19.0%	49.2%	31.7%	88.9%	11.1%	41.3%	58.7%	62.5%	27.0%	10.5%	11.7%	11.7%
Russia	550	599	56.9%	28.0%	15.0%	90.0%	10.0%	40.9%	59.1%	66.3%	21.9%	11.9%	10.0%	9.7%
Slovak Republic	200	220	41.4%	40.9%	17.7%	89.1%	10.9%	26.8%	73.2%	67.7%	22.3%	10.0%	11.8%	17.7%
Slovenia	200	223	21.1%	22.0%	57.0%	89.2%	10.8%	39.0%	61.0%	70.9%	16.6%	12.6%	7.6%	29.6%
Tajikistan	200	200	37.0%	41.0%	22.0%	90.5%	9.5%	44.0%	56.0%	61.5%	28.5%	10.0%	10.0%	12.5%
Turkey	550	559	54.4%	27.0%	18.6%	90.2%	9.8%	36.5%	63.5%	71.6%	18.8%	9.7%	9.8%	15.7%

Table 2.1 (continued)

Country	No. of Interviews		City/Town			Sector		Main activity		Size of enterprise			Foreign owned	Export
	Target	Completed	Large	Medium	Small	Private	State	Industry	Services	Small	Medium	Large		
Ukraine	550	594	36.5%	47.5%	16.0%	90.2%	9.8%	42.8%	57.2%	70.9%	19.0%	10.1%	10.9%	10.1%
Uzbekistan	300	300	29.0%	39.3%	31.7%	89.7%	10.3%	37.7%	62.3%	73.0%	17.0%	10.0%	11.0%	9.7%
Total	**7600**	**7942**												

Source: Table 3 of Synovate (2005).

66

Table 2.2   Sources and years of input–output tables used in the analysis

Year	Country	Source
2000	Albania	Horridge, Mark[1]
2000	Bulgaria	National statistical office
1999	Croatia	National statistical office
1999	Czech Republic	Czech Republic National Statistical Yearbook
1997	Estonia	Eurostat
1998	Hungary	Eurostat
2002	Kazakhstan	Hare, Paul and Naumov, Alexander (2005, p. 28)
1998	Latvia	National statistical office
2001	Lithuania	National statistical office
2000	Poland	Eurostat
2002	Romania	National statistical office
2003	Russia	National accounts of Russia
2000	Slovakia	National statistical office
2001	Slovenia	Eurostat
2003	Ukraine	National statistical office

Notes:
All input–output tables were at the NACE 2-digit level, except for those for Kazakhstan and Russia, which were at the 1-digit level and were converted to two digits using weights constructed from data on output by industries.
[1] Horridge, Mark, 'Albania Input–Output Table'. GTAP/USAID. Table downloaded from http://www.monash.edu.au/policy/archivep.htm.

3.   FINDINGS ON VERTICAL AND HORIZONTAL SPILLOVERS

Using our data, we obtain several important findings. First, we find that there is an increase in the efficiency of those domestic firms that supply industries (in their country) that have higher concentrations of foreign firms or that export a higher share of their output (that is, sell more to foreign firms outside the country). Second, we find that domestic firms that buy from foreign firms, either domestically or via imports, do not seem to gain efficiency from these vertical spillovers. Finally, only large firms gain from the presence of foreign firms in their industries; the effect was not significant for all other firms.

The overall findings may, of course, cover important differences across countries. In particular, there may be differences in countries' spillover gains (losses) that may be caused by differences in institutional factors and the business environment. Moran et al. (2005) and others, for instance, argue that a country with better property rights and more openness to market competition and FDI will attract better quality FDI (higher level technology) because, by being unconstrained, these foreign firms will be able to optimize. Moreover, several studies have shown that foreign investors tend to transfer technology within wholly owned networks of multinationals' subsidiaries rather than to joint ventures or licensees (see for example, Ramachandran, 1993, and Mansfield and Romero, 1980). Others have shown that in countries with limited rule of law, MNEs tend to shy away from joint-ownership and choose to invest in wholly owned ventures (see for example, Javorcik and Wei, 2002, who study the impact of corruption on mode of entry). Hence, this evidence seems to point to potentially stronger positive spillovers from wholly owned foreign firms than from partially owned foreign firms, since they bring with them a higher level of technology, and to indicate that the positive spillovers should be even greater in better business environments, that is, more open economies with better rule of law.

Another characteristic that may affect spillovers is the nationality of foreign investors. Javorcik et al. (2004) argue that there are two reasons why we might see nationality matter: 1) distance between host and headquarters countries can affect the share of intermediate inputs sourced by multinationals in a host country and hence affect spillovers; and 2) preferential trading agreements will cover some host countries and not others, which will also affect the extent to which intermediate inputs are purchased from the host country. In addition, the nationality of the FDI can matter because the quality of FDI (level of technology) may vary by origin. Thus FDI from more developed countries may have a higher level of technology than FDI from less advanced countries. One may conjecture that FDI from the OECD countries has higher technology than FDI from non-OECD countries and hence one would see greater spillovers from FDI from OECD than non-OECD countries.

In order to test these hypotheses, we re-estimated our production function equations with new variables for the backward, forward and horizontal linkages where the foreign presence variable is recalculated for share of output by wholly versus partially owned foreign firms and for share of output produced by FDI from OECD countries versus non-OECD countries. The findings based on these proxy variables for the 'quality of FDI' suggest that there is no difference in the productivity spillovers from wholly versus partially owned foreign firms or from FDI from OECD versus non-OECD countries. Hence, neither the hypothesis from the literature that wholly owned foreign firms have higher levels of technology than partially owned ones, nor the hypothesis that the quality of FDI from OECD countries is better than that from non-OECD seem to be borne out in terms of the estimated spillover effects.

We also test whether spillovers are higher for wholly owned firms in better business environments, following the hypothesis put forth by Moran et al. (2005).[16] We start by testing whether vertical and horizontal spillovers (without taking degree of ownership into account) vary systematically with different institutions. By institutions and business environment, we refer to openness of the economy, bureaucratic red tape and corruption. We hypothesize that spillovers are more likely to be positive when there is less bureaucratic tape or corruption and more openness to trade because better environments will attract better quality FDI, and because domestic firms in these environments will be more competitive and able to absorb technology spillovers.

The BEEPS data offer a unique opportunity to examine business environment factors determining the strength of horizontal and vertical spillovers. Not only does BEEPS have a rich set of variables that capture institutions/business environment, but importantly, this information is collected at the firm level. Moreover, BEEPS has large cross-country variation so that we do not have to rely on time-series variation to identify the effect on the institutions. Among the many variables in the BEEPS that measure institutions/business environment, we consider the following: 1) *Corruption*, measured as the percentage of total annual sales typically spent on unofficial payments/gifts to public officials (*bribes*) and contract enforcement; 2) *Red tape*, proxied by the percentage of *management's time spent with officials*; and 3) *Openness* of the economy, proxied with a variable that captures hold-up in trade (*wait-time*) by the number of days waiting at customs to get imports in and exports out.

These three variables were constructed by averaging firms' responses for the industry and country in which the firm resided. The results do not reveal any systematic patterns. Corruption is not found to have a direct or indirect effect on the efficiency of domestic firms. The length of time that a manager spends with bureaucrats has little effect on efficiency of his/her firm and on the strength of vertical or horizontal spillovers. On the other hand, the strength of the spillover varies somewhat with the hold-up time in customs but the effect is generally small. We also examine whether it is the rate of change in business conditions or the actual level of business conditions that matters and find that neither has a significant effect.

We next assess whether these business environment variables have an effect when measured at the country level rather than at the industry and country level. This approach would make sense if the effect of corruption or waiting time at customs were more nation-specific than industry-specific. We calculate a new measure of corruption as the average response rate for all firms in a country; we then rank and divide the 15 countries into three groups by level of corruption and see if this categorical variable of corruption has an interaction effect with the three linkage variables. Our results indicate that there is no systematic effect. Finally we ask whether spillovers vary systematically for wholly and partially foreign owned firms with the business environment. Again, we do not find any significant relationship.

4.   TECHNOLOGY GAP OR DISTANCE TO THE FRONTIER

Differences between plants' or firms' technology or level of human capital may also help explain the extent to which domestic firms can benefit from spillovers. Specifically, firms that are close to the technological frontier benefit more from foreign presence than firms that are far from the technological frontier. Melitz (2003) obtains similar results, although in his model foreign presence has only general equilibrium effects.

The empirical problem for testing the hypothesis with respect to the 'technology gap' is that the level of technology is not observed and thus it is hard to compute the distance to the technological frontier at the firm level. We tackle this problem in the following way. Since there is substantial anecdotal and other evidence that foreign firms are more advanced than domestic firms in the developing countries, we assume that foreign firms embody the technological frontier. Firms that are similar to foreign firms along observed characteristics are likely to have a technology close to the technology of the foreign-owned counterparts. If the observed characteristics of domestic firms are different from the observed characteristics of the foreign-owned firms, the domestic firms are likely to use a technology different from the technology used by foreign-owned firms. At the minimum, one can interpret this difference as the distance from the business practice of foreign-owned firms. To construct such a metric of discrepancy, we use standard tools from the literature on matching (for example, Rosenbaum, 2002). Specifically, we use the Mahalanobis distance for a set of firms' observable characteristics. The key findings are that only in the service sector does distance have a significant effect, indicating that domestic firms whose technology is further away from the foreign firms are less efficient and also have smaller horizontal spillovers than those that are closer to the foreign firms.

Finally, the effect of human capital (measured as the share of workers with a university or higher education) on the strength of spillovers indicates that large firms with more educated workers do indeed tend to gain positive spillovers from foreign firms in their industries. Otherwise the effect is not significant.

5.   SUMMARY AND CONCLUSIONS

Our research advances the understanding of the presence and magnitude of vertical and horizontal spillovers of MNEs in seven key areas by (a) providing much larger comparative evidence than other studies; (b) generating estimates not only for manufacturing but also for services; (c) analysing not only large but also small firms that tend to be the new entrepreneurs and engine of growth; (d) covering the recent period of 2002–2005; (e) providing a methodological advance by analysing forward and backward linkages (vertical spillovers) of MNEs with a *direct* firm-specific variable and extending the analysis of forward and backward spillovers to include the concept of selling or buying from firms outside the country; (f) shedding light on the impact of a country's institutions on the strength of vertical and horizontal spillovers; and (g) addressing the question of whether the technology or human capital gap of local firms affects the strength of spillovers.

In a set of baseline estimates we find support for the findings in the literature that there is a positive impact of *backward spillovers* and a zero effect of *forward spillovers*. We next find that both large and small firms experience efficiency gains if they supply industries with a higher share of foreign firms. However, *horizontal* spillovers turn out to be positive and significant only for large firms, and are insignificant otherwise. Whereas importing goods does not appear to have a positive effect on efficiency, exporting goods is consistently associated with increased efficiency. This is a robust finding in all specifications. Hence we identify a clear pattern that supplying a foreign firm, whether in the host country or outside the country, has knowledge spillover effects, whereas purchasing from foreign firms does not.

Our analysis of the performance effects of key institutional variables focuses on bribes (unofficial payments) to public officials, regulatory burden as measured by the time that top management spends with public officials, and the hold-up problems in the customs, proxied by the number of days the firm has to wait to get its imports in and exports out of the country. We find that by and large these aspects of the business environment do not have significant effects on performance. Specifically, corruption does not have a direct or indirect effect on efficiency of domestic firms. The length of time that a manager spends with bureaucrats has little effect on efficiency of his/her firm and on the strength of vertical or horizontal spillovers. On the other hand, the strength of the spillover varies somewhat with the hold-up time in customs, but the effect is generally small. We also tested for the hypothesis that wholly owned foreign firms have greater technology spillovers than partially owned foreign firms and that the strength of the positive spillovers of wholly owned is enhanced in countries that are open to trade and that have good rule of law. We found no support for either of those hypotheses.

Finally, we find that *distance* from the technological frontier in the service industry dampens the positive horizontal spillovers found there and that large firms with a more educated workforce gain from the presence of foreign firms in their industry.

Bringing all of these findings together, we find that spillovers are not easily found, even in a multi-country study with a large number of firms. After searching systematically for various types of spillovers, we find they are gained by the larger firms that are more capable and that place themselves in the competitive side of the product market. However, the institutional/business environment features that we have analysed (bribing, hold-up in customs and red tape) do not systematically affect the strength of spillovers, suggesting that on average firms find ways to get around these problems.

NOTES

1. University of Michigan. We would like to thank Anne Harrison, Kamal Saggi and participants of the Association for Comparative Economic Studies (ACES) sessions at the 2006 and 2007 Allied Social Science Associations (ASSA) Meetings, and Libor Krkoska and participants of the Austrian National Bank 2006 Conference for their comments. Tomislav Ladika provided excellent research assistance. We are grateful to the European Bank for Reconstruction and Development for making this research possible through funding and making available the data for our analysis.
2. There is extensive literature on this, from the seminal work of Caves (1974) to more recent work of Haskel et al. (2002) and Sabirianova et al. (2005a).
3. Foreign firms can also have other spillover effects on domestic firms, such as wage spillovers, but we focus on total factor productivity.
4. In this chapter the term MNEs will refer to foreign owned multinationals, although we recognize that domestically owned firms can also be multinational in their production and sourcing.
5. Domestic firms may again learn to achieve this on their own or be trained directly by the foreign firm.
6. The reverse hypothesis – that spillovers increase with a larger technology gap – was put forth by Findlay (1978).
7. On the other hand, there are numerous case studies which provide specific examples of how MNEs provide training and assistance to their suppliers. See, for example, Moran (2001).
8. Blalock and Gertler (2005) point out that MNEs may establish a relationship with multiple suppliers to reduce dependency on a single supplier and that this will then benefit all firms that purchase these vendors' output. Consistent with this view, Lin and Saggi (2005) show theoretically how exclusivity in the contractual relationship between a multinational and its local supplier reduces the competition among local suppliers and can lower backward linkages and local welfare relative to autarky.
9. At the moment the analysis includes firm level data from: Albania, Bulgaria, Croatia, Czech Republic, Estonia, Hungary, Kazakhstan, Latvia, Lithuania, Poland, Romania,

Russia, Slovakia, Slovenia and Ukraine. We will potentially be able to provide results for all 26 transition economies once data limitations are overcome.

10. The information in the section draws heavily from Synovate (2005). (Synovate implemented the BEEPS instrument and provided the EBRD with electronic data sets.)

11. Turkmenistan did not allow the interviewers into its country for either the second or third rounds of the BEEPS survey.

12. Manufacturing includes mining and quarrying, construction, manufacturing and agroprocessing.

13. Services includes: Transportation, storage and communications; Wholesale, retail, repairs; Real estate, business services; Hotels and restaurants; Other community, social and personal activities; and Commerce.

14. Small=2–49 employees, Medium=50–249, Large=250–9999.

15. A total of 17 083 eligible enterprises were contacted, resulting in an interview completion rate of 37.7 per cent. Respondents who either refused outright (i.e. not interested) or who were unavailable to be interviewed (i.e. on holiday, etc.) accounted for 34.6 per cent of all contacts. Enterprises that were contacted but that were non-eligible (i.e. business activity, year of establishment, etc) whose quotas were already met (i.e. size, ownership, etc.) or to which 'blind calls' were made to meet quotas (i.e. foreign ownership, exporters, etc.) accounted for 27.7 per cent of the total number of eligible enterprises contacted.

16. One argument in the literature is that horizontal spillovers will be less likely if the wholly owned firms are better able than joint ventures to protect their proprietary assets. We do have data to test this hypothesis.

REFERENCES

Aghion, Philippe, Robin Burgess, Stephen Redding and Fabrizio Zilibotti (2005), 'Entry liberalization and inequality in industrial performance', *Journal of the European Economic Association*, **3** (2–3), 291–302.

Aitken, Brian J. and Ann E. Harrison (1999), 'Do domestic firms benefit from foreign direct investment? Evidence from Venezuela', *American Economic Review*, **89**, 605–18.

Blalock, Garrick and Paul J. Gertler (2002), 'Firm capabilities and technology adoption: Evidence from foreign direct investment in Indonesia', *Working paper Department of Applied Economics and Management*, Cornell University, Ithaca, NY.

Blalock, Garrick and Paul J. Gertler (2004), 'Welfare gains from foreign direct investment through technology transfer to local suppliers', *Working paper Department of Applied Economics and Management*, Cornell University, Ithaca, NY.

Blalock, Garrick and Paul J. Gertler (2005), 'Foreign direct investment and externalities: The case for public intervention', in T.H. Moran, E.M. Graham and M. Blomström (eds), *Does Foreign Direct Investment Promote Development?*, Washington, DC: Institute for International Economics, Center for Global Development.

Borensztein, E., J. De Gregorio and J-W. Lee (1998), 'How does foreign direct investment affect economic growth?', *Journal of International Economics*, **45**, 115–35.

Caves, Richard (1974), 'Multinational firms, competition and productivity in host-country markets', *Economica*, **41** (162), 176–93.

Findlay, Robert (1978), 'Relative backwardness, direct foreign investment and the transfer of technology: a simple dynamic model', *Quarterly Journal of Economics*, **92**, 1–16.

Girma, S., D. Greenaway and K. Wakelin (2001), 'Who benefits from foreign direct investment in the UK?', *Scottish Journal of Political Economy*, **48** (2), 119–33.

Gorodnichenko, Yuriy, Jan Svejnar and Katherine Terrell (2007), 'Horizontal and vertical spillovers in transition economies: do institutions matter?', University of Michigan, mimeo.

Griffith, Rachel, Stephen Redding and Helen Simpson (2002), 'Productivity convergence and foreign ownership at the establishment level', *CEPR Discussion Paper* No. 3765.

Haddad, M. and Ann E. Harrison (1993), 'Are there positive spillovers from foreign direct investment?', *Journal of Development Economics*, **42**, 51–74.

Haskel, Jonathan E., Sonia C. Pereira and Matthew J. Slaughter (2002), 'Does inward foreign direct investment boost the productivity of domestic firms?', *NBER Working Paper* No. 8724.

Haskel, Jonathan E., Sonia C. Pereira and Matthew J. Slaughter (2004), 'The composition of FDI and protection of intellectual property rights. Evidence from transition economies', *European Economic Review*, **48** (1), 39–62.

Javorcik, Beata Smarzynska (2005), 'Does foreign direct investment increase the productivity of domestic firms? In search of spillovers through backward linkages', *American Economic Review*, **97** (3), 605–27.

Javorcik, Beata Smarzynska, and Shang-Jin Wei (2002), 'Corruption and cross-border investment: firm-level evidence', WDI working paper No. 494.

Javorcik, Beata Smarzynska and Kamal Saggi (2004), 'Technological asymmetry and the mode of foreign investment', *World Bank Policy Research Working Paper* No. 3196, Washington: World Bank.

Javorcik, Beata Smarzynska, Kamal Saggi and Mariana Spatareanu (2004), 'Does it matter where you come from? Vertical spillovers from FDI and investor nationality', *World Bank Policy Research Working Paper* No. 3449, Washington: World Bank.

Kathuria, Vinish (2001), 'Productivity spillovers from technology transfer to Indian manufacturing firms', *Journal of International Development*, **12** (3), 343–69.

Keller, Wolfgang and Stephen R. Yeaple (2003), 'Multinational enterprises, international trade and productivity growth: firm level evidence from the US', *NBER Working Paper* No. 9504, February.

Kinoshita, Yuko (2000), 'R&D and technology spillovers through FDI: innovation and absorptive capacity', *CEPR Working Paper* No. 2775.

Kokko, Ari (1994), 'Technology, market characteristics, and spillovers', *Journal of Development Economics*, **43** (2), 279–93.

Konings, Jozef (2000), 'The effects of direct foreign investment on domestic firms: evidence from firm level panel data in emerging economies', *William Davidson Institute Working Paper* No. 344.

Kosova, Renata (2004), 'Do foreign firms crowd out domestic firms? Evidence from the Czech Republic', University of Michigan Business School, Ph.D. Dissertation.

Lall, Sanjay (1980), 'Vertical inter-firm linkages in LDCs: an empirical study', *Oxford Bulletin of Economics and Statistics*, **42**, 203–26.

Lin, Ping and Kamal Saggi (2005), 'Multinational firms, exclusivity and backward linkages', unpublished paper, Department of Economics, Lingnan University, Hong Kong.

Mansfield, Edwin and Anthony Romero (1980), 'Technology to overseas subsidiaries by US-based firms', *Quarterly Journal of Economics*, **95** (4), 737–50.

Melitz, Mark (2003), 'The impact of trade on intra-industry reallocations and aggregate industry productivity', *Econometrica*, **71** (6), 1695–725.

Moran, Theodore H. (2001), *Parental Supervision: The New Paradigm for Foreign Direct Investment and Development*, Policy Analyses in International Economics 64, Washington: Institute for International Economics.

Moran, Theodore H., Edward M. Graham and Magnus Blomström (2005), *Does Foreign Direct Investment Promote Development?*, Center for Global Development, Washington, DC: Institute for International Economics.

Ramachandran, Vijaya (1993), 'Technology transfer firm ownership and investment in human capital', *Review of Economics and Statistics*, **75** (4), 664–70.

Rosenbaum, Paul R. (2002), *Observational Studies*, New York: Springer-Verlag.

Sabirianova, Klara, Jan Svejnar and Katherine Terrell (2005a), 'Foreign investment, corporate ownership and development: are firms in emerging markets catching up to the world standard?', *IZA and CEPR Discussion Paper*.

Sabirianova, Klara, Jan Svejnar and Katherine Terrell (2005b), 'Distance to the efficiency frontier and FDI spillovers', *Journal of the European Economic Association*, **3** (2–3), 576–86.

Schoors, Koen and Bartoldus van der Tol (2001), 'The productivity effect of foreign ownership on domestic firms in Hungary', presented at the EAE Conference in Philadelphia, PA, 11–14 October, 2001.

Sembenelli, Alessandro and George Siotis (2002), 'Foreign direct investment, competitive pressure and spillovers: an empirical analysis of Spanish firm level data', Centro Studi Luca D'Agliano Development Studies working paper No. 169.

Sjoholm, Fredrik (1999), 'Technology gap, competition and spillovers from foreign direct investment: evidence from establishment data', *Journal of Development Studies*, **36** (1), 53–73.

Synovate (2005), *The Business Environment and Enterprise Performance Survey (BEEPS) 2005: A brief report on observations, experiences and methodology from the survey*, Report prepared for the EBRD.

Takii, Sadayukii (2001), 'Productivity spillovers and characteristics of foreign multinational plants in Indonesian manufacturing 1990–95', ICSEAD Working Paper 2001–14, Kitakyushu, Japan: ICSEAD.

Yudaeva, Ksenia, Konstantin Kozlov, Natalia Melentieva and Natalia Ponomareva (2003), 'Does foreign ownership matter? The Russian experience', *The Economics of Transition*, **2**, 383–410.

3. The role of FDI in Eastern Europe and New Independent States: new channels for the spillover effect

Irina Tytell and Ksenia Yudaeva[1]

Foreign direct investment (FDI) is widely considered an important catalyst of economic development. Economists and policy makers believe that FDI can improve host countries' technological capacities and managerial style, both at companies receiving FDI (through direct effects) and at companies working in the same industry (through indirect spillover effects) or in upstream industries (through backward linkages). In order to strengthen these effects, governments of many developing and transition economies introduce special policies aimed at attracting FDI and/or enhancing spillovers and backward linkages. In particular, FDI regulation was a key issue in many recently negotiated preferential trade agreements and bilateral trade agreements.

Yet especially for spillover effects, this political enthusiasm is not based on rigorous economic theory and evidence. For the direct effect of FDI on productivity, the rationale is that FDI will only occur if investors have an advantage over local firms because of superior technological knowledge, better managerial techniques, distributional networks or the like. As a result, recipients of FDI should usually be more productive than domestic firms. This prediction is indeed supported by virtually all empirical studies conducted for both developing and developed countries.[2] In contrast, empirical findings on the spillover effect are mixed,[3] depending on given data samples and econometric techniques. For example, in the case of transition countries, Yudaeva et al. (2003) find positive spillover effects for Russian firms, as do Javorcik and Spatareanu (2005) and Damijan et al. (2003) for Romania. However, Djankov and Hoekman (2000), Konings (2001), Javorcik and Spatareanu (2005) and Damijan et al. (2003) observe negative effects for some other Eastern European countries. Recently, the literature started to look into less conventional channels for spillovers, such as inter-industry spillovers. In such cases the evidence obtained looks more consistent with the hypothesis of positive spillovers.

In this chapter we explore new channels of intra-industry spillovers in transition countries and appear to find spillover effects from foreign-owned firms on the production function of domestic firms. The chapter also gives special attention to the effect of institutions and education on spillovers.

For our analysis we chose Russia, Ukraine, Poland and Romania – the four largest and most populous countries of Eastern Europe, which at the same time represent a wide spectrum in terms of macroeconomic performance and institutional development. Poland, currently the richest of the four, has by far the highest unemployment rate and the lowest inflation rate. The Polish private sector has the best access to domestic credit, and the Polish government scores best in terms of general effectiveness and rule of law. Poland also has the lowest corruption levels, but the cost of starting a business and enforcing contracts is fairly high. Among the four countries, starting a business is cheapest in Romania, but enforcing contracts is costly, and Romania's private sector faces the highest domestic credit constraints. Moreover, the Romanian labour market is fairly inflexible, especially on the hiring side, and highly educated workers are in relatively short supply. Ukraine, also the poorest of the four countries, has the least flexible labour market on the firing side and ranks lowest on government effectiveness and the rule of law, while the cost of starting a business is high and corruption is widespread. At the same time, the cost of enforcing contracts is relatively moderate in Ukraine – as it is in Russia, where the cost of starting a business is not too high and the labour market is quite flexible. The Russian stock market, notably, is the most developed among the four countries. Yet Russia ranks very low in terms of rule of law, where it is on a par with Ukraine. Its corruption level is on a par with Romania, and in between Poland and Ukraine. Russia and Ukraine are also much less open to trade and foreign investment than Poland and Romania.

We use firm-level data for manufacturing companies in these countries for several recent years (1999–2003 for Poland and Romania, 1998–2002 for Russia, and 2000–2003 for Ukraine). Our data come from two sources: the national statistical authorities for Russia and Ukraine, and from the Amadeus database of Bureau van Dijk for Poland and Romania. The data for Russia and Ukraine cover large- and medium-sized industrial enterprises, while the data for Poland and Romania also include some smaller manufacturing firms.[4] Companies with foreign ownership are defined here as firms with at least 10 per cent owned by external entities, excluding those registered in popular off-shore destinations. This correction is important in our view, as the latter are likely to be domestic companies and should therefore be regarded as a potential destination, rather than a source of spillovers. In the case of Ukraine we also excluded companies owned by

Russians or representatives of other New Independent States (NIS). Data are based on the NACE industrial classification of economic activities for Poland, Romania and Ukraine. We use information about activities of Russian firms to construct a correspondence matrix between OKONH and NACE classifications, and employ NACE classification in the regression analysis for all countries in the sample.

PRODUCTIVITY EFFECTS OF FDI: STATIC SPECIFICATION

We begin by estimating a Cobb-Douglas production function for each country, including a dummy variable for firms with foreign participation. We allow the factor shares to vary between domestic enterprises and those with foreign ownership. This simple specification allows us to compare productivities and factor intensities of domestic firms and those with foreign capital. Our results show that recipients of FDI are significantly more productive than domestic firms. The size of the coefficient on FDI dummy is largest for Russia and smallest for Poland.[5]

FDI recipients are also somewhat less labour intensive and somewhat more capital intensive than domestic companies. The differences are particularly striking for Russian FDI recipients, whose labour intensity is 42 percentage points lower and whose capital intensity is 27 percentage points higher than for domestic firms. In Poland and Romania, in contrast, the difference does not exceed 7 percentage points for labour intensity and is between 4 and 5 percentage points for capital intensity.

In order to study the potential spillover effects of firms with foreign participation on domestic companies, we constructed an FDI DENSITY measure reflecting the weighted labour employed in firms with foreign capital, relative to the total labour employed in a given year, sector and region. This is a measure of foreign presence that is standard in this literature. It allows us to study horizontal spillovers, that is spillovers to enterprises within the same industry. Since we use two-digit industries to define sectors, this measure also captures some vertical spillovers, that is spillovers to enterprises in upstream industries. In addition, it reflects the likely local nature of spillovers in countries with not yet fully developed business communication networks.

Following the literature, we included our proxy for spillovers into a Cobb-Douglas production function. In the fixed-effects specification the coefficient on FDI DENSITY is positive but statistically insignificant for all four countries except Russia, where it is negative and insignificant. This result suggests that, generally, there is no evidence for spillover effects from

FDI on the productivity of domestic firms. This finding is in agreement with most of the recent empirical literature on FDI spillovers.

As already mentioned, the recent literature started to pay more attention to heterogeneity of FDI and, in particular, to potential differences in spillovers on domestic firms from export-oriented FDI and FDI aimed at supplying domestic markets (Moran, 2005; Melitz, 2005). We tested this hypothesis for Russia, the only country for which we have the necessary data. Using a dataset on international trade transactions, we identified those foreign firms that exported more than 50 per cent of their output. We computed a measure of EXPORT-ORIENTED FDI DENSITY as a share of such firms in the total employment in each year, sector and region, weighted by the size of the foreign stake. The coefficient on EXPORT-ORIENTED FDI DENSITY turned out to be positive and significant in the fixed-effects specification, while that on FDI DENSITY became negative and statistically insignificant. This result supports the idea that the positive spillover effect on productivity originates from export-oriented FDI, if at all.

In the third specification we allow production functions to be different across sectors and to be influenced by FDI DENSITY. After all, it is reasonable to expect that if a foreign presence has any effect on domestic firms, it is unlikely to be limited to productivity. Rather, technological spillovers should affect the production function of domestic firms and factor intensities in particular. If domestic firms become more technologically sophisticated as a result of their contact with foreigners, their production processes are likely to become more capital intensive and less labour intensive. This is, indeed, the case in Poland where, in sectors with 10 per cent local foreign ownership, the capital intensity of domestic firms is over 2 percentage points higher and labour intensity is over 3.5 percentage points lower than elsewhere. In Romania the difference in intensities is not statistically significant, but domestic firms appear somewhat less labour intensive when the density of foreign firms is higher. For Ukraine we do not have data on capital, but the labour intensity of domestic firms also appears to be smaller in sectors and regions with substantial foreign presence, although the difference is not significant. Surprisingly, the results for Russia are absolutely different: domestic firms are more labour intensive and less capital intensive in sectors that attract a lot of FDI.[6]

Our findings on the production function effects in Russia and Poland may reflect backward linkages between domestic and foreign firms. There is anecdotal evidence suggesting that if foreign firms work with Russian suppliers, the latter tend to provide technologically simple and often labour intensive goods. Ford, for example, assembles cars in Russia using imported components, with the exception of a few components made of rubber.

Poland, on the other hand, has a longer history of FDI inflows, giving domestic producers of the same goods time to upgrade their technologies to more capital intensive processes. Additionally, foreign investors in Poland may have become more familiar with local producers and may, therefore, trust them with production of some capital intensive components. An alternative and complementary explanation of our findings is that competition from foreign firms forces domestic firms to adjust in ways that depend on the situation in their particular country. Thus, while Polish firms upgrade their capital and technologies in order to compete in the same market with foreign entrants, Russian firms shield themselves from foreign competition by concentrating on producing unsophisticated, labour intensive goods for the less well-off segments of the population.

THE ROLE OF EDUCATION AND INSTITUTIONS IN THE TRANSMISSION OF SPILLOVERS

External factors such as the endowment of skills, measured by the education level in the host country, and the quality of the host country's institutions, can influence both the choice of technologies used by foreign investors and the capacity and incentives of domestic firms to learn from their foreign competitors. In this section we look at the effects of education and corruption on productivity of foreign firms and on the spillovers that they impart on domestic firms.

We use this regional variation to study how local educational levels influence the domestic impact of foreign firms. Our results on spillover effects show that both productivity and production spillovers, as observed in previous specifications, are pronounced only in regions with a high education level. The direction of the spillover effect may differ, though: among firms located in high-education regions, Russian firms are more labour intensive, and Polish firms more capital intensive than other domestic firms. These results suggest that education, which can be regarded as a proxy for absorptive capacity, is the major pre-condition for spillover effects on productivity or on production functions.

In the case of Russia we are able to control for the effect of corruption on FDI productivity and spillovers. We use a measure of the perception of corruption, recently reported by INDEM, a Russian anti-corruption think tank. This measure is available for 40 Russian regions, and reflects the results of a survey of households and businesses in these regions. Consistently with the findings of Yudaeva et al. (2003), foreign firms are more productive than domestic ones in regions with low corruption. In the high-corruption regions there are no differences in productivity between domestic and foreign firms. FDI DENSITY is insignificant in high-corruption regions, and negative and significant in low-corruption regions. Foreign firms in the regions with low corruption are more than twice as productive as domestic firms. Such a large productivity difference could result in crowding out local domestic firms. The overall effect on welfare can still be positive, because foreign-owned firms are so much more productive than domestic ones. There also seems to be a difference between low- and high-corruption regions in the effect of FDI DENSITY on the production function of domestic firms. The coefficient on the cross term between the log of labour and FDI DENSITY is positive and significant only in low-corruption regions, while in high-corruption regions this coefficient is positive but insignificant. Therefore domestic firms react to foreign entry by switching to more labour intensive technologies only if the corruption level is low. This may be an adjustment that Russian firms make in order to compete with highly productive foreign-owned firms. By switching to more labour intensive technologies and producing goods of low quality but at cheaper costs, domestic firms find their niche as producers for less well-off consumers. Additionally, some domestic firms may become suppliers for foreign-owned firms, and, as we argued before, foreign firms may tend to buy supplies more readily from labour intensive firms. The lack of any effects in the high-corruption regions is consistent with the following inter-pretation. Domestic firms in these regions use their connections with the local authorities to put administrative pressure on foreign-owned firms, which reduces their effectiveness. This practice reduces the competitive pressure from foreign-owned firms, which, in turn, reduces the incentives of domestic firms to adopt new technologies.

PRODUCTIVITY EFFECTS OF FDI: DYNAMIC SPECIFICATION

We now go beyond the static specification to analyse whether and how foreign presence affects the change in, rather than merely the level of, pro-ductivity of domestic firms. The dynamic panel estimation that we use allows us to control for potential endogeneity of FDI DENSITY by instrumenting it using past values. The dynamic specification allows us to include, in addition to the density of foreign firms, a measure of their productivity.

We measure total factor productivity (TFP) of individual firms as a residual from a fixed-effects estimation of the Cobb-Douglas production function, with factor shares that are allowed to vary by industrial sector. [7] We then aggregate our measure to obtain the TFP average of firms with foreign ownership in each sector and region in a given year (FDI TFP). We study dynamic effects of FDI TFP and FDI DENSITY using the following specification:

$$TFP_{i,t+1} = \alpha TFP_{i,t} + \beta FDI\ TFP_{t,s,r} + \gamma FDI\ DENSITY_{t,s,r} + \varepsilon_{i,t}$$

We estimate this equation only for domestic companies using the GMM[8] method of Blundell and Bond (1998). Regression results show that the productivity of foreign firms is indeed positively associated with the productivity of domestic firms in the same sector and region in the following year. The coefficient on FDI TFP is positive for all four countries and statistically significant for Russia and Romania. In other words, the productivity of domestic firms tends to grow in regions where firms with FDI are more productive. This finding is in contrast with the effect of mere foreign presence: the coefficient on FDI DENSITY is negative in three out of four countries and statistically significant in Romania. Thus it appears that foreign entry slows the productivity growth of domestic firms, possibly because they lose market share yielding to increased competition.

We argued above that effects of foreign presence may change as foreign capital accumulates. Namely, foreign firms may initially focus on labour intensive activities in order to benefit from low labour costs in the host countries, but shift to more advanced technologies as their weight and experience in the area grows. They may also be unwilling initially to outsource high technology jobs to local producers, but as they invest more in their relationship with domestic firms, they may trust the locals with producing more sophisticated components. We incorporate this potential threshold effect into our analysis by adding a variable that equals FDI DENSITY if the latter exceeds 50 per cent, and zero otherwise. Our results show that the coefficients on FDI DENSITY and FDI DENSITY over 50 per cent are of different signs in three out of four countries. Both are statistically significant in Romania, where the productivity-reducing effect of foreign presence is much smaller in sectors and regions dominated by foreign firms (-0.366 as compared to -1.052). This is consistent with our notion of threshold effect, although the spillover effect in FDI-abundant sectors and regions is still negative. It is possible that it takes not only a large foreign presence, but also a longer period to see any positive spillover effect; unfortunately our panel is too short to tell. Interestingly, the signs on FDI DENSITY and FDI DENSITY over 50 per cent are reversed in Russia, although both are statistically insignificant.

Our results from static specifications suggest that the effect of foreign entry may manifest itself in the change of the production function of domestic firms, rather than simply in higher total factor productivity. To examine this issue in a dynamic setting, we look at the effects that foreign presence and foreign productivity have on the capital–labour ratio of domestic firms:

$$Log(K/L)_{i,t+1} = \alpha Log(K/L)_{i,t} + \beta FDI\ TFP_{t,s,r}$$
$$+ \gamma FDI\ DENSITY_{t,s,r} + \varepsilon_{i,t}$$

The outcome of our estimations is as follows. For Poland and Romania, higher productivity of foreign companies is associated with higher capital–labour ratios of domestic firms in the same sector and region in the following year. This is consistent with the idea that more productive foreign firms generate more pronounced positive effects on domestic firms. A higher density of foreign companies, however, is associated with lower capital–labour ratios in the following year in both countries. This is consistent with the notion that foreign entry, rather than driving technology transfer, forces domestic firms to compete by focusing on cheaper, low technology goods for the less well-off segments of the domestic population. This finding does not necessarily contradict the results we obtained above using a static specification. Since in the dynamic regressions we control for the productivity of foreign firms, our measure of their density is largely divorced from their efficiency. While highly efficient foreign entrants are a possible source of knowledge spillovers, the sheer number of foreign firms is most likely to affect domestic producers through increased competition. An alternative explanation would suggest that our static results reflect reverse causation. In other words, foreign companies in Poland and Romania are attracted to more capital intensive segments of these economies, but once established, they drive domestic firms into more labour intensive activities. In Russia, neither FDI TFP, nor FDI DENSITY is significantly associated with the change in productivity of domestic firms. Ukraine is excluded from these estimations due to the lack of data on capital.

CONCLUSIONS

The literature on FDI and their effects on domestic firms usually concentrates on productivity differences between firms with foreign ownership and domestic firms, and on resulting productivity spillovers. At the same time, theoretical considerations used to justify empirical analyses usually state that firms with foreign ownership should possess different technologies and that their entry should prompt domestic firms to upgrade technologically. Therefore, the theory may be re-interpreted as suggesting that firms with foreign ownership have different production functions than domestic firms and that FDI stimulates production function change by domestic firms. In addition, more productive foreign firms with superior technologies should have a larger impact on both the productivity of domestic firms and their production function.

Based on evidence from four transition countries – Russia, Ukraine, Poland and Romania – this chapter confirms this new interpretation of the theory. In the more developed countries with better institutions and larger FDI inflows (Poland and Romania), foreign presence is associated with higher capital intensity and lower labour intensity of domestic firms. The absorptive capacity of domestic firms is also important: the evidence of the production function change toward more capital intensive technologies is strongest in areas where the labour force is more educated.

In contrast, in the countries with worse institutions and correspondingly smaller FDI inflows (Russia[9]), foreign presence is associated with lower capital intensity and higher labour intensity of domestic firms. The shift to more labour intensive technologies happens primarily where foreign capital is more abundant. Domestic firms may choose this adaptation in order to secure a separate market for themselves by specializing in serving relatively poor segments of the population. This effect may also reflect a reluctance of foreign firms to outsource anything but the production of simple, labour intensive components to domestic suppliers. The reason for such reluctance may be a lack of confidence in the quality of domestically produced goods and the ability of local firms to deliver on time. The production function effect is observed only in the relatively more educated and the less corrupt regions. In highly corrupt regions, foreign firms do not exhibit any productivity advantage over domestic firms, possibly as a result of the attitude of local authorities, which in turn is lobbied for by domestic producers.

As far as conventional productivity spillovers are concerned, we failed to find evidence of their presence, except in a few special cases. In Romania, foreign presence leads to lower productivity of domestic firms after one year, but this effect is present only in low education regions and appears to wear out as more foreign capital is accumulated. In Ukraine, foreign presence is associated contemporaneously with higher output of domestic firms in high education regions. In Russia, negative spillovers occur in the less corrupt regions, where foreign firms are more than twice as productive as domestic firms. Also, importantly, export-oriented foreign firms in Russia generate positive spillovers on domestic firms. Since such foreign firms bring cutting-edge technologies to host countries, the scope for knowledge spillovers is higher for those domestic firms that compete with or work as suppliers for export-oriented foreigners. More generally, own productivity of foreign firms matters: domestic companies show higher next-year productivity, as well as larger next-year capital–labour ratios, where foreign entrants are more productive.

NOTES

1. The authors thank Sergei Golovan for outstanding research assistance. Financial support for this project and access to the Amadeus database was provided by the EBRD. The views expressed in this chapter are those of the authors and not necessarily those of the EBRD or of other institutions with which the authors are affiliated. A more detailed description of the results is available on www.cefir.ru. Irina Tytell (International Monetary Fund) was a visitor at the Centre for Economic and Financial Research (CEFIR at NES) while parts of this chapter were written. Ksenia Yudaeva is Director of Research at the Centre for Strategic Research (Moscow, Russia). She started writing the paper while Director for Policy Studies at the Centre for Economic and Financial Research (CEFIR at NES), and Scholar in Residence, Carnegie Moscow Centre.
2. The survey of the literature is provided by Lipsey (2004), Lipsey and Sjöholm (2005).
3. A detailed survey of the spillover literature can be found in Lipsey and Sjöholm (2002) and Blomström and Kokko (1998, 2003).
4. For Poland and Romania, we used the data for Amadeus top 1.5 million firms, which include firms that satisfy at least one of the following size criteria: operating revenue equal to at least EUR 1 million, total assets equal to at least EUR 2 million, number of employees equal to at least 15.
5. Tables with regression results are omitted from this version of the chapter. They can be found in a long version, available at www.cefir.ru.
6. We cannot, at this stage, fully exclude the possibility of reverse causality, i.e. that foreign companies are attracted to more capital intensive and less labour intensive parts of the domestic economy in Poland, and to less capital intensive and more labour intensive parts of the domestic economy in Russia. We return to this issue at a later stage in the chapter.
7. We experimented with an alternative measure of TFP based on stochastic frontier estimation, again with factor shares that vary by sector. Effectively, the stochastic frontier approach allows for firm fixed effects with industry-specific estimated growth trends. However, we encountered convergence problems when running these estimations on Russian and Ukrainian data. For Poland and Romania, the two measures were very highly correlated, suggesting that the fixed-effects approach is sufficiently accurate.
8. GMM = generalized method of moments.
9. The absence of data on capital in the Ukraine makes the analysis of production functions there problematic.

REFERENCES

Blomström, Magnus and Ari Kokko (1998), 'Multinational corporations and spillovers', *Journal of Economic Surveys*, **12** (2), 1–31.
Blomström, Magnus and Ari Kokko (2003), 'The economics of foreign direct investment incentives', *NBER Working Paper* 9489, Cambridge, MA: National Bureau of Economic Research.
Blundell, Richard and Stephen R. Bond (1998), 'Initial conditions and moment restrictions in dynamic panel data models', *Journal of Econometrics*, **87**, 115–43.
Damijan, Jose P., Mark Knell, Boris Majcen and Matija Rojec (2003), 'The role of FDI, R&D accumulation and trade in transferring technology to transition

countries: Evidence from firm panel data for eight transition countries', *Economic Systems*, **27**, 189–204.

Djankov, S. and B. Hoekman (2000), 'Foreign investment and productivity growth in Czech enterprises', *World Bank Economic Review*, **14** (1), 49–64.

Javorcik, Beata Smarzynska and Mariana Spatareanu (2005), 'Disentangling FDI spillover effects: What do firm perceptions tell us?', in Theodore H. Moran, Edward M. Graham and Magnus Blomström (eds), *Does Foreign Direct Investment Promote Development?*, Washington, DC: Institute for International Economics.

Konings, J. (2001), 'The effect of direct foreign investment on domestic firms', *Economics of Transition*, **9** (3), 619–33.

Lipsey, Robert E. (2004), 'Home- and host-country effects of foreign direct investment', in Robert E. Baldwin and L. Alan Winters (eds), *Challenges to Globalization*, Chicago: University of Chicago Press.

Lipsey, Robert E. and Fredrik Sjöholm (2002), 'Foreign firms and Indonesian manufacturing wages: an analysis with panel data', NBER Working Paper 9417, Cambridge, MA: National Bureau of Economic Research.

Lipsey, Robert E. and Fredrik Sjöholm (2005), 'The impact of inward FDI on host countries: Why such different answers', in Theodore H. Moran, Edward M. Graham and Magnus Blomström (eds), *Does Foreign Direct Investment Promote Development?*, Washington, DC: Institute for International Economics.

Melitz, Mark J. (2005), 'Comment', in Theodore H. Moran, Edward M. Graham and Magnus Blomström (eds), *Does Foreign Direct Investment Promote Development?*, Washington, DC: Institute for International Economics.

Moran, Theodore H. (2005), 'How does FDI affect host country development? Using industry case studies to make reliable generalizations', in Theodore H. Moran, Edward M. Graham and Magnus Blomström (eds), *Does Foreign Direct Investment Promote Development?*, Washington, DC: Institute for International Economics.

Yudaeva, Ksenia, Konstantin Kozlov, Natalia Melentieva and Natalia Ponomaryova (2003), 'Does foreign ownership matter? Russian experience', *Economics of Transition*, **11** (3).

4. Blessing or curse? An industry-level analysis of FDI effects on productivity and wages in CEECs

Jesús Crespo Cuaresma, Carmen Fillat Castejón, Maria Antoinette Silgoner and Julia Woerz[1]

Despite the abundance of research on the host country effects of FDI, the empirical literature on the topic remains ambiguous. There are a large number of studies working with economy-wide data on FDI, which mostly find positive productivity spillover effects from FDI on the host economy (Blomström et al., 1996; Blonigen and Wang, 2005; Borensztein et al., 1998). There are, however, also examples for negative effects on productivity (Akinlo, 2004) or no spillovers (Carkovic and Levine, 2005). Most of the above studies stress the importance of host country heterogeneity, and many authors explicitly take into account differences in the stage of development between home and host country.[2] More recently the macroeconomic evidence has been supplemented by firm-level studies, again with inconclusive results.

The effect of FDI on productivity growth is one of the elements determining wage developments in FDI host countries and thus also the convergence process of income levels. Most empirical studies on the link between FDI and wage growth use firm-level data and focus on single or a small number of countries.[3] The general finding is that foreign-owned firms pay higher wages than domestic firms, even at comparable qualification levels. The evidence on wage spillovers from foreign to domestic firms is, however, far less conclusive.

In this chapter we study the effects of FDI on productivity developments in host countries at the industrial level. We postulate that the effects of FDI – after controlling for host country heterogeneity as has been done in the existing literature – will further depend on the specific industry that receives FDI. We then investigate the link between FDI and wage growth for a set of CEECs, explicitly distinguishing between that part of wage growth that is directly related to productivity developments and the wage mark-up, defined as the part of wage growth that exceeds or falls short of productivity growth.

1. DATA SET

The data set contains observations for 28 to 35 countries,[4] six industries (food; textiles, wood and paper; petroleum, chemicals, rubber and plastics; metals and mechanical machinery; electrical machinery; transport equipment) and 14 years (1987–2000) for the following indicators: output, employment, gross fixed capital formation, inward FDI stock data, exports, imports and wages. Later on in this chapter we will use more recent data for CEECs only (1998–2002) to look at the specific effects of FDI in this region. We combined data from several sources (UNIDO, UN COMTRADE, OECD, wiiw, ASEAN Secretariat). Woerz (2005) gives a detailed description of the dataset.

The ratio of inward FDI stock to output varies across industries, years and countries. For the complete sample, the FDI-to-output ratio ranges from far below 1 per cent in the textiles and wood industry in Japan to more than 100 per cent in the industry group comprising fuel, rubber, plastics and chemicals in Indonesia. Over time, the FDI-to-output ratio has risen on average, but even more so in variance, reflecting the increasing internationalization of production at different rates for all countries and industries. While Asian countries on average show higher shares of FDI in total industry output, they also exhibit more variation across individual countries than OECD members.

Entering the picture at a much later point in time, Central and Eastern European Countries (CEECs) show again substantially higher FDI-to-output ratios, yet with considerably less variation across countries. Thus, this region experienced a uniformly high inflow of foreign capital into manufacturing due to a general lack of domestic capital and the disruption of state-owned companies, with many inefficient firms exiting the market.

Table 4.1 illustrates the regional and industrial heterogeneity through the weighted averages of inward FDI stocks to output ratios for different country groups towards the end of the studied period. The highest FDI to output ratio is in general found in the petroleum, chemical, rubber and plastic industry. CEECs are the only region with the highest FDI-to-output ratio in the transport industry. Apart from the general strong role of FDI in petroleum, chemicals, rubber and plastics, all regions differ with respect to the importance of FDI in individual industries. Thus, the data support our argument about the two sources of heterogeneity in the relationship between FDI and output or productivity.

While FDI and output patterns do not show a high correlation in OECD members and in Emerging Asia, the four Asian Tiger economies and CEECs exhibit closely matching FDI and output structures. In the case of the four Tiger countries, where the observation period extends over 20 years, the sequencing of industry patterns suggests that high FDI shares in electrical machinery have resulted in subsequently high output shares in the industry.

Table 4.1 FDI-output ratios, 1998–2000

	Advanced OECD	Catch-up OECD	4 Tigers	Emerging Asia	CEEC
Food	4.6	10.5	7.1	2.9	13.7
Textiles/Wood	7.4	7.7	4.6	11.8	12.2
Petrol/Chemicals	15.7	16.3	16.1	30.4	15.4
Metals/Mechanicals	5.7	13.3	4.5	9.0	9.1
Electrical machinery	6.6	8.3	12.4	11.1	13.7
Transport equipment	3.6	9.5	4.6	6.7	18.6

Source: Woerz (2005).

For the CEECs, the time period is too short for any conclusions. However, the distribution of FDI across industries is distinct from the distribution found for other country groups, like OECD and Asia. CEECs show a higher share of FDI in the food industry, but also in the transport industry.

2. FDI AND PRODUCTIVITY GROWTH

Our empirical specification for testing the relationship between FDI and productivity growth, accounting for different forms of heterogeneity, is similar to the specification used in Nair-Reichert and Weinhold (2001) but extended to include industry-specific FDI. We assume that total factor productivity of country c in industry i and time t, A_{cit}, is determined by previous investment in physical capital in each sector as given in equation (4.1):

$$A_{cit} = f(DI_{cit-1}, FDI_{cit-1}) = DI_{cit-1}^{\phi} FDI_{cit-1}^{\theta} \tag{4.1}$$

where *DI* stands for domestic investment and *FDI* stands for foreign direct investment. We use equation (4.1) in a standard Cobb-Douglas production function, with time-varying endowments of capital and labour, after having taken logs and first differences yielding equation (4.2):

$$\Delta y_{cit} = \phi \Delta di_{cit-1} + \theta \Delta fdi_{cit-1} + \alpha \Delta k_{ct} \tag{4.2}$$

where Δy_{cit} is the growth of industry i's output per employee in country c and time t. Hence, the growth rate of output per employee is a function of previous growth of investment (both domestic and foreign) in the respective industry and country, and of changes in the country's capital-to-labour ratio k. We will capture these changes in capital-to-labour ratio by country-specific time-varying effects.[5] Consequently, the following econometric model is to be estimated over our sample of countries, industries and years:

$$\Delta y_{cit} = \alpha + \beta_{1i}\Delta fdi_{cit-1} + \beta_{2i}\Delta di_{cit-1} + \beta_{3i}\Delta ex_{cit-1} + \mu_i + \gamma_{ct} + \varepsilon_{cit} \quad (4.3)$$

where μ_i are industry-specific effects, γ_{ct} are country-specific time trends and ε_{cit} is the basic error component. Δy_{cit} refers to growth of output per employee in the respective country, industry, and time period. Δfdi and Δdi are the growth rates of foreign and domestic capital used in production respectively.[6] The growth of the export share in output Δex controls for outward orientation through trade. FDI is hardly ever observed in isolation (especially in the manufacturing sector) but always in combination with a certain openness of the industry to international competition. All right-hand side variables are lagged by one time period to avoid a simultaneity bias between output growth and the explanatory variables in the results. Endogeneity between FDI and productivity growth is an important aspect which is often mentioned and confirmed in the literature (for example Bellak, 2004). In the above specification, we control explicitly for industry- and country-specific effects. Thus, the specific modelling of the error term in the panel is a first step to control for both types of heterogeneity – across countries and across industries simultaneously.

The results, reported in the first column of Table 4.2, show no significant effect from FDI in any industry. In the second specification, we interact FDI with the domestic investment share of the receiving industry. The effect of foreign capital may depend on the existing amount of investment, that is a certain amount of investment in an industry is necessary for absorbing the external effects of FDI. Also, this interaction reflects the need of structural matching between foreign and domestic investment. The results from column 2 in Table 4.2 indicate that FDI leads to increased productivity growth only in the presence of high overall investment shares in labour- and resource-intensive industries. Industries like food processing, textiles and woods, and petroleum, chemicals, rubber and plastics show negative direct effects but positive marginal effects in combination with a sufficient level of investment in the host country.

3.   ARE CEECs DIFFERENT?

Like few other countries, CEECs have experienced a rapid transformation of their output and trade patterns over the past decade, and FDI has played a decisive role in this transformation process. FDI inflows in these countries

Table 4.2   GLS estimation for productivity effects, total sample

Variable	Industry	(1)		(2)	
		Coeff.	t-stat	Coeff.	t-stat
Δfdi	Food	−0.0050	*(−0.74)*	−0.2333***	*(−11.56)*
	Textiles/Wood	−0.0066	*(−1.12)*	−0.1455***	*(−12.24)*
	Petrol/Chemicals	0.0025	*(0.70)*	−0.0956***	*(−6.00)*
	Metals/Mechanicals	−0.0006	*(−0.20)*	−0.0178	*(−0.85)*
	Electrical machinery	−0.0005	*(−0.10)*	0.0212	*(1.17)*
	Transport equipment	1.99E-08	*(0.09)*	0.0146	*(1.47)*
Δdi	Food	−0.0008	*(−0.10)*	−0.2698***	*(−11.34)*
	Textiles/Wood	1.7166***	*(14.69)*	1.0016***	*(8.94)*
	Petrol/Chemicals	0.6251***	*(5.39)*	0.2270**	*(1.96)*
	Metals/Mechanicals	−0.1010**	*(−2.37)*	−0.2165**	*(−1.72)*
	Electrical machinery	−0.0981	*(−1.28)*	−0.0800	*(−1.11)*
	Transport equipment	−0.0131	*(−0.52)*	−0.0601	*(−1.59)*
Δex	Food	2.4770***	*(141.47)*	1.9097***	*(38.04)*
	Textiles/Wood	1.2470***	*(12.89)*	0.6314***	*(6.65)*
	Petrol/Chemicals	0.3142***	*(3.70)*	0.2184***	*(2.86)*
	Metals/Mechanicals	0.0963	*(0.88)*	0.0669	*(0.69)*
	Electrical machinery	−0.0306	*(−0.28)*	−0.0408	*(−0.44)*
	Transport equipment	−0.0157	*(−0.36)*	−0.0133	*(−0.35)*
$\Delta fdi*di$	Food			4.9062***	*(11.81)*
	Textiles/Wood			3.8318***	*(14.98)*
	Petrol/Chemicals			1.9430***	*(6.26)*
	Metals/Mechanicals			0.4185	*(0.81)*
	Electrical machinery			−0.2997	*(−1.25)*
	Transport equipment			−0.2933	*(−1.47)*
CONST		0.2616*	*(1.80)*	0.2901**	*(2.41)*
Observations		1138		1138	
Adjusted R-squared		96.15		97.28	

Notes:
GLS Random effects model; country-trend and industry dummies are included, but not reported here.
*, **, *** indicates significance at the 10%, 5%, 1% significance level, respectively.
t-statistics computed with robust standard errors in parenthesis.

Source: Own calculations.

Table 4.3   Results for CEECs

Variable	Industry	(1)		(2)	
		Coeff.	t-stat	Coeff.	t-stat
Δfdi	Food	−0.1924	*(−0.94)*	−0.1859	*(−0.86)*
	Textiles/Wood	−0.0250	*(−0.12)*	−0.0919	*(−0.18)*
	Petrol/Chemicals	0.2150	*(1.02)*	0.2814	*(0.98)*
	Metals/Mechanicals	−0.0257	*(−0.17)*	0.0488	*(0.29)*
	Electrical machinery	0.0274	*(0.12)*	0.1154	*(0.45)*
	Transport equipment	0.0155	*(0.08)*	0.3609	*(0.35)*
Δdi	Food	−0.2200	*(−0.65)*	−0.5524	*(−1.39)*
	Textiles/Wood	0.2052	*(0.73)*	0.0430	*(0.10)*
	Petrol/Chemicals	0.0831	*(0.49)*	−0.1942	*(−0.56)*
	Metals/Mechanicals	−0.0890	*(−0.85)*	−0.0472	*(−0.22)*
	Electrical machinery	0.6359**	*(2.35)*	−0.5876	*(−1.06)*
	Transport equipment	0.2297	*(1.46)*	0.1820	*(0.55)*
Δex	Food	0.1703	*(0.24)*	−0.6158	*(−0.63)*
	Textiles/Wood	−0.0734	*(−0.11)*	−0.2419	*(−0.32)*
	Petrol/Chemicals	1.0602***	*(3.73)*	0.9970***	*(3.04)*
	Metals/Mechanicals	0.4517	*(1.50)*	0.3919	*(1.11)*
	Electrical machinery	0.6559*	*(1.86)*	−0.4435	*(−0.75)*
	Transport equipment	0.2093	*(1.16)*	−0.0595	*(−0.07)*
$\Delta fdi*di$	Food			3.5140	*(1.09)*
	Textiles/Wood			−0.5540	*(−0.35)*
	Petrol/Chemicals			0.3667	*(0.57)*
	Metals/Mechanicals			−0.0757	*(−0.11)*
	Electrical machinery			12.6335**	*(2.47)*
	Transport equipment			−0.0242	*(−0.22)*
CONST		0.0754	*(1.19)*	0.0351	*(0.57)*
Observations		55		55	
Adjusted R-squared		75.33		77.27	

Notes:
Dependent variable is productivity growth.
*, **, *** indicates significance at the 10%, 5%, 1% significance level, respectively.
t-statistics computed with robust standard errors in parenthesis.

Source: Own calculations.

were closely connected to the process of privatization.[7] Using our estimating framework, we will investigate the effect of FDI in this region.

Table 4.3 summarizes the results. FDI exhibits again a significant growth-promoting effect in only a few industries. In the first specification, without interaction terms, no significant influence from FDI growth is found in any industry. When interacting FDI with investment, the electrical machinery industry emerges as the only industry where FDI has spurred growth in interaction with high investment levels.

The results are remarkable in two ways. First, the observation period for this group of countries is shorter than for the sample as a whole. In general, one would expect to see effects from FDI on productivity growth only after a certain time lag. These countries already show a significant correlation after a very short time period. Second, in Central and Eastern Europe, FDI has a significant influence in fewer industries, but – in contrast to the full sample before – in the manufacture of electrical machinery. Significant growth effects are observed in this more high tech and skill intensive industry. Again, the existence of a sufficient domestic investment share is important.

4.   FDI AND WAGE GROWTH IN CEECs

The link between FDI and productivity growth that was investigated in the previous section is of key importance for the convergence process of income levels in the CEECs. In the run-up to EU membership and after successful EU entry these countries experienced intensified trade and FDI flows. If FDI implies an import of new technologies or managing skills and thus promotes productivity growth, we can assume that these gains in productivity are – at least partly – passed on to the employees in the form of higher wages. In this case FDI plays a central role in accelerating the catching-up process of income levels in CEECs.

We study this link between FDI and wage growth in detail for a set of nine CEECs in the years 1998 to 2002. In this period, FDI inflows reached a peak that was only topped – after suffering a backlash in 2003 – in the years after EU accession. Gains in productivity growth would imply a positive relationship between FDI and wage growth. The *productivity channel* is, however, only one of the possible channels that link FDI and wage developments. Theory suggests that FDI may also have an impact on that part of wage growth that is not directly related to productivity developments. We define as the wage mark-up the difference between wage growth and productivity growth, which can therefore take positive as well as negative values. There are two additional channels through which FDI may affect the wage mark-up and thus ultimately wage growth.

The *wage premium channel* implies that foreign-owned firms have an incentive to pay higher wages to their employees than domestic firms. One reason for such a wage premium may be a segmentation of the local labour market so that foreign firms have to pay higher wages to attract the best qualified workers. Alternatively, employees in foreign firms may receive more initial training, so that employers seek to reduce the turnover rate by paying a positive wage premium. All these arguments point again to higher wages in industries and countries that receive more FDI.

Contrary to the first and second channel, the *competition channel* establishes a negative effect of FDI on wage growth. If firms or industries that receive more FDI funds are also more open, they will be more exposed to international competition. This limits the bargaining power of labour and restrains the room for firms to distribute large wage mark-ups. In very open industries this competition channel may dominate the wage premium channel so that the wage mark-up turns negative.

It is the sum of the effects of these three channels that determines the overall link between FDI and wage growth. Causality may, however, also run the other way round when FDI is attracted by those firms or industries with most favourable unit labour cost developments. This potential endogeneity will have to be taken into account for the empirical estimation.

In this section we use industry-level data on nine CEECs[8] in the period 1998 to 2002. We investigate the overall link between FDI and wage growth, but also explicitly distinguish between the different channels: the productivity channel, the wage premium channel and the competition channel.

The link between FDI and productivity growth was extensively studied in the last section. Figure 4.1 shows a simple scatter plot in which one point stands for wage growth and productivity growth in one industry of one country in our sample, at one point in time. Pure eyeball econometrics seems to confirm that industries or countries that experience higher productivity growth also show higher wage growth, in line with the hypothesis of the first channel. Figure 4.2 illustrates the link between FDI and the wage mark-up. Countries and industries in our sample have experienced positive as well as negative wage mark-ups. Visual inspection can, however, not identify a robust link between FDI and the wage mark-up. This is not surprising given that the wage mark-up represents the sum of two channels with opposing effects: the wage premium and the competition channel. It is one of the objectives of this section to disentangle these two effects.

We assume a purely competitive labour market in which – at the aggregate level – real wage growth is exactly compensating for productivity growth so that $\Delta w_{cit} = \Delta y_{cit}$, where w_{cit} is the log of the real wage in industry i of country c at time t, and y_{cit} is the log of labour productivity. This implies that on aggregate the wage mark-up is zero. Substituting the right-hand side by labour productivity growth as implied by a conventional Cobb-Douglas production function with constant returns to scale, we get

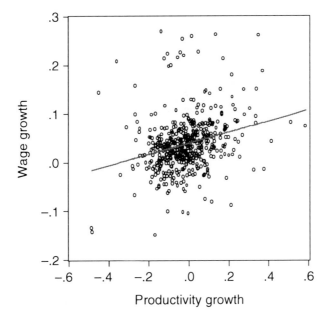

Source: Own calculations based on wiiw data.

Figure 4.1 *Wage growth and productivity growth*

$$\Delta w_{cit} = \Delta a_{cit} + \alpha(\Delta K_{cit} - n_{cit}), \tag{4.4}$$

where a_{cit} stands for technological progress (in logs), K_{cit} represents the (logged) capital stock and n_{cit} is employment growth. Equalizing the growth rate of the capital stock with the total investment share (as percentage of output) and furthermore equalizing total investment with the sum of domestic investment and foreign direct investment, results in the following specification for the empirical estimation:

$$\Delta w_{cit} = \beta_1 di_{cit} + \beta_2 fdi_{cit} + \beta_3 n_{cit} + \varepsilon_{cit}, \tag{4.5}$$

where the random error ε_{cit} is assumed to be formed by a country-specific effect, a random shock with industry-specific variance, and a time effect which is common to all countries and industries in the sample.

We estimate equation (4.5) with Generalized Least Squares (to correct for industry-specific heteroskedasticity), including both country and time dummies that also control for country-specific differences and common shocks to technological progress (Δa_{cit}). To account for the potential

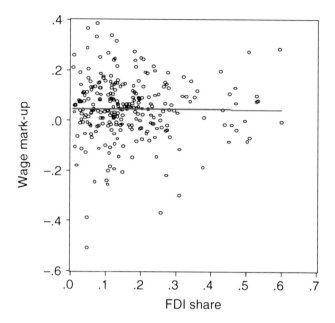

Source: Own calculations based on wiiw data.

Figure 4.2   FDI and the wage mark-up

endogeneity of the FDI inflows with respect to wage growth we also estimate the model using industry-specific trade levels (imports over output
and exports over output) as instruments for FDI in the estimation.

   The results from Table 4.4 indicate that both domestic and foreign investment have a significantly positive effect on real wage growth.[9] An increase
of FDI by 10 per cent raises wage growth by 0.8 percentage points. The
point estimate for domestic investment appears to be somewhat lower, but
an F-test indicates that we cannot reject the hypothesis that the two
coefficients for *di* and *fdi* are equal. The positive impact of FDI on real
wage growth confirms the central role of FDI for the catching-up process
of income levels in CEECs.

   To shed some light on the single channels behind the link between FDI
and wage growth, we have a closer look at the wage mark-up. A non-zero
wage mark-up implies a deviation from the basic assumption that, on
aggregate, wage growth exactly compensates for productivity growth. We
try to explain these deviations by those factors that were directly implied by
the wage premium and the competition channel. We therefore regress the
wage mark-up on FDI, openness and an interaction term between FDI and

Table 4.4   Basic regression results

Variable	GLS	IV-GLS
di	0.056* (1.81)	0.057** (2.48)
fdi	0.078** (2.11)	0.080** (2.42)
n	−0.060 (−0.98)	−0.060 (−0.95)
Observations	266	266
Adjusted R-squared	0.122	0.139

Notes:
*, **, *** indicates significance at the 10%, 5%, 1% significance level, respectively.
t-statistics computed with robust standard errors in parenthesis.

Source: Own calculations based on wiiw data.

Table 4.5   Regression results with wage mark-up as dependent variable

Variable	GLS
op	0.013 (1.30)
fdi	0.219** (2.23)
fdi ×op	−0.068* (−1.89)
Observations	266
Adjusted R-squared	0.136

Notes:
*, **, *** indicates significance at the 10%, 5%, 1% significance level, respectively.
t-statistics computed with robust standard errors in parenthesis.

Source: Own calculations based on wiiw data.

openness, so as to explicitly capture the effect of differential exposure to external competition.

$$\Delta w_{cit} - \Delta y_{cit} = \delta_1 op_{cit} + (\delta_2 + \delta_3 op_{cit}) fdi_{cit} + \varepsilon_{cit}, \qquad (4.6)$$

The positive and significant coefficient for *fdi* (δ_2) in Table 4.5 appears to confirm the hypothesis that firms in sectors that receive more FDI pay higher wages in the form of a wage premium in order to reduce employees' turnover rate. At the same time, the negative coefficient for the interaction term (δ_3) suggests that sectors that receive FDI but that are also more open, are more heavily exposed to external competition, limiting the bargaining power of labour and thus reducing the marginal effect of FDI on the wage mark-up.

The sum $(\delta_2 + \delta_3 op_{cit})$ determines the overall link between FDI and the wage mark-up. A look at single industries reveals that in relatively closed sectors such as the food or textiles industries the wage mark-up is positive throughout. By contrast in more open industries such as the transport equipment, electric machinery or metal industries, the wage mark-up takes significantly negative values in a substantial number of periods. This indicates that in these more open industries external competition significantly limits the room for enterprises to distribute positive wage premiums. To the extent that open industries tend to have more domestic investment, the effect of FDI on productivity found in section 3 (and thus on wages) will be counterbalanced by this effect to a certain extent. Overall the results appear to be in line with the hypothesized channels behind the link between FDI and wage growth.

CONCLUSIONS

This chapter has analysed the impact of FDI on the economic performance and on wage developments in FDI host countries. As a general result we found that there is substantial heterogeneity in this relationship arising from both cross-country differences and industry characteristics. More specifically, FDI was confirmed to play a special role in CEECs. While in the larger sample, including OECD members and Asian countries, FDI exerts a positive influence on productivity growth in low-skill, labour-intensive industries, it is in the skill- and technology-intensive production of electrical machinery (concentrated in Hungary) where FDI has significant positive effects in CEECs. Further, we could see a positive effect of FDI on wages in the region. However, the differential between wage growth and productivity growth (wage mark-up), being determined by two opposing effects, turned out to be influenced positively only in those industries that are less exposed to international competition.

NOTES

1. Jesús Crespo Cuaresma, University of Innsbruck, Department of Economics. Carmen Fillat Castejón, Universidad de Zaragoza, Facultad de Economía, Dpto. Economía Aplicada. Maria Antoinette Silgoner, Oesterreichische Nationalbank, Foreign Research Division. Julia Woerz, Wiener Institut für Internationale Wirtschaftvergleiche (wiiw). Julia Woerz acknowledges funding of this research through Jubiläumsfonds der Oesterreichischen Nationalbank, Project No. 10214.
2. For instance, Blomström et al. (1996) identify minimum threshold levels for the stage of development which has to be attained by the host country in order to profit from inward FDI.

3. Examples are Aitken et al. (1996) on Mexico, Venezuela and USA; Lipsey and Sjöholm (2004) on Indonesia; Driffield (1996) on the UK; Faggio (2003) on Poland, Bulgaria and Romania; Lipsey (2004) on developing countries more generally; and Onaran et al. (2006) on a set of five CEECs.
4. The sample is divided broadly into advanced OECD members (Australia, Austria, Denmark, Finland, France, Germany, Iceland, Ireland, Italy, Japan, The Netherlands, Norway, Sweden, Great Britain, USA), and different groups of catching up countries: OECD members (Greece, Mexico, Portugal, Spain, Turkey), the four Asian Tigers (Taiwan, Hong Kong, Korea, Singapore), Emerging Asia (Indonesia, Malaysia, Philippines, Thailand) and CEECs (Croatia, Czech Republic, Hungary, Latvia, Poland, Slovak Republic, Slovenia).
5. Since we are thinking of economies that are in transition rather than in a steady state (i.e. catching-up economies like the Central and Eastern European countries and emerging Asian countries) we do not assume a constant capital-to-labour ratio.
6. Given that industries with very small initial FDI levels often exhibited extremely high FDI growth rates, we are using the growth rate of the inward FDI stock-to-output ratio as our explanatory variable. The same normalization is used for domestic investments.
7. Privatization policies differed across individual CEECs. While Hungary pursued a policy of early privatization via the capital market, thus attracting large FDI inflows to all sectors, the voucher privatization in, for example, the Czech Republic implied that foreign capital was kept out of the country for a relatively long time period. Poland started to privatize state-owned firms at a later point in time; thus FDI inflows occurred at a later stage.
8. Croatia, Czech Republic, Estonia, Hungary, Latvia, Lithuania, Poland, Slovak Republic and Slovenia.
9. The broadly similar results in both columns seem to indicate that endogeneity is not seriously biasing our estimation results.

REFERENCES

Aitken, B., A. Harrison and R.E. Lipsey (1996), 'Wages and foreign ownership: A comparative study of Mexico, Venezuela, and the United States', *Journal of International Economics*, **40**, 345–71.

Akinlo, E. (2004), 'Foreign direct investment and growth in Nigeria: an empirical investigation', *Journal of Policy Modeling*, **26** (5), 627–39.

Bellak, C. (2004), 'How domestic and foreign firms differ and why does it matter?', *Journal of Economic Surveys*, **18** (4), 483–514.

Blomström, M., R.E. Lipsey and M. Zejan (1996), 'Is fixed investment the key to economic growth?', *Quarterly Journal of Economics*, **111** (1), 269–76.

Blonigen, B.A. and M. Wang (2005), 'Inappropriate pooling of wealthy and poor countries in empirical FDI studies', in T. Moran, E. Graham and M. Blomström (eds), *Does Foreign Direct Investment Promote Development?*, Washington, DC: Institute for International Economics, pp. 221–44.

Borensztein, E., J.D. Gregorio and J.W. Lee (1998), 'How does foreign direct investment affect economic growth?', *Journal of International Economics*, **45** (1), 115–35.

Carkovic, M. and R. Levine (2005), 'Does foreign direct investment accelerate economic growth?', in T. Moran, E.M. Graham and M. Blomström (eds), *Does Foreign Direct Investment Promote Development?*, Washington, DC: Institute for International Economics, pp. 195–220.

Driffield, N.L. (1996), *Global Competition and the Labour Market*, Amsterdam: Harwood Academic Publishers.

Faggio, G. (2003), 'Foreign direct investment and wages in Central and Eastern Europe', *FLOWENLA Discussion Paper* 10, Hamburg Institute of International Economics.

Lipsey, R.E. (2004), 'The labour market effects of US FDI in developing countries', *Employment Strategy Papers* 2004/6.

Lipsey, R.E. and F. Sjöholm (2004), 'FDI and wage spillovers in Indonesian manufacturing', *Weltwirtschaftliches Archiv*, **140** (2), 321–32.

Nair-Reichert, U. and D. Weinhold (2001), 'Causality tests for cross-country panels: a new look at FDI and economic growth in developing countries', *Oxford Bulletin of Economics and Statistics*, **63** (2), 153–71.

Onaran, Ö., E. Stockhammer, D. Bohle and B. Greskovits (2006), 'The effect of FDI and foreign trade on sectoral manufacturing industry wages in the Central and Eastern European Countries: A panel data analysis', mimeo.

Woerz, J. (2005), 'Industry patterns in output, FDI and trade – a regional comparison of CEECs to OECD and East Asia', *wiiw Statistical Report No. 2*, The Vienna Institute for International Economic Studies.

5. How do FDI inflows affect the productivity of domestic firms? The role of horizontal and vertical spillovers, absorptive capacity and competition[1]

Marcin Kolasa

INTRODUCTION

Foreign direct investment (FDI) is believed to bring positive spillovers to domestic firms in the recipient country. The idea is that the presence of multinational corporations, which are among the most technologically advanced firms, can facilitate the transfer of technological and business know-how. At the same time, empirical studies aimed at measuring the size of spillovers from FDI in developing and transition economies have yielded mixed results (see meta-analysis in Görg and Greenaway, 2003).

The aim of this chapter is to add to the understanding of externalities associated with FDI in a host transition country by exploiting unique and extensive firm-level panel data covering the Polish corporate sector. In particular, we look for possible spillovers to domestic firms from foreign-owned companies operating in the same industry (horizontal spillovers), downstream industries (backward spillovers) and upstream industries (forward spillovers). We also try to examine how the size of these externalities depends on the absorptive capacity of domestic firms and on competitive pressures. Contrary to most of the previous related studies, our data set includes not only manufacturing companies, but also covers services.

EMPIRICAL MODEL

Similarly to some earlier papers on the topic (see for example Javorcik, 2004), our strategy to examine the existence of spillovers from FDI is to estimate a firm-level production function augmented by three terms measuring foreign presence in the same sector and in upstream or downstream industries. These measures are constructed by treating a firm as foreign if more than a half of its equity is owned by non-residents. In order to mitigate the possible bias resulting from omission of unobserved variables, the production function is estimated in first differences, with a full set of time- and firm-specific dummies (see Haskel et al., 2002).

Additionally, we expand our baseline model to examine whether the absorptive capacity of domestic enterprises and competitive pressures facilitate spillovers from FDI. We do so by interacting the three variables capturing foreign presence with two measures of firm-level innovation intensity (one based on intramural R&D expenditures, the other relying on a broader definition of innovation effort, including knowledge acquisition from external sources) and with the Herfindahl-Hirschmann index of market concentration.

We deal with the possible heteroskedasticity by using robust estimates of the variance–covariance matrix. In order to avoid a bias arising from merging microdata with aggregated variables (see Moulton, 1990), we allow for the possibility that the residuals are correlated across firms within year-industry cells.

DATA

The main data sources are yearly balance-sheet and profit-and-loss reports of non-financial enterprises, collected by Poland's Central Statistical Office. The reporting duty applies to all enterprises employing at least ten workers. The dataset constitutes an unbalanced panel, spanning the period 1996–2003. The number of establishments per year varies from 25 171 in 1998 to 14 878 in 2002, adding up to 147 479 observations for the whole sample. The final sample used in estimations consists of 94 691 observations and includes domestic firms only. The firm-level dataset is supplemented by industry-level statistics (available at a two- or three-digit level of aggregation), including price indexes and input–output tables.

RESULTS

Our main results (five final specifications) are reported in the respective columns of Table 5.1. Detailed results, including preliminary regressions and unrestricted specifications (containing insignificant variables) are available from the author upon request. We find positive and significant coefficients on proxies for horizontal and backward spillovers. Both

Table 5.1   Spillovers from foreign direct investment – summary results

Regressors	Coefficients (standard errors)				
	1	2	3	4	5
Horizontal	0.040*	0.040*	0.040*	0.039*	0.036*
	(0.021)	(0.021)	(0.021)	(0.021)	(0.021)
Backward	0.208**	0.208*	0.208**	0.199*	0.320**
	(0.106)	(0.106)	(0.106)	(0.105)	(0.128)
R&D intensity		0.215***			
		(0.049)			
R&D intensity x Backward		10.106***	13.523***		
		(2.384)	(2.661)		
R&D intensity x Forward			7.070***		
			(2.864)		
Innovation intensity				0.035***	
				(0.006)	
Innovation intensity x Horizontal				1.059***	
				(0.547)	
Concentration x Backward					−3.136**
					(1.387)
Concentration x Forward					1.830*
					(0.957)
Number of observations	94 691	94 691	94 691	94 691	94 691
R^2 (adjusted)	0.541	0.541	0.541	0.542	0.541

Notes: The dependent variable is a first-differenced log of gross output. Other (unreported) variables include first-differenced logs of inputs (materials, labour, capital), firm and year dummies.
***, ** and * denote significance at 1%, 5% and 10%, respectively.

Source: Own calculations.

horizontal and backward effects are economically meaningful; however, the size of the latter seems to be substantially stronger (see column 1 in Table 5.1).

The results obtained suggest that domestic firms involved in R&D activities benefit more from foreign presence in downstream and upstream industries than others (see columns 2 and 3), while the broadly defined innovation expenditures turn out to be conducive to higher horizontal spillovers (see column 4). These results are consistent with the hypothesis that the technological gap between domestic firms and their direct competitors from abroad is too large for the former to exploit additional spillovers relying only on their own R&D-based absorptive capacity. However, the extent of benefits reaped by domestic firms from foreign presence can be increased if they upgrade their stock of knowledge reaching out for (and adopting) the fruit of other firms' innovation effort (embodied in patents, licences, software and so on).

We next try to examine how competition affects the productivity of domestic firms and what role it plays in accounting for the extent of spillovers from foreign presence (see column 5). Our results suggest that higher competition is associated with larger spillovers from foreign presence in downstream industries, while higher concentration (and lower competition) seems to be consistent with larger spillovers from foreign presence in upstream sectors.

Given the possible channels through which spillovers from FDI operate, it is reasonable to expect that their extent may depend on whether foreign investors enter the host country by setting up fully-owned subsidiaries or rather by letting the local capital participate in the business (for example joint ventures). In order to examine this issue, we redefine our measures of foreign presence by treating a firm as foreign if it is fully-owned (and not majority-owned as before) by non-residents. Now we do not find any unconditional spillovers to domestic firms. Only firms increasing their absorptive capacity seem to benefit from foreign investment. We also do not find any significant role for competition in facilitating the extent of spillovers.

In order to verify whether our main results are robust to alternative assumptions, we perform a number of checks, involving various specifications of production function and estimation methods. We find our main results broadly unchanged.

CONCLUSIONS

Although this chapter confirms the existence of positive productivity externalities associated with foreign investment, policy implications are not straightforward. On the one hand, our results provide some rationale for the use of investment incentives focusing on foreign firms. On the other hand, with many countries competing for FDI, there is the risk of over-bidding, that is the risk of granting subsidies surpassing the level of spillover benefits. One should also bear in mind that subsidies create market distortions, which may lead to welfare losses.

Our findings of significant backward spillovers should not necessarily be viewed as a call for policies enforcing links between foreign investors and domestic suppliers, such as local content requirements. While they might potentially have positive welfare effects on the host country, the empirical evidence of effectiveness of such policies in developing countries is rather mixed. It should also be taken into account that these and similar restrictions may in fact discourage foreign investment.

In our view, the clear implications of this chapter are consistent with the suggestions of Blomström and Kokko (2003). First, there are reasons to support policies strengthening the absorptive capacity of domestic firms. Second, reforms increasing competition, particularly in sectors supplying technologically advanced firms, should benefit a country's growth as well. Finally, it is worth pursuing more general policies that not only attract foreign investors, but that are also beneficial to domestic companies (like enhancing modern infrastructure, increasing the quality of institutions and so on).

NOTE

1. This section is based on an early draft of the paper, of which the full and revised version was published in the *Journal of International Trade and Economic Development*, March 2008.

REFERENCES

Blomström, M. and A. Kokko (2003), 'The economics of foreign direct investment incentives', *NBER Working Paper* 9489.

Görg, H. and D. Greenaway (2003), 'Much ado about nothing? Do domestic firms really benefit from foreign direct investment?', *Discussion Paper* 944, IZA, Bonn.

Haskel, J.E., S.C. Pereira and M.J. Slaughter (2002), 'Does inward foreign direct investment boost the productivity of domestic firms?', *NBER Working Paper* 8724.

Javorcik, B. Smarzynska (2004), 'Does foreign direct investment increase the productivity of domestic firms? In search of spillovers through backward linkages', *American Economic Review*, **94** (3), 605–27.

Moulton, B.R. (1990), 'An illustration of a pitfall in estimating the effects of aggregate variables on micro units', *Review of Economics and Statistics*, **72** (2), 334–8.

6. Home country spillovers of FDI: some results and discussion of estimation issues

Priit Vahter and Jaan Masso[1]

1. INTRODUCTION

Compared to the analysis of host country effects of FDI, the home country effects of FDI have been researched less extensively. Still, this issue has provoked significant interest among policy makers in developed countries. After all, investing directly in foreign businesses has often, and very often with no reason, been blamed for adverse effects on the home economy. Studies discussing the effects of FDI in the home country – that is the source country of FDI – have focused overwhelmingly on the effects on the investing parent firm. Examples include Lipsey (2002), Criscuolo and Martin (2003) as well as Barba Navaretti and Venables (2004), who stressed that the spillovers of FDI to the investor's home country have mostly been left out of the analysis and that there is a need to fill this gap in research.

This chapter summarizes a study in which we compared the spillover effects of both inward and outward FDI on corporate productivity. The full version of the study, including a more detailed description of the methodology, can be found in Vahter and Masso (2006). The main novelty in our approach is that we also address spillover effects of outward FDI which may occur outside the investing firms on the rest of the home country. Additionally, we concentrate on effects resulting in both the manufacturing and the services sector. Previous studies, as a rule (except, for example, Griffith, 2004 on the UK), only considered the effects of FDI in the manufacturing sector.

We employ a rich enterprise-level panel dataset of the population of all Estonian firms (up to approximately 41 000 firms per year) from the Estonian Business Register, covering the period from 1995 to 2002.

Estonia has been a transition economy that has witnessed continued rapid growth and has attracted significant amounts of inward FDI per capita. Moreover, the outward FDI from the Central and Eastern European countries (CEECs) in general, and from Estonia in particular to its neighbouring countries has risen significantly in recent years. Estonia was already ranked first in 2001–2003 among the CEECs by the ratio of its outward FDI to total capital formation (UNCTAD, 2004). Thus there could be some reason to expect, in addition to inward FDI spillovers, that some spillovers occur from firms that have undertaken outward FDI.

Our finding about the direct effect of FDI is that both receiving FDI into the firm and making outward FDI is associated with higher corporate productivity. At the same time, significant self-selection effects are also found among firms.

However, we do not find much evidence of positive horizontal spillovers via outward or inward FDI that is robust to the specification of the model. The results vary according to the different specifications, being either statistically insignificant or, in some cases, positive.

2. HOME AND HOST COUNTRY EFFECTS OF FDI

Similarly to the host country effects[2] we can divide the home country effects of FDI into 'own-firm effects' and spillovers. Own-firm effects are the effects that investing abroad has on the performance characteristics of a multinational corporation's home firm. In addition to that, *horizontal* or *vertical spillover effects*[3] can materialize, that is, the presence of multinational firms (MNCs) can influence the performance of other local firms and other MNCs active in the home economy.

The theoretical predictions about the direct effects outward FDI has on the performance of the investing firm and the potential spillover effects it has on other firms in the investor's home country are, however, not as clear-cut as in the case of inward FDI. The effects of inward FDI are covered in many chapters of this volume and in earlier papers (see, for example, Lipsey, 2002; Lipsey, 2006; Blomström and Kokko, 2003); thus we concentrate here on outward FDI.

To begin with, investing directly abroad is a matter of self selection (see Helpman et al., 2004), as is the recipient's decision to open up to FDI. Apart from the self-selection effect, establishing a foreign affiliate may positively affect the productivity of the MNC in its home country (see also Kokko, 2006; Barba Navaretti and Castellani, 2004). This may occur through:

- opening a new channel for international knowledge sourcing (including technological, managerial, host country conditions/market-related knowledge);

- exploiting firm-level scale economies;
- changing the composition of production inputs (specialization effect) and taking advantage of the international division of labour within a MNC (Barba Navaretti and Castellani, 2004).

The first of these effects, knowledge transfers, may also result in positive spillover effects on other national firms in the investor's home economy. The transferred knowledge may not be about technology[4] alone but also about marketing, foreign market-related information or information that will make it easier for other firms to become multinational as well.

The channels through which outward FDI may affect the productivity of other firms in the investor's home country (that is the spillovers) are arguably similar to those of inward FDI.[5] These spillovers basically include demonstration and worker mobility effects. In general, we can expect these spillover effects from the presence of other MNCs to be positive (unless there is some adverse effect on former suppliers in the home economy, for example because the investor switched to new suppliers from the host economy).

One relevant idea from the previous literature on host country spillovers is that the magnitude of host country spillovers may depend a lot on the absorptive capacity of local firms (Cohen and Levinthal, 1989). This is likely also to be the case for home country spillover effects.[6] Thus the external effects of outward FDI may be, for example, larger for firms that are themselves multinationals, as these firms have more international experience and may thus be more able to absorb potential benefits via spillovers.

Some empirical papers on home country effects, while focusing mainly on the effects on the investing firm, could be considered as studies of spillover effects. The most recent example is the book *Multinational Firms, Innovation and Productivity* by Castellani and Zanfei (2006), who find that domestic multinationals have a positive impact on non-internationalized domestic firms.

Other former studies, however, tend to concentrate on only part of the spillover effect of outward FDI by analysing patent citation data (for example Globerman et al., 2000), which severely limits the scope of the analysis. Given that only some knowledge can be patented, a sizeable share of the potential spillover effects may potentially be left out of the analysis. In addition, this approach cannot be used in our case for Estonia due to the very low level of patenting activity among local firms in this country.

One recent contribution to filling the gap in the literature on home country spillovers, finally, is a paper by Bitzer and Görg (2005), but they use country- and sector-level data rather than firm-level data from OECD countries.[7]

3. METHODOLOGY

At first, we estimate total factor productivity (hereinafter TFP) as a residual from the logarithmic form of the Cobb-Douglas production function by using the Levinsohn–Petrin (2003) procedure, accounting for endogeneity of inputs and, additionally, allowing different coefficients of logs of capital and labour in the production function for different sectors (at NACE 2-digit level). In a second step, we regress the log of TFP (denoted as tfp_{ijt}; i is the index for firm, j for industry, t for time) on the FDI spillover variable(s), sector dummies α_j, time dummies α_t and other control variables (X_{ijt}; these include Herfindahl index, firm size variable and region dummies).

$$tfp_{ijt} = \beta_1 X_{ijt} + \beta_2 OUTFDI\_spillover_{ijt-1} + \alpha_i + \alpha_j + \alpha_t + \varepsilon_{ijt} \quad (6.1)$$

This equation is estimated both in levels and (first) differences. As we do not have much confidence in the applicability of conventional measures of vertical spillovers in our context, we look at the 'horizontal' ones. The 2-digit-level division of sectors has often been used by different authors in the empirical literature on vertical spillovers of inward FDI. A well-known example is the article by Javorcik (2004). However, such a small number of sectors (in the manufacturing industry we have about 14 sectors in a 2-digit-level division) may not be enough to study this type of spillover adequately. Arguably, a large share of the spillovers may occur within each of these 2-digit individual sectors – that is, more between the sub-sectors of the wood processing industry than, for example, between the wood processing and the chemical industries. The existing 2-digit-level input–output tables for Estonia and other countries, moreover, indicate that the largest weight in these tables tends to be on the diagonal, which means that the bulk of a sector's vertical relations is limited to the same rather broadly defined sector. Unfortunately, for many countries (including Estonia) more detailed input–output tables have not been available. Thus we do not engage in the estimation of vertical spillovers here. In this chapter we present the results of horizontal spillovers using a 3-digit-level division of sectors. Corresponding 2-digit-level results are available for the same time period from Vahter and Masso (2006).

4. ESTONIAN OUTWARD AND INWARD FDI

Estonia has been a transition economy that has implemented radical economic reforms, witnessed rapid economic growth and is known for attracting substantial amounts of inward FDI per capita. The ratio of inward FDI stock to GDP reached 93.6 per cent in 2005 (UNCTAD, 2006). With this ratio (and by per capita stock of FDI) Estonia outperforms other attractive locations for FDI in the Central and Eastern European region.

Unlike many other CEECs, Estonia does not provide special incentives for foreign investors but treats them the same as domestic investors. The features attracting foreign investors include its geographical proximity to Sweden and Finland, relatively low production costs and, since 2000, a special tax regime with zero corporate income tax on reinvested earnings.

Moreover, in recent years, outward FDI from CEECs in general and from Estonia in particular to its neighbouring CEECs has risen significantly. Already in 2001–2003 Estonia ranked first among CEECs on the basis of its ratio of outward FDI to total capital formation (UNCTAD, 2004) and by 2005 the outward FDI stock to GDP ratio amounted to 15 per cent. This shows why Estonia can be a suitable case for studying the home country effects of FDI. Surveys addressing the motives of Estonian companies to invest abroad have indicated that market-related motives prevail (Varblane et al., 2001).

5.   EMPIRICAL ANALYSIS OF THE EFFECTS OF FDI ON TOTAL FACTOR PRODUCTIVITY

In our analysis we use yearly balance sheet and income statement data for the population of Estonian firms from the Business Register of Estonia for the period 1995–2002. The calculations in Vahter and Masso (2006) based on the same panel show that foreign-owned firms, and even more so firms engaging in outward FDI, are on average larger than the rest.

The descriptive statistics in Table 6.1 confirm that the highest level of productivity (including TFP), wages and capital intensity in the manufacturing industry can be found in foreign-owned firms that have themselves invested abroad from Estonia. The second group on the basis of productivity (both by labour productivity calculated as sales per employee or value added per employee and by log of TFP; see Table 6.1) are domestically-owned firms that have invested abroad themselves. Foreign-owned firms that have not invested abroad from Estonia rank third. The lowest level of productivity can be found in domestically-owned firms that have not invested abroad from Estonia. All top three ranking groups have much higher labour productivity ratios than the domestically-owned firms operating only at the national level.

Table 6.1   Average labour productivity, capital intensity, wages ('000 EUR) and log of TFP in 2002 for different groups of firms

Inward FDI	Outward FDI	Sector	Wage	K/L	Log(TFP)	Y/L	VA/L
No	No	Services	2 (4)	11.1 (4)	9.6 (4)	25.2 (4)	7.2 (4)
Yes	No	Services	5.2 (3)	17.9 (3)	10.5 (3)	53.6 (3)	14.9 (3)
No	Yes	Services	5.9 (2)	63.6 (1)	11 (2)	65.9 (2)	19.3 (2)
Yes	Yes	Services	7.3 (1)	31.9 (2)	11.1 (1)	80.7 (1)	23 (1)
No	No	Manuf.	2.4 (4)	3.5 (4)	9.3 (4)	18.7 (4)	6.3 (4)
Yes	No	Manuf.	4.5 (3)	12.2 (3)	9.8 (3)	34.3 (3)	10.9 (3)
No	Yes	Manuf.	5.3 (2)	10.5 (2)	10.1 (2)	46.6 (2)	14.2 (2)
Yes	Yes	Manuf.	5.8 (1)	14.8 (1)	10.6 (1)	66.5 (1)	23.4 (1)

Notes:
The number in parenthesis is the respective group's rank among the four groups in the particular indicator.
VA/L – value added per employee; K/L – capital intensity, Y/L – sales per employee.

Source: Own calculations based on panel data of Estonian firms 1995–2002.

In Vahter and Masso (2006) we also tried to address the issue of potential selection bias. The main finding there was that there is some self-selection, as better firms tend to receive inward FDI or engage in outward FDI. However, there also appeared to be some causal positive direct effects of FDI on subsidiary or parent firm productivity. Thus some positive spillovers to the rest of the economy might be expected as well.

We estimated the equation (6.1) both at levels and (first) differences for the period 1995 to 2002. For the level results of estimating equation (6.1) please refer to Vahter and Masso (2006), who incidentally demonstrate that the results yielded by the specification of equation (6.1) in differences differ from results estimated with similar augmented production functions in differences (that did not account for the endogeneity of inputs). In comparison, the results presented here in Table 6.2 paint a somewhat more positive (yet still ambiguous) picture of outward FDI's horizontal spillovers than alternative specifications that do not address some of the important econometric problems in estimating the production function.

The specification in Table 6.2 accounted for the endogeneity of inputs in the first stage of the estimation process. The only robust finding in this framework as compared to the alternatives presented in Vahter and Masso (2006) is the positive spillover effect inward FDI has on other foreign affiliates' TFP in the services sector (see specification 1 in Table 6.2) – with

Table 6.2 Spillover effect of FDI, first differences; spillover variable is based on total assets of firms and defined at 3-digit NACE level

Dep. variable is Δt/p	Only inward 1		Only outward 2		Both 3	
	Manuf.	Services	Manuf.	Services	Manuf.	Services
Δ(INFDI_spillover)$_{t-1}$	0.003	0.009			0.014	0.022
	(0.053)	(0.041)			(0.051)	(0.04)
Δ(INFDI_firm · INFDI_spillover)$_{t-1}$	0.079	0.154*				
	(0.101)	(0.085)				
Δ(OUTFDI_spillover)$_{t-1}$			0.162	0.182*	0.164	0.178*
			(0.156)	(0.095)	(0.156)	(0.095)
Δ(OUTFDI_firm · OUTFDI_spillover)$_{t-1}$			0.06	−0.145		
			(0.613)	(0.559)		
ΔHerfindahl	−1.046**	−2.085***	−1.017**	−2.082***	−1.016**	−2.078***
	(0.510)	(0.575)	(0.511)	(0.573)	(0.511)	(0.573)
Δln(size)	−0.057*	−0.02	−0.057*	−0.019	−0.057*	−0.019
	(0.029)	(0.015)	(0.029)	(0.015)	(0.029)	(0.015)
Constant	−1.417***	−0.487**	−1.466***	−0.485**	−1.417***	−0.488***
	(0.525)	(0.244)	(0.314)	(0.245)	(0.314)	(247)
Sector dummies	Yes	Yes	Yes	Yes	Yes	Yes
Year dummies	Yes	Yes	Yes	Yes	Yes	Yes
Location dummies	Yes	Yes	Yes	Yes	Yes	Yes
Observations	9598	32 230	9590	32 197	9590	32 197
R²	0.062	0.017	0.062	0.017	0.062	0.017

| Do the signs and significance of spillovers change if 2nd and 3rd differences are used? | Not for 2nd, but yes (+ effect) for 3rd diff. | No significant effects found if 2nd and 3rd diffs are used | 2nd diff.: no; 3rd diff.: + effect of INFDI and – of OUTFDI | The same results in 2nd and 3rd differences | Not for 2nd, but yes (+ both effects) for 3rd diff. | The same in 2nd and 3rd differences |

Notes:
Spillover variables are defined at 3-digit NACE level.
The robust standard errors are in parentheses.
***, **, * denote statistical significance at the 1, 5 and 10 per cent level, respectively.

Source: Own calculations based on panel data of Estonian firms 1995–2002.

the caveat that this finding is actually not robust to choice of time difference. Longer time differences – that is second or third differences – will give more emphasis to more persistent changes in FDI penetration and reduce noise in the data (for longer time differencing in inward FDI spillover analyses see, for example, Javorcik, 2004). Longer time differences do not yield significant coefficients for spillover variables in the services sector column. For the manufacturing sector the results on inward FDI spillovers also vary with the choice of time difference. There appear to be no significant coefficients for spillover variables in column 1 for manufacturing in Table 6.2 when the first and second difference is used. However, a small significant effect is found if the third difference is employed.

The robust finding from this table is that the presence of MNCs has a positive significant effect on other firms (both national firms and MNCs) working in the same services sub-sector. This finding actually contradicts results from the level equations, suggesting that outward FDI has substantially smaller effects, and that inward FDI has several positive significant effects (see, for more results, Vahter and Masso, 2006). However, we find the results from the first (and second and third) difference estimation of equation (6.1) more reliable than the levels estimation. The findings of a potential positive evidence for the presence of firms with outward FDI seem to be robust to the choice of shorter or longer time differences.

Our analysis has outlined the multitude of difficulties hampering the analysis of spillover effects from inward and outward FDI in the production function framework. These different findings stress the need to subject the spillover effect results to many cautious robustness checks. Accounting for endogeneity of production inputs and allowing for greater heterogeneity of production yielded significantly different outcomes from the augmented production function case where both these issues are treated in a simplistic way. An augmented production function assumed the technology of firms to be homogeneous while not accounting for the endogeneity of inputs. In addition to that, in Vahter and Masso (2006) we showed that the choice of the spillover variable may affect the results (2-digit versus 3-digit-level variable, the spillover variables as calculated based on the assets, employees or sales of firms). The use of the sales-based measure may be less beneficial than the others as the sales numbers of MNCs and foreign affiliates may be distorted by the transfer pricing activities of these companies. There is a clear need to differentiate between the potential receivers of spillovers, as other foreign affiliates (in the inward FDI spillovers' case) or other MNCs (in the outward FDI spillovers' case) might benefit more from knowledge externalities than the local firms with less international experience. Finally, the robustness checks with both longer and shorter time differences may yield important further (and sometimes different) information about the existence and strength of spillovers.

In conclusion, the findings about spillover effects of outward FDI depend on the kind of estimation framework used. We rank more highly estimation frameworks that account for endogeneity of inputs and heterogeneity of coefficients of inputs like capital and labour across sub-sectors, and which at the same time estimate the relationships, not only in levels, but in longer and shorter time differences to check their robustness. These results (see Table 6.2) also show the possibility of some positive external effects created by outward FDI in the services sector.

6.   CONCLUSIONS

The main contribution of this chapter is that it addresses the so far largely discarded topic of spillover effects from outward FDI to the rest of firms in the investor's home country. The results in Vahter and Masso (2006) show that both inward and outward FDI in Estonia are positively related to the productivity of the firm receiving or engaging in FDI. These results also imply a significant self-selection effect for firms receiving FDI (both in manufacturing and services) or for firms investing directly abroad (that is firms with higher productivity attract inward FDI or are more likely to engage in outward FDI).

However, the results on the spillover effects from inward and outward FDI are quite diverse for different specifications of the model or the specification (calculation) of the spillover variable. Our most preferred specification – which accounts for endogeneity of inputs, allows for heterogeneity of technology across sectors and looks at effects in shorter and longer time differences – finds outward FDI to have some positive external effects. However, these very mixed results show that the coefficients of spillover variables must be interpreted with caution, especially when considering the policy implications for special FDI incentives or generalizing the results for other countries. Different assumptions about the specification of the relationship between FDI and TFP of firms may lead to significantly different results.

The scarcity of robust statistical evidence on the spillover effects via outward FDI based on our data does not mean that there are no positive effects at all. The effects of FDI are certainly quite diverse for different host or home countries, different sectors and in different time periods, and are most likely to depend on the type of FDI. Favourable effects from the proximity of some types of multinationals are likely to occur for some groups of firms with high absorptive capacities.

In the future, better availability of input–output tables could potentially shed more light on the analysis of vertical spillovers of FDI. However, different detailed input–output tables for different years of the panel are probably needed for the analysis of vertical spillovers, the use of only one input–output table and thus the assumption that these input–output relations do not change much in time is very often not likely to be a viable proposition.

NOTES

1. Priit Vahter: School of Economics, University of Nottingham; Jaan Masso: Faculty of Economics and Business Administration, University of Tartu, Estonia. This study was largely undertaken while Priit Vahter was an economist at the Research Department of Eesti Pank (Bank of Estonia). The authors are grateful for valuable comments and suggestions by Holger Görg, Ari Kokko, Urmas Varblane, Davide Castellani, Aurelijus Dabušinskas, Ele Reiljan, Harald Lehmann, Kalev Kaarna and seminar participants from the Research Department and the Economics Department of Eesti Pank. We thank Piret Anton from the Balance of Payments Department of Eesti Pank for substantial help with data on outward FDI in Estonia. Jaan Masso acknowledges financial support from the Republic of Estonia Ministry of Education and Research target financed project No. 0182588s03. Priit Vahter acknowledges support from grant projects No. 5840 and No. 6493 from the Estonian Science Foundation. Please address correspondence to Priit Vahter, School of Economics, University of Nottingham, University Park, Nottingham, NG7 2RD, UK. E-mail: lexpv@nottingham.ac.uk. The authors acknowledge financial support from the EU 6th framework project CIT5-CT-028519 'U-Know'.
2. For earlier studies on productivity-related host country effects in Estonia see, for example, Sinani and Meyer (2004), Damijan and Knell (2005) or Vahter (2005).
3. Horizontal spillovers are the effects of FDI on other firms in the same sector (to the competitors); vertical spillovers are the effects on suppliers and clients of the firm that has FDI.
4. In the case of Estonia, technology-related know-how from outward investment is probably not very important, as the technological level of the main host countries of Estonian FDI, Latvia and Lithuania, is not significantly different from Estonia. We would, in this context, rather expect spillovers in the form of improved host market-related know-how (for example the knowledge about local customers).
5. For an overview of the literature on spillovers of inward FDI, see, for example, Görg and Strobl (2001).
6. It is possible that the amount of positive effects of outward FDI in the home economy may increase as the home country's economy grows and the absorptive/learning capacity of national firms grows as well. A sufficient level of absorptive capacity among national firms may be a necessary condition for benefiting from possible positive spillovers from outward FDI in Estonia and in the home countries in general (see, for example, Cohen and Levinthal, 1989).
7. Bitzer and Görg (2005) investigate the productivity effects of both inward and outward FDI and find, on average, a negative correlation between a country's stock of outward FDI and productivity. However, this is the average effect. Also, a positive relationship is found for several OECD countries in their article. Their results underline that the effects of FDI depend a lot on the characteristics of the home (or host) countries of investment.

REFERENCES

Barba Navaretti, G. and A.J. Venables, with F.G. Barry, K. Ekholm, A.M. Falzoni, J.I. Haaland, I.K.H. Midelfart and A. Turrini (2004), *Multinational Firms in the World Economy*, Princeton, NJ: Princeton University Press.

Barba Navaretti, G. and D. Castellani (2004), 'Investments abroad and performance at home: evidence from Italian multinationals', *CEPR Discussion Paper* No. 4284.

Bitzer, J. and H. Görg (2005), 'The impact of FDI on industry performance', Economics Working Paper Archive at WUSTL, series *International Trade*, No. 0505003.

Blomström, M. and A. Kokko (2003), 'Human capital and inward FDI', *Stockholm School of Economics Working Paper* No. 167, Stockholm School of Economics, Stockholm, Sweden.

Castellani, D. and A. Zanfei (2006), *Multinational Firms, Innovation and Productivity*, Cheltenham, UK and Northampton, MA, USA: Edward Elgar.

Cohen, W. and D. Levinthal (1989), 'Innovation and learning: The two faces of R&D', *Economic Journal*, **99** (397), 569–96.

Criscuolo, C. and R. Martin (2003), 'Multinationals, foreign ownership and US productivity leadership: Evidence from the UK', Royal Economic Society Annual Conference 2003 from *Royal Economic Society, Working Paper* No. 50.

Damijan, J.P. and M. Knell (2005), 'How important is trade and foreign ownership in closing the technology gap? Evidence from Estonia and Slovenia', *Review of World Economics*, **141** (2), 271–95.

Globerman, S., A. Kokko and F. Sjöholm (2000), 'International technology diffusion: evidence from Swedish patent data', *Kyklos*, **53** (1), 17–38.

Görg, H. and E. Strobl (2001), 'Multinational companies and productivity spillovers: A meta-analysis', *The Economic Journal*, **111** (475), 723–39.

Griffith, R. (2004), 'Foreign ownership and productivity: new evidence from the service sector and the R&D lab', *Oxford Review of Economic Policy*, **20** (3), 440–56.

Helpman, E., M.J. Melitz and S.R. Yeaple (2004), 'Export versus FDI with heterogeneous firms', *The American Economic Review*, **94** (1), 300–16.

Javorcik, B. Smarzynska (2004), 'Does foreign direct investment increase the productivity of domestic firms? In search of spillovers through backward linkages', *The American Economic Review*, **94** (3), 605–27.

Kokko, A. (2006), 'The home country effects of FDI in developed economies', *SSE EIJS Working Paper* No. 225.

Levinsohn, J. and A. Petrin (2003), 'Estimating production functions using inputs to control for unobservables', *Review of Economic Studies*, **70** (2), 317–41.

Lipsey, R.E. (2002), 'Home and host country effects of FDI', *NBER Working Paper* No. 9293, Cambridge, MA: National Bureau of Economic Research.

Lipsey, R.E. (2006), *Measuring the Impacts of FDI*, Paper presented at the CEEI 2006 Conference of the Oesterreichische Nationalbank in Vienna.

Sinani, E. and K. Meyer (2004), 'Spillovers of technology transfer from FDI: the case of Estonia', *Journal of Comparative Economics*, **32** (3), 445–66.

UNCTAD (2004), *World Investment Report*, New York and Geneva: United Nations, UNCTAD.

UNCTAD (2006), *World Investment Report*, New York and Geneva: United Nations, UNCTAD.

Vahter, P. (2005), 'Which firms benefit more from inward foreign direct investments?', *Bank of Estonia Working Paper* No. 2005-11, Tallinn, Estonia: Bank of Estonia.

Vahter, P. and J. Masso (2006), 'Home versus host country effects of FDI: searching for new evidence of productivity spillovers', *William Davidson Institute Working Paper* No. 820.

Varblane, U., T. Roolaht, E. Reiljan and R. Jüriado (2001), 'Estonian outward foreign direct investments', *University of Tartu Economics & Business Administration Working Paper* No. 9, Tartu, Estonia: University of Tartu.

7. Effects of FDI on industry structure: a host country perspective

Katja Zajc Kejžar[1]

1. INTRODUCTION

An important task in shaping the policy towards inward FDI is to know how inward direct investment and multinational enterprises' (MNCs) operations affect market structure and the process of industrial evolution and restructuring in a host country. After all, the entry of foreign firms (either through exports or FDI) disturbs the existing equilibrium in a host country, increases the intensity of competition within that country[2] and may provoke different offensive and defensive response strategies from local firms. As a result of the pro-competitive effect of foreign firm entry, monopolistic distortions may be reduced, and the price–cost margins of host country firms may be depressed. Local firms are then forced to cut production, and the least efficient ones may even have to exit the market ('crowding-out effect'). On the other hand, a foreign firm's activity in a host country might trigger positive productivity spillovers on local firms. Recently, it has frequently been observed that industry consolidation induced by changes in foreign competition is accompanied by heightened merger activity.

Due to the importance of firms' strategic motives when deciding on FDI, and the fact that MNCs mainly enter industries with relatively high barriers to entry and concentration (Caves, 1996; and see Blomström and Kokko, 1998, for a survey), a full understanding of market structure and welfare effects requires an industrial organization approach that takes into account the strategic behaviour and interactions between foreign affiliates and local competitors and the possible attempts they make to modify the structure of the industry. Since the mid-1980s, several models have appeared that examine firms' choices between different modes of foreign entry (for example exports, FDI, licensing) and that determine the equilibrium market structure as the solution of a multi-stage game between international oligopolists.[3] Most of these models consider either that there is only one (potential) local rival or that host country firms are symmetric.

These assumptions, however, contradict recent empirical studies that empha-size the co-existence of relatively large and persistent differences in produc-tivity levels among firms in the same industry and provide evidence that the exit/entry process and within-industry re-allocations contribute significantly to average productivity growth and constitute an important mode of indus-trial restructuring (see Olley and Pakes, 1996; Roberts and Tybout, 1996; Pavcnik, 2002).

My aim is therefore to relax the assumption of symmetrical firms and provide new theoretical insights into the market structure and welfare effects that follow the incorporation of heterogeneous firms into oligopo-listic interaction models. Further, I aim to test these theoretical predictions empirically on the Slovenian manufacturing sector data for the 1994–2003 period in which Slovenia experienced fast and substantial trade and invest-ment liberalization.

2. SOME THEORETICAL AND EMPIRICAL FINDINGS ON THE INDUSTRY STRUCTURE EFFECTS[4]

In exploring these effects, a simple partial-equilibrium multi-stage game is set up in which a foreign firm (a potential MNC) decides in the first stage whether to export, set up a subsidiary in the host country (FDI) or not to expand abroad, while, in the second stage of the game, given the choice made by the foreign firm, two asymmetrical local firms (high- and low-cost firm) simultaneously choose quantities (a Cournot assumption) and thus decide on their exit/stay strategy. The model accounts for different channels through which MNC activity potentially affects a host country: (1) through a change in the population of firms (foreign-owned firms/MNCs tend to be disproportionately productive; 'direct technology transfer'); (2) through the exit of less efficient firms (as domestic prices tend to fall due to increased foreign competition, high-cost producers are potentially forced to exit the market); (3) by re-allocation of resources and output from less to more productive firms; and (4) through within-firm improvements in productivity as a result of 'productivity spillovers' on host country firms.

Within the model, it is shown that foreign firm entry creates a selection effect, which leads to the re-allocation of market shares across firms within the industry and an increase in the probability of the exit of the least pro-ductive (efficient) firms in the host economy. Results of the model confirm that firm-level heterogeneity in the host country influences the foreign firm's decision about the mode of serving the host country market. In the absence of productivity spillovers, the general conviction was confirmed that the higher the degree of heterogeneity, the more likely is an entry via FDI (or, by analogy, the higher the productivity advantage over the host country firms, the more likely is an entry via FDI) and, hence, the exit of the least efficient host country firm. The relationship is not as straightforward when there is an interaction involving spillover effects. In particular, foreign firms are discouraged from entering the host country market by establishing a subsidiary where strong spillover effects are anticipated.

The welfare analysis reveals that even in the worst-case scenario, in which productivity spillover effects are absent, the foreign firm repatriates all its profit and the entry of a MNC leads to the exit of the inefficient local firm, FDI can still improve total welfare. Moreover, the conclusion that investment liberalization under free trade positively affects host country welfare if the free-trade market share of the foreign firm is sufficiently large is independent of the crowding-out of local firms. Several effects are at play here. On the one hand, FDI increases both allocative efficiency (the entry of a competitive firm brings prices down) and productive efficiency (an inefficient firm is replaced by a more efficient one). On the other hand, under the very conservative hypothesis that all profits earned by the foreign firm are repatriated, the exit of a domestic firm will decrease the domestic profit component of welfare. This lower profits effect decreases in strength relative to the 'larger consumer surplus' effect when, without FDI, the market share of the exporting foreign firm would be larger: in this case, which coincides with lower transportation costs, the domestic profits would be low anyhow.

The extension of the model with the possibility that local firms react to the foreign firm's entry by merging[5] demonstrates that investment liberalization may well trigger consolidation via a merger since the approval of a domestic merger by an antitrust authority is more likely where a foreign firm enters via FDI compared to the export entry mode, and also the firms' incentive for domestic merger is greater. The intuition is that as the market shares of host country firms are lower when a foreign firm enters via FDI, resulting in lower pre-merger mark-ups, the required reduction of marginal costs is lower in order for the price to fall and for the antitrust authority to approve the merger. However, the larger the anticipated synergies from domestic mergers, the less likely it is that a foreign firm would choose FDI as a mode of entry.

Empirical evidence for the Slovenian manufacturing sector in the 1994–2003 period also confirms that entry of foreign firms stimulates the firm selection process within the industry and encourages mergers between firms from the same industry and region. The selection process is characterized by the least efficient firms experiencing a drop in their survival probability upon a foreign firm's entry. On the other hand, more efficient and more skill-intensive firms do not experience any pronounced 'static' crowding out with respect to the increased probability to exit. In addition, a foreign firm's entry seems to stimulate the selection process not only within the industry but also through backward linkages in the upstream-supplying industries as indicated by less skill-intensive firms' increased probability of exiting when the concentration of foreign firm activity in backwardly-linked industries rises.

3.   CONCLUDING REMARKS ON POLICY IMPLICATIONS

As demonstrated, investment liberalization under free trade has an ambiguous impact on the welfare of a host country; hence, there is no unique optimal policy towards inward FDI. However, most countries have liberalized their FDI regulations since the early 1980s, and many are now actively trying to encourage inward foreign investment by providing a range of incentives. Following the model described above, the conditions that appear to be crucial for welfare-enhancing subsidy are: (1) pre-FDI market shares of foreign-owned firms are sufficiently high (this is the case when export costs and foreign firm's marginal production costs are relatively low compared to marginal costs of host country firms); (2) the subsidy required to induce FDI is lower than its maximum eligible level (this is more likely the higher the cost disadvantage of local rival firms compared to MNC and market size of the host country, and the lower the fixed plant costs); (3) presence of positive productivity spillovers. Other factors that also affect the partial-equilibrium welfare effects of a subsidy are: (1) the degree of repatriation of profits; (2) the export propensity of foreign affiliates (the higher the export propensity of foreign affiliates, the less intensive is the competition effect, all else being equal); and (3) the degree of product differentiation.

NOTES

1. Faculty of Economics, University of Ljubljana, Kardeljeva pl. 17, 1000 Ljubljana, Slovenia, katja.zajc@ef.uni-lj.si.
2. Competition also intensifies if the foreign firm was exporting prior to establishing local production in the host country market because, by avoiding export costs, the foreign firm's competitive position is improved.
3. Among others, Horstmann and Markusen (1987, 1992), Smith (1987), Motta (1992), Sanna-Randaccio (1996), Petit and Sanna-Randaccio (2000) studied the host country impacts by considering export versus FDI decisions.
4. For model derivation and econometric analysis see Zajc Kejžar (2006a, b).

5. The game is modified in such a way that in the second stage host country firms simultaneously decide whether they want to propose a merger. They have an incentive to merge if their joint profit would be higher than the sum of their profits without merging. If they decide to propose a merger, then in the third stage of the game the antitrust authority has to decide whether to approve or reject the proposed merger (according to the consumer surplus standard).

REFERENCES

Blomström, Magnus and Ari Kokko (1998), 'Multinational corporations and spillovers', *Journal of Economic Surveys*, **3** (12), 247–77.

Caves, Richard E. (1996), *Multinational Enterprise and Economic Analysis*, Cambridge: Cambridge University Press, Second Edition.

Horstmann, Ignatius J. and James R. Markusen (1987), 'Strategic investments and the development of multinationals', *International Economic Review*, **28**, 109–21.

Horstmann, Ignatius J. and James R. Markusen (1992), 'Endogenous market structures in international trade (natura facit saltum)', *Journal of International Economics*, **32**, 109–29.

Motta, Massimo (1992), 'Multinational firms and the tariff-jumping argument: a game theoretic analysis with some unconventional conclusions', *European Economic Review*, **36**, 1557–71.

Olley, S. and A. Pakes (1996), 'The dynamics of productivity in the telecommunications equipment industry', *Econometrica*, **64** (6), 1263–97.

Pavcnik, Nina (2002), 'Trade liberalization, exit, and productivity improvements: evidence from Chilean plants', *The Review of Economic Studies*, **69**, 245–76.

Petit, M.L. and F. Sanna-Randaccio (2000), 'Endogenous R&D and foreign direct investment in international oligopolies', *International Journal of Industrial Organization*, **18**, 339–67.

Roberts, Mark J. and James R. Tybout (eds) (1996), *Industrial Evolution in Developing Countries: Micro Patterns of Turnover, Productivity, and Market Structure*, Oxford: Oxford University Press.

Sanna-Randaccio, F. (1996), 'New protectionism and multinational companies', *Journal of International Economics*, **41**, 29–51.

Smith, A. (1987), 'Strategic investment, multinational corporations and trade policy', *European Economic Review*, **31**, 89–96.

Zajc Kejžar, Katja (2006a), *Effects of Foreign Direct Investment on Industry Structure: A Host-Country Perspective*, doctoral dissertation, Ljubljana: University of Ljubljana, Faculty of Economics.

Zajc Kejžar, Katja (2006b), 'The role of foreign direct investment in the firm selection process in a host country: evidence from Slovenia', *William Davidson Institute Working Paper* No. 841, Ann Arbor: University of Michigan, The William Davidson Institute. [http://www.wdi.umich.edu/files/Publications/WorkingPapers/wp841.pdf].

PART II

Where is FDI going? Global trends and patterns

8. Why FDI? Re-inventing economic geography in times of globalization

Peter Mooslechner

'The world is flat . . . The global competitive playing field was being leveled. The world was being flattened.' (Friedman, 2006)

'Recent decades have seen momentous changes in the economic geography of the world. Political transitions and economic liberalization have brought formerly closed countries into the world economy.' (Venables, 2006)

'The global economic community, and economic policymakers in governments and global institutions alike, has yet to fully understand the most fundamental economic development in this era of globalization – the doubling of the global labor force.' (Freeman, 2005)

'We live in an age of outsourcing. . . . Some firms have gone so far as to become "virtual" manufacturers, owning designs for many products but making almost nothing themselves.' (Grossman and Helpman, 2005)

Four leading international economists directly address one of the fundamental economic policy questions – 'globalization' – from quite different perspectives in their recent work, singling out aspects held essential from their points of view. This, on the one hand, underlines the complicated and multifaceted nature of globalization; on the other hand it reflects the challenge globalization creates for economic theory as well as, in particular, for economic policy making.

It is no surprise then that globalization may have become – no, has indeed become *the* buzz word of the early twenty-first century in the media and in public debate. Over time, the term has been used increasingly superficially, thoughtlessly and inaccurately. However, the fact that 'globalization' has turned into a household word shows that large parts of the population attach importance to it as a phenomenon which affects their lives, by which they are moved. If one takes people's attitude and the potential effects of globalization seriously, it becomes clear that globalization and its perception pose a significant challenge for the world's political systems, especially in the realm of economic policy.

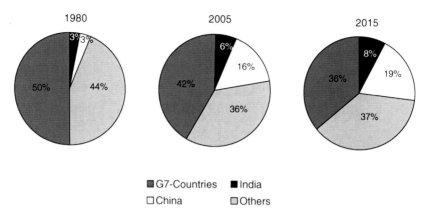

Source: IMF-Forecast, Consensus Economics.

Figure 8.1   *Globalization – indication: increasing share of China and
India in the world economy (shares of global output
1980–2015, purchasing power parity)*

One of those aspects of the globalization process that many people per-
ceive to be momentous and disquieting at the same time is China's and
India's increasingly powerful role in the world economy. In an extreme
oversimplification, this development is often viewed as indicative of a
power shift in the global economic and political landscape, which will entail
negative consequences for the established industrialized nations of the
world, specifically for Europe. As shown by the IMF (Figure 8.1), China
and India each accounted for roughly only 3 per cent of total global output
in 1980 (in terms of purchasing power parities). By 2005, this share had
already reached 22 per cent and, according to IMF estimates, it is expected
to reach 27 per cent by 2015.

At the same time, Europe underwent a fundamental change in its political and economic landscape since the end of the cold war and the opening
up of Central, Eastern and South-Eastern Europe starting in the late 1980s.
In parallel to this 'enlargement' of Europe's economic geography,
European economic integration transformed the western part of the conti-
nent from a group of economically rather separated national states into an
integrated single market, thereby completely changing the nature and the
functioning of the existing economic systems.[1]

New economic geography – or, as Venables (2006) proposes: 'geographical economics' – undertakes a theoretical attempt to develop an integrated theory of location, capable of dealing with the new challenges this
restructuring of the world economy constitutes. The key building block of

geographical economics is the recognition that proximity is good for productivity, growth and development. Mobile factors – firms and possibly workers – will go where productivity is high, and by so doing tend to further raise productivity, creating a new and permanently changing landscape of growth centres.

Some of the key determinants of national and regional prosperity are truly exogenous, ranging from nature and geography to the political and institutional history of countries. But, on top of these, there is a clear need for a theory of the location of economic activity. International trade theory is part of the story. In addition, the new economic geography approach suggests that globalization – perhaps best characterized by Friedman's (2006) 'flattening of the world' image – causes dispersion of activity: some countries will experience rapid growth (at least for some time) while others will lag behind (at least for some time). The catching-up process going on in Central, Eastern and South-Eastern Europe as well as, compared to other regions of the world, exceptionally high growth rates in Asia, are clear signs of the empirical relevance of this view.

FDI FLOWS TO CESEE AS A CHARACTERISTIC TOOL OF INTEGRATION AND GLOBALIZATION

The countries of Central, Eastern and South-Eastern Europe (CESEE) have undergone a significant process of transformation towards market economies. Inflows of FDI into this region are of crucial importance for the success of their transformation and for their integration into the world economy. Foreign investors are usually seen to potentially benefit from access to new markets and cheap factor inputs primarily. For host countries, FDI offers the potential for additional income and employment, increases competition, and supports the creation of a market economy environment. At the same time, uncertain framework conditions do not always allow FDI to turn into a success. Therefore, it is by no means clear that the envisaged objectives for undertaking and attracting FDI will be achieved eventually. For both the firm granting FDI and the firm receiving FDI, there is a substantial risk of FDI projects failing. In the end, the success or failure of FDI will depend, first, on the reasons why all relevant parties expect an FDI project to be an attractive undertaking benefiting all sides, and second, on the degree to which these initial motives can be achieved in reality.

The decade up to 2005 saw particularly strong growth of direct investments in Central and Eastern European countries. According to (updated) UNCTAD estimates, the ten new EU member states in 2005 on average

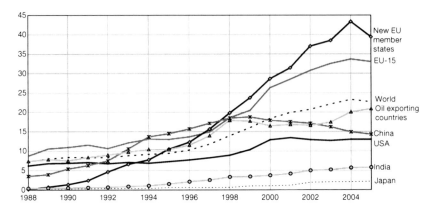

Source: UNCTAD (2006), IMF (GDP for new EU member states 2004 and 2005 and for oil exporting countries 2004 and 2005 excl. Iraq).

Figure 8.2   FDI: stocks of FDI inflows in per cent of GDP by region 1988–2005

show a stock of FDI inflows of about 40 per cent of GDP, a level far beyond the world average and even the popular examples of China and India (Figure 8.2). This growth is mainly regarded as being driven by the process of integration into the European Union, the elimination of the barriers to FDI and the – economic, legal and institutional – progress of the transition process perceived in those economies (Bevan and Estrin, 2004). However, the countries in CESEE are far from homogeneous and both the level and growth of FDI differ across these countries. In terms of cumulative FDI inflows per capita (in USD), the EU-8 countries of the region (see Table 8.1) receive more than twice the average inflow of the SEE-8 countries (including Bulgaria and Romania), with FDI levels varying strongly within the two country groups as well.

Not surprisingly, CEE countries have on average attracted a higher amount of foreign capital than SEE countries, given the well-known differences in starting points as well as in political and economic developments. Obviously, this discrepancy cannot be fully explained by traditional FDI determinants because transition-specific factors certainly play an important role in the investment decision. An example like Croatia, which has attracted rather high FDI inflows, underlines the importance of country-specific factors in understanding the perceived incentives for firms to channel their FDI activities into a particular country.

It seems to be a fair characterization that the economic integration of the CEE countries into the EU has been achieved to a significant extent. Current FDI flows to CEE may now reflect a second, deeper phase of integration

Table 8.1   Cumulative FDI inflows per capita (in USD)

Country	FDI inflow
Czech Republic	5061
Estonia	4674
Hungary	4229
Latvia	1827
Lithuania	1423
Poland	1866
Slovak Republic	2556
Slovenia	1536
Total EU-8 Average	**2714**
Bulgaria	1575
Romania	1110
Croatia	2376
Albania	535
Bosnia and Herzegovina	516
FYR of Macedonia	639
Montenegro	1024
Serbia	725
Total SEE-8 Average	**1134**
CIS and Mongolia Total	**254**

Source: EBRD.

compared to the previous period and compared to the characteristics of FDI flows to SEE countries. However, countries with favourable initial conditions have, in general, attracted more FDI than more risky and poorer performing countries or countries with a higher degree of legal, political, economic or institutional uncertainty. FDI flows to CEE come largely from the EU, with Germany and Austria being among the main investors. The proximity of these countries to the EU as well as their overall policy target of joining the EU as soon as possible has surely stimulated market-seeking investment of EU-based firms. At the same time, the privatization process of formerly state-owned enterprises in these countries has considerably fostered FDI-acquiring existing firms. Greenfield FDI, for a long time rather the exemption than the rule, will now gain in importance in the second phase as the privatization process will phase out in most of the CEE countries (Sinn and Weichenrieder, 1997).

Overall, relative to their size, the CEE countries today are the most successful countries in attracting FDI. This is due to their relatively high market potential, their closeness to the EU-15 countries, and the legal and economic environment they have developed over the last 15 years. They are attractive for FDI even if their unit labour costs are already high compared to other potential host countries. SEE countries are in a quite different position. They mainly benefit from a still low unit labour cost, but most of them are small and less attractive from a market access perspective. For some time, their lagged transition process combined with a risky economic environment was a major obstacle for FDI. This has changed now and SEE countries today are among the most attractive group of target countries for European FDI projects.

Looking ahead, EU enlargement can be expected to raise the market potential of CEE countries, including the most recent new EU member states, Bulgaria and Romania, because of permanent higher growth rates (catching-up) and because of a reduction in the 'economically relevant distance' to the other EU countries. At the same time, the successful process of integration into the EU can be expected to reduce differences in unit labour cost between CEE countries and EU-15 countries, leading to a decrease in existing comparative cost advantage. With some delay, both effects will also gain importance in SEE countries, fostering a tendency to increasing investments motivated by market access and decreasing FDI driven by cost considerations. These tendencies, once again, will fundamentally alter the relevant landscape of production location in an enlarged Europe, putting the now catching-up and FDI-attracting countries under pressure to develop new comparative advantages to gain in competitiveness. Increasingly they will have to capture a share of investment in research, development and innovation to address this medium- and long-term objective.

ECONOMIC GLOBALIZATION – TWO BASIC THEORETICAL PERSPECTIVES

As the example of FDI flows and their determinants shows, globalization is driven by various influences (Fischer, 2003), not least the preferences and objectives of businesses and consumers, which, in turn, are guided by many different factors. These include the attractiveness of a broad range of (relatively cheap) goods and services, unlimited travelling possibilities as well as the 'exotic' character of products, countries and people from geographically remote regions. At the same time, globalization is a politically motivated (and enabled) process (Porter, 1990), which has been consciously shaped and promoted through trade and capital liberalization, the opening-up of markets and especially regional economic integration (as in the case of the EU).

If one looks at the history of economic theory, globalization is but the logical consequence of the historically evolved division of labour, which is crucial to long-term welfare effects. As early as in 1776, Adam Smith described the fundamental importance of the division of labour as a driving factor of productivity growth and industrialization. In identifying comparative advantages to be reaped through external trade, David Ricardo added the decisive international dimension to economic discourse. Representatives of modern economic theory, such as Paul Krugman, have since highlighted market integration, product differentiation and international returns to scale as key growth factors in modern market economies.

Recently, however, Paul Samuelson (2004) has made it clear that blind euphoria about globalization processes may be as misguided as utter rejection. Samuelson underlines the importance of the distribution problem linked to globalization; after all, integration, as a rule, produces winners and losers alike. In theory, it appears possible to offset losses through realized gains. However, in practice the possibility of achieving this theoretical balance boils down to a political issue that is without doubt one of the most sensitive issues in the entire globalization debate. Samuelson thus addresses one of the pivotal points of the current debate. Policy makers need to address the fact that many people expect to be negatively affected by globalization without being compensated by positive effects, even if global welfare should increase. This distribution perspective is the reason why globalization is not primarily an economic but a political issue.[2]

As mentioned before, globalization (in the narrow economic sense) can be interpreted as the (logical?) consequence of a long-term development process, if viewed from a historical perspective. The development of the modern market economy, which evolved from absolute economic autarky ('Robinson Crusoe'), via barter, money and eventually credit economies, was characterized by the gradual emergence of essential economic functions.

Similarly to the division of labour, the evolution of barter, money and credit financing went hand in hand with significant welfare gains. Thanks to these welfare gains, nobody would ever seriously consider reversing the establishment of barter and money or demanding the abolition of credit financing. Globalization now adds a new, geographical dimension to this historical process, which is expected to yield further productivity gains. If this assessment of the situation is correct, by the end of this century, globalization will have become a welcome feature of our economic system which is taken for granted, just as money and credit financing are today.

All in all, the global division of labour and the global mobility of production factors can be assumed to produce welfare gains, as they increase allocative efficiency, widen choices for producers and consumers and contribute to faster knowledge transfer (European Commission, 2005; CEPR,

2006). Of course, the notion that globalization creates more wealth 'for everyone' only holds in theory. In reality, there will be winners and losers, but, generally speaking, gains will exceed losses, theoretically making it possible to compensate 'losers'. If politicians want the general public to embrace the globalization trend, they will have to face the crucial challenge of actually making this sort of compensation happen (Bernanke, 2006).

MOTIVES – THE DRIVING FORCES BEHIND FDI

In the view of the media and in public discussion, FDI flows from developed countries to emerging markets is driven – almost exclusively – by low production costs, mainly low wages, and low tax rates. Pressure on wages, reduction in employment and loss of competitiveness are perceived by the population in FDI home countries as, in their view, obvious threats of globalization, market integration and FDI activities. From a (dynamic) economic point of view, this widely held opinion is in stark contrast to theoretical as well as empirical results. The main factor behind these differences in perception seems to be a lack in understanding correctly the nature and role of (economic) motives as driving forces behind FDI decisions.

In order to compensate for the high costs of operating abroad, a firm must reap significant advantages from engaging in a FDI project and going international. In practice, a broad range of micro- and macroeconomic determinants similarly determine a firm's willingness and ability to undertake FDI: ownership, location and internationalization advantages are seen as the most relevant factors for FDI (Dunning, 1993). The ownership advantages come in several forms, all based on the concept of knowledge-based or firm-specific assets. The sources of location advantages differ primarily with the type of multinational involved. Horizontally structured firms produce the same goods and services at different places internationally. They invest abroad to avoid trade costs associated with exporting from their home country to sometimes distant foreign markets. These trade costs can be expected to be high, in particular when the host market is large and when it is far away (Markusen, 1995). Firms with a vertical organizational structure fragment their production process geographically by stages of production. In these cases the main motive behind FDI is related to cost reduction, to take advantage of lower wages or, more generally, input costs of production in other countries. It makes particular sense when the stages of production use different factor intensities and/or when countries differ regarding the availability of factor resources and/or factor prices, in many cases cheap(er) labour.[3]

Table 8.2   FDI motives of Austrian companies (in per cent)

	Wage cost	Taxes	Market	Inputs – Raw materials	Other
1989	1.8	1.9	72.7	2.3	21.2
1990	1.9	2.0	71.2	2.8	22.0
1991	2.6	1.9	70.6	2.7	22.2
1992	2.3	1.6	71.9	2.5	21.6
1993	2.6	2.2	79.3	2.4	13.6
1994	3.5	2.1	75.4	2.7	16.3
1995	3.7	2.2	75.2	2.5	16.4
1996	3.6	2.3	73.1	2.2	18.9
1997	4.0	2.0	71.7	2.9	19.5
1998	3.4	2.0	72.2	2.8	19.5
1999	3.4	1.7	71.9	2.9	20.2
2000	3.1	2.2	71.7	2.4	20.6
2001	3.1	2.2	71.4	2.4	20.9
2002	3.4	2.1	71.5	2.5	20.4
2003	3.1	2.2	70.2	2.7	21.8
2004	3.4	2.1	69.5	2.7	22.4
Of which:					
Hungary	6.9	0.5	68.5	3.0	21.1
Czech Republic	8.0	0.0	70.3	1.3	20.4
Slovak Republic	9.1	2.1	68.5	0.7	19.6
Poland	1.4	0.0	74.5	9.2	14.9
Croatia	1.1	0.0	78.5	1.1	19.4

Source: OeNB.

An important task of economic theory is to connect these advantages in a consistent way to develop an overall framework for understanding all the relevant influences leading to FDI decision making. In empirical studies the impact on FDI is usually dominated by the market potential in the targeted host country. Other comparative advantages as well as – particularly in the case of CESEE – transition-specific determinants, for example privatization issues or institutional uncertainty, also determine FDI flows.[4]

The overriding importance of market access and market potential is evident from the structure of motives expressed by Austrian firms which have undertaken FDI projects abroad.[5] Continually, 70 per cent or more of these firms name market access as their main motive to engage in FDI, while they declare wages (about 3 per cent) and taxes (about 2 per cent) to be of minor importance. The prospect of market access motivated the most recent Austrian FDI projects in selected CESEE countries to an even higher extent, whereas taxes were apparently virtually irrelevant. In contrast, Hungarian, Czech and Slovak firms declare wages to be of above average importance.

With motives being the key drivers of all participants shaping FDI decision making, a large body of literature deals with theories of investors' motives for undertaking FDI, based on market imperfections, theories of internationalization and theories of choice and firm strategies. Absolute and comparative advantages, the direct control of foreign operations in a less known foreign environment and, more generally, establishing a better knowledge of foreign markets are the key issues in this respect. Geographical distance, the fundamental complication behind all these factors, is tackled first by trading goods from one country to the other and later on by establishing subsidiaries and branches or by acquiring existing entities. Complementary to market seeking, the internationalization of production assets and the internationalization of factor sources can also be understood as a risk-minimizing strategy from the point of view of a firm – transforming itself from a locally oriented enterprise into an internationally active, eventually globally acting, corporation. Enhancing the competitive advantage of a firm in the medium- and long-term is the final rationale of all these attempts.

Investors' motives for undertaking FDI ideally coincide with host countries' motives for attracting FDI. In addition, the motives for target companies to become acquired by foreign investors are obviously important in cases of non-greenfield investment. Host countries are mainly interested in broadening their productive capacity, increasing efficiency and productivity, fostering employment and importing organizational as well as technological skills. FDI-receiving firms try to internalize these advantages to strengthen their competitive position at the 'cost' of substituting domestic through foreign ownership. Ideally all these aims, which need not be conflicting ones theoretically, can be realized in a successful FDI project. Unfortunately, things are much more complicated in reality. Uncertainty about the true motives for FDI as well as uncertainty about framework conditions in FDI host countries and conflicting interest contribute to making FDI projects probably one of the most complicated kinds of undertaking. Foreign direct investment, unlike portfolio investment, involves a long-term relationship between the parent and the affiliate, and it reflects a lasting interest in the host economy.

A recently published European Commission Survey illustrates the general issue of rules as a determinant of business activities (Table 8.3). For the EU-15 countries, (new) rules for establishing a business in other EU countries did not have an impact on the behaviour of the clear majority of firms (63 per cent no impact + 16 per cent not concerned). Very similarly, it seems

Table 8.3 *How did rules for establishing a business in other EU countries have an impact on your business activities (in per cent)?*

		Positive Impact	No Impact	Negative Impact	(Not Concerned)	(Don't Know)
Businesses in EU-15		12	63	6	16	4
Businesses in New EU-10 Member States		10	30	1	52	6
	Of which:	Very Important	Rather Important	Rather Un-important	Not At All Important	(Not Relevant – Don't Know)
	EU Companies Investing in Your Business	8	10	7	14	60
Impact of Enlargement on Activities		Positive Impact	No Impact	Negative Impact		(Don't Know)
	Access to New Markets	54	37	4		5
	Productivity	46	44	6		4
	Profitability	34	39	21		6
	Cost of Wages	21	46	29		4
	Cost of Raw Materials	19	40	33		9

Source: European Commission Flash Eurobarometer 2006.

that businesses in the new EU-10 member states see this as irrelevant to their own business. Interestingly enough, for EU companies investing in the new member states this is also not considered to be very important (7 per cent + 14 per cent not important + 60 per cent not relevant). Concerning the impact of enlargement activities more directly, a majority of firms (54 per cent) see access to new markets as a positive impact. The assessment is also positive overall for productivity and, to a lesser extent, for profitability, whereas cost of wages and cost of raw materials are perceived to have developed negatively because of this enlargement effect.

TOWARDS A 100 PER CENT FOREIGN-OWNED ECONOMY?

One of the obvious 'side effects' of growing FDI flows and stocks, although mostly neglected in the FDI literature itself, is the change in ownership structure in FDI host countries. If a foreign investor acquires an existing company, the transfer from domestic to foreign ownership is at the heart of the transaction, directly changing the previous ownership-structure of capital stock in the direction of foreign ownership. In the case of greenfield FDI the change in ownership structure takes place via a foreign-owned addition to the capital stock of the host country.

Recent experience has shown that the interaction of privatization and FDI has resulted in an almost complete restructuring of the ownership structure in CESEE countries. Overall, foreign ownership – which was almost non-existent in these areas 20 years ago – has increased substantially or has even become the dominant ownership category in many countries. In specific countries and sectors, foreign ownership has even reached or is approaching 100 per cent – for example in banking and/or financial services in the Baltic States or in the Czech Republic.[6] Therefore, the question of the consequences of these fundamental changes definitely needs to be addressed when tracking the developments of FDI flows and stocks (Demsetz and Lehn, 1985).

Empirical studies focusing on enterprise performance have consistently concluded that foreign firms appear to have been considerably more profitable than domestic firms. For example, total factor productivity has been found to increase more in firms with foreign direct investment and more still in firms with foreign ownership. Most of the economic literature emphasizes the positive spillover effects of FDI, namely advances in productivity, technical expertise and business competence, through the transfer of these elements from foreign to domestic enterprises and through the labour force as a whole, augmenting the human capital base. In addition, it has also been shown that productivity in the economy as a whole has risen in tandem with FDI inflows, leading to the policy conclusion that low productivity growth can be associated with a relative lack of foreign investment (Davies and Lyons, 1991).

Of course, these results are convincing with regard to a situation of raising foreign ownership starting from a very low or perhaps medium level.

In particular, the beneficial effects of FDI and an increasing share of foreign ownership will unfold in an economy characterized by low productivity and a less efficient use of capital. But the question becomes increasingly puzzling under conditions where foreign ownership has already reached a comparable high share: think of a world characterized by complete foreign ownership – every existing firm is 100 per cent owned by a foreigner, and there is no domestic ownership in any country. Nobody will expect the world productivity level to be higher in this hypothetical case than when some degree of domestic ownership is left. Similarly, a conquest of an FDI host country by an FDI home country would not be expected to automatically depress efficiency and/or productivity in the combined area of these two countries because of the implied decrease in the degree of foreign ownership.

Theoretical as well as empirical studies offer few economic criteria to differentiate foreign ownership from domestic ownership (Friedman, 1995). In discussing a theoretically desirable ownership structure of a country, the dimension of domestic versus foreign ownership is only one out of many – and it is not at all clear that it is the most important one. For example, the question of strategic ownership commitment, as expressed by the contrast between management- and ownership-controlled corporate structures, seems to be of much more importance in many cases. But given the many times narrower confines of capital markets in smaller countries, the problem is once again typically reduced to the question of how much foreign ownership seems to be 'acceptable'. Economic theory can contribute little towards solving the implied dilemma. Only by considering substantial market imperfections, that is differences in the behaviour of foreign and domestic owners under the same framework conditions, may arguments be derived for or against foreign ownership. In reality, limiting foreign ownership is an economic policy perceived desirable by many countries for a number of different reasons.

Even in the US, foreign influence in a so-called 'key sector' – such as banking – is 'officially' viewed critically (United States GAO, 1996), although no explicit economic rationale is given (Tyson, 1991). Traditional economic arguments used in favour of limiting foreign ownership could be external effects, which in the case of banking would relate primarily to the banks' specific position in the transmission process of monetary policy and to financial stability considerations. Very recently a rather wide range of strategic sectors was defined in Russia based on criteria like security and confidentiality, ranging from energy to military as well as basic metals, to limit foreign ownership.[7] The OECD (2006) illustrates the currently rising concerns in many countries regarding cross-border mergers and acquisitions by pointing out three areas – national security, access to resources and public utilities – as the main criteria for restricting foreign ownership in many countries, including highly developed ones.

Finally, in addressing the question of foreign ownership, one should take into account that the consequences of foreign ownership may significantly differ by sector. In theory, the consequences of FDI and foreign ownership are typically derived for the manufacturing industry. Yet banking and many financial services, including those in high-end market segments, are basically customer-oriented services, above all financial products requiring a considerable amount of personal consulting. For as long as these product features apply, the product must be supplied mainly at the place where demand occurs. In spite of the rapid development of modern communication technologies, it must be assumed that the factor mobility of financial institutions is likely to remain comparatively low. Unlike manufacturing companies, banks are limited in their efforts to separate production from demand in the spatial dimension. This rather limits the employment and income risks that might result from foreign ownership. Nevertheless, suppliers of financial services can and do shift central functions internationally, particularly high-end service components (ranging from product development to market analysis) and back-office tasks susceptible to standardization (outsourcing of data processing).

Overall, analysing FDI developments from roughly 1985 to 2005 and, in particular, the changing landscape of FDI in Europe due to the ongoing integration process of CESEE countries with the EU, it becomes very clear that the related change in ownership structures will create one of the important new policy challenges for the future. More research is definitely needed on this specific topic to understand better what the consequences of this will be for the functioning of economic systems in times of globalization.

CONCLUDING REMARKS

Globalization has clearly changed the (economic) geography of the world and nowadays poses an obvious new challenge to economic policy. Many people in the industrialized world feel personally affected by this phenomenon and its potential effects on their lives. In Europe the (ongoing) process of economic integration and EU enlargement, following the opening-up of Central and Eastern Europe, is shaping the changing landscape of competitive advantage. One of the main tools that companies can use to adapt to this new situation is FDI. As a consequence, FDI flows and stocks have risen markedly over the last decade. Contrary to the main focus of the discussions in the media and in the public, the main driving motive for this development is market access – firms struggling to explore the available new market potential in the catching-up countries of Central, Eastern and South-Eastern Europe. But FDI of this kind is not only to the benefit of the firms investing in foreign markets; empirical evidence suggests that, in general, home and host countries are benefiting simultaneously. For the host country the envisaged advantages range from higher growth potential and employment to R&D spillovers and increased competition. The home country may profit from a better competitive position regarding its production because of an improved division of labour, lower input costs and economies of scale due to market enlargement. Overall, FDI has definitely changed the geography of production all over Europe; at the same time, the rise of China and India in the world economy is significantly adding to the geographical reallocation of the world's capital stock. Widely neglected, the significant increase in FDI stocks has, at the same time, changed, and will continue to change the ownership structure in FDI-receiving countries, in particular in smaller ones. Although the bulk of the literature agrees on the beneficial effects of foreign ownership on productivity and efficiency, it is silent on the consequences of almost completely 'foreign-owned countries'. As the situation has developed close to this status at least in some countries and/or in particular sectors, it has become clear that this will create one of the important new policy challenges for the functioning of economic systems in the forthcoming future.

NOTES

1. See Denis et al. (2006), Stiglitz (2002), Taylor (2006) and the report of the Working Group of the Capital Markets Consultative Group (2003) for an encompassing treatment of the relevant issues.
2. The crucial importance of this aspect has recently been underlined by Bernanke (2006): 'The challenge for policymakers is to ensure that the benefits of global economic integration are sufficiently widely shared (. . .).'
3. See Lipsey et al. (1995) as well as Riess and Uppenberg (2004) for analyses of the internationalization of production.
4. On the empirical results on the determinats of FDI see, for example, Lankes and Venables (1996) and Blonigen (2005).
5. For an in-depth analysis of Austrian FDI to CEE see Altzinger (1998) and Sieber (2006).
6. In banking the share of total assets of branches and subsidiaries from abroad for 2005 according to OeNB calculations – already reaches more than 90% in Estonia, Slovakia and the Czech Republic, whereas in EU-15 the highest share with the exception of Luxembourg (94.5%) lies at 58.4% (Finland) and the average of the euro area is 16.3% only.
7. See *Neue Zürcher Zeitung*, 'Russland definiert strategische Sektoren', 1 February 2007, p. 10.

REFERENCES

Altzinger, W. (1998), 'Austria's foreign direct investment in Central and Eastern Europe: "Supply based" or "market driven"?', *University of Economics Vienna Working Paper* No. 57, April.

Bernanke, B. (2006), 'Global Economic Integration: What's New and What's Not?', Federal Reserve Bank of Kansas City's 30th Symposium, Jackson Hole, Wyoming, August.

Bevan, A. and S. Estrin (2004), 'The determinants of foreign direct investment into European transition economies', *Journal of Comparative Economics*, **32** (4).

Blonigen, B.A. (2005), 'A review of the empirical literature on FDI determinants', *NBER Working Paper* 11299, May.

CEPR (2002), 'Making sense of globalization', *Policy Paper* 8, London.

CEPR (2006), *Global Integration and Technology Transfer*, London: Centre for Economic Policy Research.

Davies, S.W. and B.R. Lyons (1991), 'Characterising relative performance: the productivity advantage of foreign owned firms in the UK', *Oxford Economic Papers*, **43** (4).

Demsetz, H. and K. Lehn (1985), 'The structure of corporate ownership: causes and consequences', *Journal of Political Economy*, **93** (6).

Denis, C., K. McMorrow and W. Röger (2006), 'Globalisation: trends, issues and macro implications for the EU', *European Economy. Economic Papers*, **254**, July.

Dunning, J.H. (1993), *Multinational Enterprises and the Global Economy*, Wokingham: Addison-Wesley.

European Commission (2005), 'Rising international economic integration – opportunities and challenges', *The EU Economy 2005 Review*, 11 November.

Fischer, S. (2003), 'Globalisation and its challenges', *American Economic Review*, **93** (2), May.

Freeman, R. (2005), 'What really ails Europe (and America): the doubling of the global workforce', www.theGlobalist.com (3 June).

Friedman, B.M. (1995), 'Economic implications of changing share ownership', *NBER Working Paper*.

Friedman, Th.L. (2006), *The World Is Flat. The Globalized World in the Twenty-first Century*, London: Penguin Books Ltd.

Grossman, G.M. and E. Helpman (2005), 'Outsourcing in a global economy', *Review of Economic Studies*, **72**.

Helpman, E. and P. Krugman (1985), *Market Structure and Foreign Trade*, Cambridge: MIT Press.

International Monetary Fund (IMF) (2006), *World Economic Outlook*, April, IMF.

Krugman, P. (1991), *Geography and Trade*, Cambridge, MA: MIT Press.

Lankes, H.-P. and A.J. Venables (1996), 'Foreign direct investment in economic transition: the changing pattern of investments', *Economics of Transition*, **4** (2).

Lipsey, R.E., M. Blomström and E. Ramstetter (1995), 'Internationalized production in world output', *NBER Working Paper* 5385.

Markusen, J.R. (1995), 'The boundaries of multinational enterprises and the theory of international trade', *Journal of Economic Perspectives*, **9** (2).

OECD (2006), *International Investment Perspectives*, Paris: OECD.

Porter, M.E. (1990), *The Competitive Advantage of Nations*, New York: Free Press.

Riess, A. and K. Uppenberg (2004), 'The internationalisation of production: moving plants, products, and people', *EIB Papers*, **9** (1).

Samuelson, P.A. (2004), 'Where Ricardo and Mill rebut and confirm arguments of mainstream economists supporting globalization', *Journal of Economic Perspectives*, **18** (3), 135–46.

Sieber, S. (2006), 'Direktinvestitionen österreichischer Unternehmen in Ost-Mitteleuropa', *WIFO-Monatsberichte*, **8**.

Sinn, H.W. and A.J. Weichenrieder (1997), 'Foreign direct investment, political resentment and the privatization process in Eastern Europe', *Economic Policy*, April.

Stiglitz, J. (2002), *Globalization and Its Discontents*, New York: W.W. Norton & Company.

Taylor, A. (2006), 'Globalization. A Historical Perspective', Lecture held at the 34th Economics Conference of the Oesterreichische Nationalbank, 22–23 May.

Tyson, L.D. (1991), 'They are not us – why American ownership still matters', *The American Prospect*, Winter.

UNCTAD (2006), *World Investment Report*, New York and Geneva: United Nations.

United States, General Accounting Office (GAO) (1996), 'Foreign banks: assessing their role in the US banking system: report to the ranking minority member, Committee on Banking, Housing, and Urban Affairs, US Senate', GAO/GGD-96-26, Washington, DC: The Office.

Venables, A.J. (2006), 'Shifts in economic geography and their causes', *Federal Reserve Bank of Kansas City Economic Review*, Fourth Quarter.

Working Group of the Capital Markets Consultative Group (2003), *Foreign Direct Investment in Emerging Market Countries*, September.

9. Recent FDI trends: implications for investment policy

Blanka Kalinova[1]

Since the slump in 2001–2003, foreign direct investment (FDI) has recovered briskly. World FDI inflows increased by some 20 per cent in each of the years 2004–2006 and are estimated to have reached a level of over USD 1 trillion the last year, the second or third highest amount on record. FDI developments continue to be driven by a number of traditional determinants, such as natural and human endowments and market size, but they are also increasingly influenced by new factors, in particular the growing importance of novel forms of international investment and the emergence of new players. Conversely, FDI may arguably have been held back by a resurgence of investment protectionism. This chapter summarizes recent OECD investment policy initiatives launched in response to the challenges created by the changing world FDI landscape, notably the OECD's FDI restrictiveness index and its Policy Framework for Investment.

DISTINCTIVE FEATURES OF RECENT FDI TRENDS

OECD countries are the major source of FDI flows, representing around 60 per cent of world FDI inflows and more than 80 per cent of outflows (for some of the statistical challenges see Box 9.1). The OECD area as a whole remains a net outward direct investor with net outflows amounting to USD 95 billion in 2005 (see Figure 9.1). In 2005, the main FDI recipients among OECD countries were the United Kingdom (USD 164 billion), followed by the United States (USD 110 billion) and France (USD 64 billion). The most active OECD outward investors in 2005 were the Netherlands (USD 119 billion), France (USD 116 billion) and the United Kingdom (USD 101 billion).

While OECD countries continue to dominate world FDI flows, the share of non-OECD countries has been increasing from 18 per cent of world FDI inflows in 1988–1990 to 36 per cent in 2003–2005. However, FDI is still concentrated on a limited number of beneficiaries: six emerging market

---

BOX 9.1   FDI STATISTICS DO NOT CAPTURE ALL
ASPECTS IN CORPORATE INVESTMENT
BEHAVIOUR

Many new corporate sector developments and cross-border transactions are not yet fully and adequately captured by FDI statistics.
Efforts to raise the coverage and coherence of statistics towards
agreed standards are an ongoing concern of the OECD and its
Workshop on International Investment Statistics. Extending these
standards to non-OECD countries is another important objective.

Revising data definitions to better reflect the changing corporate
landscape is a further critical undertaking. The revised OECD
Benchmark Definition of FDI – under discussion with the IMF and
other responsible international agencies at the time of writing,
seeks to address the following statistical shortcomings.[2]

- Separate purely 'pass through' investment from 'genuine' FDI,
  that is identify the ultimate home or host country enterprise.
- Allocate FDI to sectors of activity according to the non-
  resident's field of activity (and not according to the activity of
  the non-resident enterprise as it is current practice).
- Take into account new forms of international investment,
  including investment in intangible assets.

---

economies are among the top 20 FDI recipients (that is China, Hong Kong,
Singapore, Russia, Brazil and India).[3] As for direct investment originating
in OECD countries, Singapore remains the largest recipient in cumulative
terms, followed by China and Brazil.

FDI developments in the decade since the mid-1990s have been marked by
several distinctive features. First, in many OECD countries mergers and
acquisitions (M&A) now account for more than half of total FDI. This FDI
component, traditionally the most reactive to changes in the business climate,
has been particularly dynamic in response to improved corporate profitability
and low borrowing costs. Second, sharp sectoral divergences emerged – and
then disappeared. In the years leading up to 2000, direct investment flows
were totally dominated by the high technology and public utilities sectors.
During the recent rebound of FDI, no particular sector has so far stood out.

That said, a broader and more gradual shift in sectoral balances seems
to have taken place. An increasing share of services in FDI flows is now

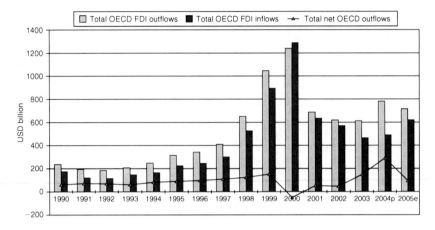

Source: OECD Investment Newsletter, No. 2/2006, October 2006.

Figure 9.1   FDI flows to and from OECD countries, 1990–2005

a well confirmed trend: two-thirds of the OECD's outward FDI position is
in this sector. A second distinctive feature is the increasing number of
players, not only in terms of countries, but also with respect to the number
of multinational enterprises (MNEs). From some 7000 in the 1970s, their
number has increased to 70 000 today. A third aspect is the growing importance of intellectual assets, which has led to more international investment
in knowledge-based assets. Finally, low transport and communications
costs have given rise to more complex cross-border strategic alliances and
co-operation arrangements, which allow new synergies and competencies
to develop faster and in a more flexible way compared not only to greenfield
investment but also to M&A.

FACTORS INFLUENCING THE ALLOCATION OF FDI

Traditional 'non-policy' factors continue to play an important role in world
FDI developments, in particular market size, availability of physical and
human capital, geographical distance and costs of transport and communications. The economic recovery in OECD countries and continuing robust
growth in major emerging market economies has also significantly contributed to recent FDI dynamism. As already noted, improved corporate
profitability and low borrowing costs explain for a large part the recent boom
in cross-border M&A activities. The importance of some of the non-policy
factors may even have increased. Lower transport and communications

costs, technological innovation, changing intra-firm organization and co-ordination have all influenced the patterns of FDI and globalization more generally.

Without underestimating the role of non-policy barriers, the OECD as a forum for policy makers focuses its analysis and recommendations on policy barriers. The main distinction should be made between general restrictions and FDI-specific barriers. General product and labour market regulations act as barriers to entry and increase the cost of business for domestic and foreign operators alike. While not specifically discriminating against foreign investors, these general regulations have significant distorting and diverting effects on FDI. FDI-specific restrictions range from all-out bans or limitations on foreign ownership to less restrictive notification or screening procedures and operational restrictions imposed on foreign-owned firms. According to OECD estimates, aligning product market regulations and FDI restrictions with those of the most liberal member country (the United Kingdom) could increase the area's total direct inward position by 20 per cent.[4]

FDI RESTRICTIVENESS INDEX

Developed by the OECD, the methodology of the FDI restrictiveness index allows FDI-specific restrictions in different countries to be compared.[5] The methodology distinguishes three types of open (formal) restrictions affecting foreign investors:

- Restrictions on foreign entry in terms of limitations on foreign ownership
- Approval and screening procedures
- Post-entry management and other operational restrictions

Restrictiveness is measured on a 0–1 scale, with 0 representing full openness and 1 corresponding to prohibition of FDI. The index covers 9 sectors and 11 sub-sectors, including business services, financial services, telecommunications, construction, tourism, distribution, transport, electricity and manufacturing. As with most methodologies seeking to quantify essentially qualitative aspects, there are a number of important qualifications regarding the reported FDI restrictiveness scores. The index takes into account only overt regulatory restrictions and not the actual enforcement of statutory restrictions. Such an approach could penalize countries which are more transparent in self-reporting restrictions. The OECD estimates nevertheless provide some interesting insights, in particular:

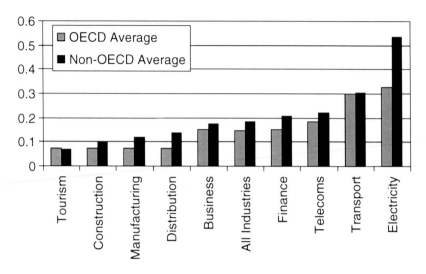

Source: OECD's FDI Regulatory Restrictiveness Index: Revision and Extension to more Economies; Investment Working Paper No. 4/2006, OECD, Paris, December 2006.

Figure 9.2   FDI restrictiveness index by industries, OECD and non-OECD average

- The sectoral pattern of the analysed sectors is broadly similar across countries: electricity and transport are the most restricted industries, followed by telecommunications and financial services. In contrast, manufacturing, tourism, construction and distribution are generally less restricted both in OECD and non-OECD countries (see Figure 9.2).
- Among OECD countries, the European members are the most open countries, partly reflecting EU integration.
- For non-OECD countries, OECD estimates are more varied: Eastern European economies (the Baltic States) and some Latin American countries (Chile and Argentina) have low scores, whereas China, India and Russia show the highest scores (see Figure 9.3).

MAIN POLICY CHALLENGES ARISING FROM THE CHANGING FDI LANDSCAPE

In response to the changing FDI landscape, the international investment community faces three major policy challenges: (i) integrating new players and encouraging them to respect international investment standards and

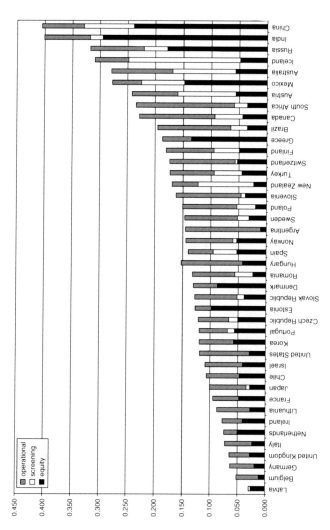

Note: * This aggregated index covers the following sectors and sub-sectors: business (legal, accounting, architectural and engineering services), telecommunications (fixed line telephony and mobile telephony), construction, distribution, finance (insurance and banking), tourism, transport (air, water and road), electricity and manufacturing.

Source: OECD's FDI Regulatory Restrictiveness Index: Revision and Extension to more Economies; Investment Working Paper No. 4/2006, OECD, Paris, December 2006.

*Figure 9.3   FDI regulatory restrictiveness index by type of restrictions**

disciplines, (ii) helping less developed countries to develop their policy capacity for investment, and (iii) balancing legitimate security and other essential interests with the resurging risk of FDI protectionism. These three areas are now at the centre of the OECD Investment Committee's work.

POLICY FRAMEWORK FOR INVESTMENT

With the objective to contribute to the effective implementation of the United Nations Monterrey Consensus on Financing for Development, the OECD has developed a Policy Framework for Investment (PFI) aimed at assisting governments in designing and implementing good policy practices for attracting and maximizing benefits of investment.[6] It represents a comprehensive, multilaterally backed investment policy tool for identifying the most important issues governments should address to improve the investment climate and enhance the contribution of investment to development. The PFI contains 82 questions to governments in 10 policy areas, which are recognized to be critical for building a sound environment for all investors, from domestic small enterprises to multinational enterprises (see Figure 9.4).

While the questions addressed by the PFI vary from theme to theme, three essential principles apply throughout: (i) policy coherence, (ii) transparency and accountability, and (iii) regular evaluation of policies. Designed as a flexible instrument that can be adapted by governments to their specific needs and objectives, the PFI provides a common platform for

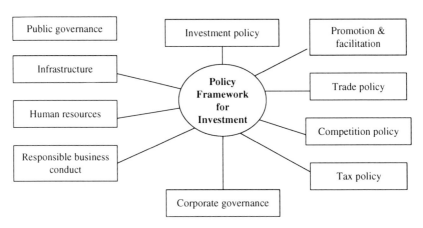

Source: OECD Policy Brief: The Policy Framework for Investment, OECD, September 2006.

Figure 9.4   Policy Framework for Investment

BOX 9.2   OECD POLICY DIALOGUE WITH MAJOR NON-OECD MEMBERS

The OECD is strengthening its partnership with key non-member countries through the policy dialogue with major players, in particular Russia and China. In 2006, the OECD undertook Investment Policy Reviews in co-operation with the authorities of these countries, encouraging them to enhance policy transparency and adopt international investment standards.[7] The OECD also pursues several regional investment initiatives, involving South-Eastern Europe (SEE),[8] African countries (NEPAD)[9] and the Middle East and North Africa (MENA)[10] region. All these programmes use peer dialogue to promote a sound investment climate both domestically and internationally, based on best policy practices.

---

dialogue and peer review. Several regional initiatives are already using the PFI for this purpose (see Box 9.2). The PFI complements other OECD initiatives directed at businesses, in particular the OECD Guidelines for Multinational Enterprises.

PREVENTING INVESTMENT PROTECTIONISM

Several countries have recently taken steps to discourage foreign takeovers of incumbent enterprises, invoking arguments such as energy security and safeguard of national interests, which go beyond traditional national defence and national security concerns. Tightening national practices towards cross-border M&A partly responds to security concerns emerging in the aftermath of 11 September 2001 and perceived risks for energy supply. Another source of concern is takeovers by entities from non-OECD countries, in some cases wholly or partially state-owned and/or with non-transparent ownership and corporate governance structures.[11] It should, however, be noted that the role of these countries as outward investors still remains relatively modest. In 2005 the 'BRICS countries' (Brazil, Russia, India, China and South Africa) represented 3.4 per cent of annual FDI outflows.

Whereas the legitimate rights of governments to defend national interest and deal with security and other economic risks should not be denied or ignored, recent events do entail a risk of triggering a defensive spiral of national measures. The OECD has been encouraged to initiate the work in this area, in particular to establish an inventory of national investment policy practices in the area of national security and other essential interests in OECD and non-OECD countries. It will also analyse relevant issues such as policies towards takeovers by foreign government-controlled entities, identification of ultimate beneficiary owners and the procedural fairness of regulatory requirements for participants in cross-border corporate take-overs. Employing its internationally recognized analytical expertise and policy approaches, based on peer review and policy dialogue, the OECD is well placed to prevent an FDI 'backlash' and contribute to safeguarding an open international investment environment.

NOTES

1.   Blanka Kalinova is a senior economist at the OECD. The chapter is based on ongoing work of the Investment Division, Directorate of Financial and Enterprise Affairs. The author wishes to thank her colleagues, in particular Hans Christiansen, for their valuable comments. The opinions expressed in this chapter do not necessarily reflect official positions of the OECD and its member countries.
2.   OECD Investment Newsletter, Issue 2/2006, 'Progress towards better FDI statistics', Paris, October 2006.
3.   The Economic Intelligence Unit/Columbia Program on International Investment: 'World investment prospects to 2010: Boom or backlash?', London, 2006.
4.   OECD Economic Outlook, no. 73/2003; Chapter VIII: 'Policy influences on Foreign Direct Investment', Paris, June 2003.
5.   OECD Investment Working Paper 4/2006: 'OECD's FDI regulatory restrictiveness index: Revision and extension to more economies', Paris, December 2006.
6.   The Policy Framework for Investment, OECD Policy Brief, Paris, September 2006, available at www.oecd.org/publications/Policybriefs.
7.   Investment Policy Review of China: 'Open policies towards mergers and acquisitions', OECD 2006; Investment Policy Review of the Russian Federation: 'Enhancing policy transparency', OECD, 2006.
8.   Investment Compact for South-East Europe, set up in February 2000, is a part of the Stability Pact for South-Eastern Europe. It seeks to support the improvement of the business environment in SEE countries through sharing policy experience, peer review and dialogue. For more information: www.investmentcompact.org.
9.   Launched with the New Partnership for Africa's Development (NEPAD) in 2003, the NEPAD-OECD Investment Initiative uses peer dialogue and experience with best policy practices to assist African countries to create a sound investment climate. It also seeks to enhance the role of official development assistance in supporting investment and increasing regional capabilities with public–private partnership in utilities. www.oecd.org/daf/investment/africa.
10. The MENA programme (www.oecd.org/mena/investment) seeks to mobilize investment – foreign, regional and domestic – as a driving force for growth, stability and prosperity through the Middle East and North Africa (MENA) region.
11. International Investment Perspectives, Chapter 1: 'Trends and recent developments in Foreign Direct Investment', OECD Paris, 2006.

10. Trends in FDI: the Austrian perspective

René Dell'mour

This chapter aims at presenting the Austrian perspective on global trends in foreign direct investment. It starts with a brief look back into recent history and then highlights several characteristics of the current situation of direct investment in Austria and abroad.

Figure 10.1 captures foreign direct investment (FDI) flows in relation to GDP. It is taken from the Austrian Balance of Payment (BOP) statistics and includes data going back to the 1960s: 40 to 50 years ago direct investment abroad was almost non-existent, while direct investment in Austria remained in the range of 0.3 to 0.4 per cent of GDP.

The situation did not change very much until the late 1980s. Investment flows remained low by international standards, as represented by the dots in Figure 10.1. Austria continued to show a negative FDI balance,

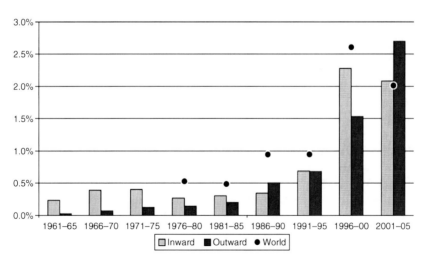

Source: OeNB, UNCTAD (2005).

Figure 10.1 FDI flows in relation to GDP

which means investment flows into Austria were bigger than outward flows.

Of course, this situation was caused by a number of factors. After World War II, capital was scarce and capital imports were urgently needed. But there were limitations to capital imports: on the one hand, fairly large parts of the Austrian economy were directly or indirectly state-owned; on the other hand, there has always been a certain amount of mistrust vis-à-vis foreign owners. Another important reason for the relatively low levels of FDI was the dominance of small- and medium-sized companies in Austria and the correspondingly 'thin' market on the stock exchange. Finally, one should not forget that Austria was situated on the periphery of the Western world, bordering on the Iron Curtain.

In 1989 the picture changed dramatically within one month, when the first part of the Iron Curtain between Austria and Hungary was torn down on 27 June and Austria officially applied for membership of the European Union on 17 July.

There had already been some earlier signs of a 'climatic' change in favour of direct investment. At the beginning of the 1980s, a much debated investment project by General Motors had taken off and turned out to be a big success. Around the same time, in 1982, the 'Austrian Business Agency', Austria's investment promotion agency, was established. Outward investment started growing too but frequently investors were criticized for not investing 'at home', and consequently a number of these projects finally failed.

Yet in 1989, FDI suddenly started skyrocketing and in the early 1990s Austria experienced a net outflow of FDI for the first time. This upturn was fully in line with a worldwide tendency towards growing numbers of mergers and acquisitions. While worldwide direct investment flows peaked in 2000, investment in Austria stagnated at high levels, and Austrian direct investment abroad even continued to grow.

Where does Austria stand now after this recent boom in cross-border investment? Figure 10.2 presents an international comparison based on UNCTAD's annual World Investment Report. Data on direct investment are, of course, not fully comparable. Despite many efforts to harmonize definitions and compilation procedures, in some cases bilateral comparisons – even within the EU – show significant discrepancies. Nevertheless, one still may say that Austria's FDI position has come close to the world average, with a slight outward bias.

As with the foreign trade statistics, relatively low levels of integration prevail for large countries and higher percentages for smaller countries. High-income countries tend to have a positive outward balance, while transition countries, for example, typically have a negative one. Switzerland and

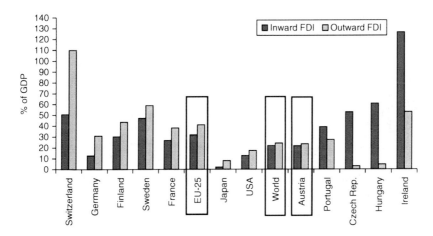

Source: UNCTAD (2005).

Figure 10.2 FDI stocks at end-2004

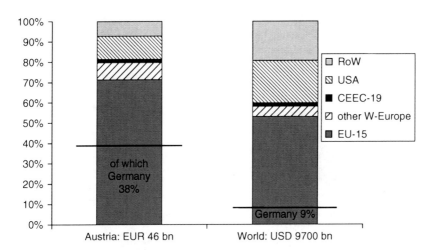

Source: OeNB, UNCTAD (2005).

Figure 10.3 Inward FDI stocks by source country

Ireland represent two extremes, both of which have proven to be viable strategies for economic success.

Looking at the regional details of inward and outward direct investments adds some useful information. Figure 10.3 compares direct investment stocks in Austria at the end of 2004 with global direct investment stocks broken down by country of origin. What immediately catches one's eye is the dominance of EU investors in Austria, implying that investment from the USA and other non-European OECD countries is relatively low. Investment from emerging economies, transition economies or OPEC countries is rather insignificant in Austria.

A closer look at the details identifies Germany as the main investor in Austria. While German investors account for roughly 9 per cent of world-wide FDI according to UNCTAD, their direct investment share in Austria is 38 per cent. Only a few years ago this share peaked at approximately 47 per cent. Although this predominance can be explained by geographical proximity, language and historical relations, it is still remarkable that one single country should hold such a major share. Spain's share in Portuguese FDI and French FDI in Belgium, for instance, are significantly lower. The only case of a similar predominance seems to be Swedish investment in Estonia. The fact that such a major share is held by just one investing country may partly explain why concerns about undue influence by foreigners on the Austrian economy continue to be raised.

The regional structure of Austrian direct investment abroad also has distinct characteristics. The most striking feature of Austrian direct investment abroad is again the overwhelming share accounted for by European countries (see Figure 10.4). While less than half of worldwide direct investment stocks are hosted by Europe, about 85 per cent of Austrian shareholdings

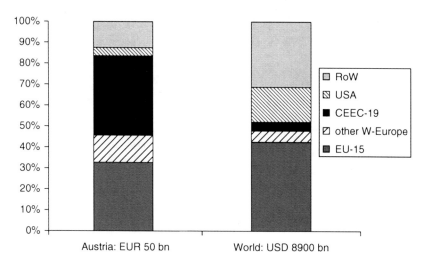

Source: OeNB, UNCTAD (2005).

Figure 10.4   Outward FDI stocks by host country

are located within Europe. Austrian FDI has a clear focus on Central, Eastern and South-Eastern Europe, which for analytical purposes includes the new members of the EU. Starting from virtually nothing, the CEEC-19 have attracted 50 per cent of the numbers of investment enterprises, 38 per cent of the capital invested abroad and 72 per cent of employment in Austrian affiliates abroad.

By contrast, the relative importance of the 'old' EU members has declined from more than 50 per cent of capital invested in the early 1990s to only one third in 2004. Within Western Europe it is yet again Germany which attracts Austrian investors most strongly; in fact, Germany is still the single most important target area for direct investment abroad.

Investment *outside* Europe is very limited. Some big manufacturing enterprises invest in Asia, taking advantage of cheap labour; others set up production facilities to access the US market. Then, there are holding companies and banks established in certain off-shore centres, relatively small trade companies almost everywhere, and a limited number of investments in raw materials.

Figure 10.5 tracks the interesting step-by-step expansion of Austrian enterprises into CEECs. The graph represents the development of employment figures, as they seem to be a useful proxy for indicating economic activity.

Target country number one was Hungary. Austrian investors had started their first economic activities in Hungary even *before* 1989. In the year of the fall of the Iron Curtain, Austrian direct investment statistics already

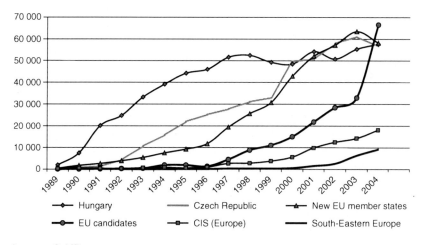

Source: OeNB.

Figure 10.5   Going eastward (employment in FDI enterprises)

registered close to 100 investments with around 2000 employees. Investment activities peaked as early as in 1990/91 and employment figures started levelling off in the mid-1990s. Of course, Austria continues to invest money in Hungary, for example through reinvestment of profits, and there are new investments too. Nevertheless, these investments seem to be offset by rationalization and productivity gains, which have led to stagnating employment figures since 1997.

With a time lag of about two years, Austrian enterprises started investing in another neighbouring country, which was still called Czechoslovakia at the time. The number of new investments peaked even before the separation into the two successor states on 1 January 1993, creating the Czech and the Slovak Republic. Due to several large investments, the Czech Republic reached similar employment levels as Hungary in 2000.

The third line in Figure 10.5 represents the sum of six countries: Poland, Slovakia, Slovenia and the three Baltic states (all of them are now members of the EU, two of them neighbouring countries of Austria). Here, the development was slightly less dynamic, which could be attributed to different country-specific reasons, like distance, size or regulatory framework. Clearly, the growth phase of Austrian affiliates' economic activity in these three countries concentrates on the second half of the 1990s. While in the case of Hungary and the Czech Republic investments were strongest even *before* the two countries applied for EU membership, one can assume a correlation with the accession perspective in the case of these new member states.

A positive effect of potential EU membership on Austrian investment abroad can clearly be seen in the next group comprising Croatia, Bulgaria and Romania. In 1999 the EU started negotiating with Bulgaria and Romania, and it is precisely around that time that investments in this region picked up. Privatization, together with improved regulatory and economic conditions, laid the ground for some of the biggest Austrian foreign investments ever.

Austrian investment is definitely less advanced in the European part of the Community of Independent States (CIS). In 2004, employment in Austrian affiliates, mostly in Russia and Ukraine, reached almost 20 000. It is still an open question whether Austrian investment in that region will ever reach the same levels as in Central Europe. I have some doubts that Russia is a realistic target for many Austrian investors. There will be fierce competition regarding investment among multinationals all around the world, and I cannot see specific advantages for Austrian investors in this respect. It might be somewhat different in the case of Ukraine. Not everybody is aware that Lviv, centre of the western Ukraine, was once the fourth-largest city of the Austro-Hungarian Empire. So, the often cited argument of historical links and cultural relations would hold even in the case of Ukraine. Currently, we can observe steadily growing volumes of investment in Ukraine, and according to Ukraine's statistics Austria ranked third among foreign investors at the beginning of 2006, just ahead of the USA.

Finally, the development of Austrian employment in the Western Balkans is shown in Figure 10.5. Until recently it was almost non-existent due to political and economic circumstances. But since 2001 more and more money has been invested in a growing number of projects, mainly in Bosnia and Herzegovina and in Serbia and Montenegro.[1] Assuming that economic and political reforms progress, this region could become a growth area for Austrian direct investment in the future.

According to data from partner countries collected by the Vienna Institute for International Economic Studies, Austria is currently the most important investor in Bulgaria, Bosnia, Slovenia and Croatia and ranks second or third in six further CEECs (the reference dates differ from 2004 to 2005 since data are published by national authorities with different time lags).

When we name some of the important investors in Eastern Europe, for example Siemens, Henkel, Billa or even Bank Austria, it becomes apparent that not all Austrian investment abroad is purely Austrian in a narrow sense. *Regional headquarters of multinational enterprises* have always played an important role in the Austrian economy. In the years before 1989, their activities mainly focused on trade with CEECs, but during the transition process many of them turned into regional headquarters which are also responsible for investment and the management of affiliates in the region.

There are no specific statistics on regional headquarters, but Austrian direct investment statistics can provide some insights as to why they might be important. Figures 10.6, 10.7 and 10.8 are related to this topic.

Figure 10.6 shows the development of the number of direct investment enterprises in Austria. It has been hovering slightly above the 2500 mark since 1998. By matching inward and outward surveys, one can identify those enterprises which make investments abroad. There are around 200 of them, represented by the small lighter columns, amounting to less than 10 per cent of the total. Even if we take into account that these numbers are only a lower limit and that the true figures might be somewhat higher due to indirect ownership structures, this does not seem to be a lot.

If we look into the amounts of capital involved, the picture changes dramatically (see Figure 10.7). Bridgeheads (regional headquarters) are steadily gaining importance. In 2004, more than 50 per cent of *inward* direct investment in Austria was attributable to enterprises, which were *outward* investors at the same time.

The important role of regional headquarters in Austria can also be looked at from the opposite angle, that is from the *outward* direct investment

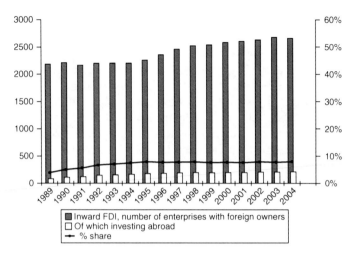

Source: OeNB.

Figure 10.6   The role of bridgeheads (regional headquarters)

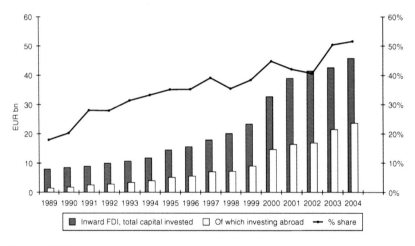

Source: OeNB.

Figure 10.7   The role of bridgeheads (capital invested in Austria)

perspective. Figure 10.8 captures the development of employment in Austrian affiliates abroad in the last 15 years. Employment in affiliates abroad grew more than 12-fold, from less than 30 000 in 1989 to 370 000 in 2004. Again, the lighter columns indicate the importance of bridgeheads,

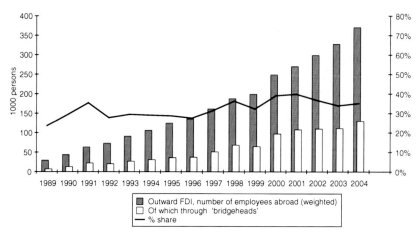

Source: OeNB.

Figure 10.8   The role of bridgeheads (employment abroad)

representing resident investors which are influenced or controlled by non-resident owners. As one can see from the black line, at least 40 per cent of the economic activity abroad is related to this type of intermediate investor.

Finally, it may be worthwhile showing a breakdown of the Austrian FDI structure by economic activity and briefly addressing the question concerning whether Austrian FDI can be characterized as horizontal or more vertical (see Figure 10.9).

The Austrian questionnaire on FDI asks about the main motives for foreign direct investment, and 'market access' proved to be by far the most important factor for both inward and outward FDI. This could be interpreted as *horizontal* FDI, which basically means doing the same job somewhere else. The most important share of Austrian direct investment abroad, that is investment in the financial sector, is clearly of that type. Austrian banks have successfully entered the fast-growing markets in Central and Eastern Europe offering the same services they have been offering at home. In the manufacturing sector we can also find examples of clearly horizontal FDI, for instance in the brickmaking trade, where transportation costs are relevant, or in the case of highly specialized niche areas like the construction of cable cars, the production of die-casting machinery or railway equipment.

For many years inward FDI had taken advantage of relatively low labour costs in Austria, but meanwhile this location-specific advantage has

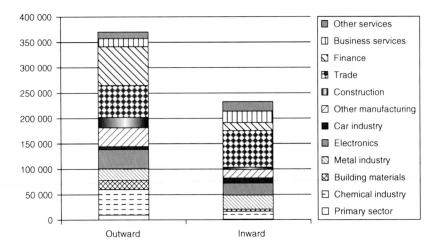

Source: OeNB.

Figure 10.9   *Employment in direct investment enterprises by economic activity*

disappeared. Nowadays, FDI in Austria is either looking for specific skills and know-how or it is simply an extension of the home market as is the case with many German firms.

Nevertheless, there are also signs of *vertical* FDI, which means international division of labour between countries. This particularly applies to direct investment in Austria. Big multinational enterprises have set up plants in Austria which are closely linked to worldwide production processes. This is true for the automobile industry where the activities range from assembly and parts supply to engineering, research and development. The same can, for instance, also be observed in the pharmaceutical industry, which has set up or bought highly specialized producers or research facilities in Austria.

It is more difficult to find traces of vertical FDI on the outward side, although differences in factor endowment between Austria and its eastern neighbours are significant. The main reason for the scarce occurrence of vertical FDI is most likely size: investors – apart from regional headquarters – are usually not big enough for a far-reaching international division of labour. At least some investors in Central and Eastern Europe report that cheap labour is an important motive for their investment, and there are a number of medium-sized enterprises which have outsourced certain labour-intensive steps of their production to neighbouring countries. The high labour intensity of direct investment in CEECs – when compared to investments in Western Europe – underlines the importance of the availability of labour force for investment.

To sum up, one can say that Austrian FDI is a *recent* phenomenon, which started around 1990. It is *centred in Europe*, with Germany as the dominant investor and CEE as the most favoured target area. The range of direct investment abroad has grown steadily, starting off in Austria's immediate neighbour countries; investments outside Europe are still very limited though. One could call this process 'globalization on a regional scale'. Austria has to play a role in the worldwide division of labour through direct investments in Austria (vertical FDI), but investment abroad seems to be mostly of the horizontal type. *Bridgeheads* or *regional headquarters* represent a big share of Austrian direct investment and they are – almost by definition – relevant in inward and outward investment at the same time.

NOTE

1. Separate data for Serbia and Montenegro will become available in 2007.

REFERENCE

UNCTAD (2005), *World Investment Report*, New York and Geneva: United Nations.

11. Is China's FDI coming at the expense of other countries?

Barry Eichengreen and Hui Tong[1]

1. INTRODUCTION

China's emergence has been perhaps the single most important new development affecting the world economy at the outset of the twenty-first century. By some estimates the country contributed more than a quarter of the growth of global GDP in the early years of the new millennium. It is the world's sixth-largest trader, supplying more than 6 per cent of global exports. It is a leading destination for foreign direct investment by producers seeking to capitalize on its large domestic market and low labour costs.

Much of this attention has focused on how China is affecting the advanced economies. But China's impact on developing countries is equally profound. As an exporter of labour-intensive manufactures, China competes with other developing countries with a comparative advantage in labour-intensive manufactured goods. As a magnet for foreign investment, China has allegedly made it more difficult for other emerging markets to attract FDI. Thus, when FDI inflows into the Mexican maquiladora sector dropped from USD 3 billion in 2000 to USD 2 billion in 2003, there was a tendency to blame the emergence of China as a more attractive low-cost production and export platform (United Nations, 2004, p. 61).

But China is also a growing market for the exports of other countries. It is the fastest-growing foreign market for countries like Brazil that are major exporters of raw materials. Chinese companies are integrated into global supply chains, assembling components produced in other parts of the world and producing components and materials that are assembled and finished in other countries. As we have shown in a previous study (Eichengreen et al., 2004), the growth of capacity and demand in China, rather than making other developing countries less attractive as platforms for production, could make them more attractive to the extent that they succeed in producing for the Chinese market and integrating into the same supply chains.

The point applies in principle to FDI. To reap the full benefits of building assembly plants in China, firms may also need to invest in component production in Singapore or Malaysia. The increase of FDI in China may thus encourage additional FDI in other countries rather than crowding it out.

In this chapter we seek to shed further light on these issues. We ask whether China's emergence as a low-cost production and export platform and its attractions as a destination for FDI made it more difficult for other countries to attract FDI. Which countries and regions have seen FDI inflows diverted toward China, and which source countries are responsible for the shift? Or does China's FDI-fuelled growth, by making neighbouring countries a logical platform for producing for the Chinese market and stimulating the development of regional supply chains, in fact heighten their attraction as destinations for FDI?

The framework for our analysis is the gravity model of bilateral FDI flows. We augment the standard specification to include Chinese FDI receipts from the same source country. The identification strategy – using the distance between China and the source country as an instrument for Chinese FDI receipts – builds on that used in our previous study of trade flows. And, as in our previous study of exports, our results for FDI are surprising.

2. FOREIGN DIRECT INVESTMENT SINCE 1990

Since the early 1990s, China has become a major destination for foreign direct investment. In 2005, the country had the third-largest inflow of FDI, after only the United Kingdom and the United States (United Nations, 2006). This increase has occurred in the context of the global growth of FDI. Net FDI flows to developing countries rose steadily over the 1990s and the early part of this decade, from USD 21 billion in 1989, to USD 179 billion in 1999, and to USD 281 billion in 2005 (World Bank, 2006). The bulk of these flows went to a handful of countries, notably China, Brazil, Argentina and Mexico. The economies of Central and Eastern Europe also attracted growing amounts of FDI over the course of the decade but starting from low levels, reflecting the early difficulties of transition.

The main sources of FDI remain Europe, the US and Japan. Europe was the source of nearly 60 per cent of global FDI inflows in the 1990s. Much of this was intra-European FDI, reflecting the incentives for consolidation provided by the creation of the single market. In addition, toward the end of the decade the advent of the euro, by enhancing the liquidity of European financial markets and providing more finance for mergers and acquisitions, encouraged European FDI flows to other parts of the world. US FDI also increased in the second half of the 1990s, reflecting the liquidity of US financial markets and impact of globalization. After surging at the end of the 1980s in response to the appreciation of the yen, Japanese FDI declined in the 1990s as the economy entered its slump. More recently, South–South FDI flows have grown in importance. FDI from developing economies reached USD 133 billion in 2005, representing about 17 per cent of world outward flows. The value of the stock of FDI from developing economies was estimated at USD 1.4 trillion in 2005, or 13 per cent of the world total (United Nations, 2006). Asia's newly developing countries have engaged in growing FDI in China. China and South Africa are now major investors in Africa. There is also much talk of Chinese FDI in Latin America.

FDI in China picked up after 1993, reflecting the further liberalization of the economy, exchange rate unification, and inflation stabilization. Inflows first exceeded USD 30 billion in 1994 and ranged from USD 36 billion to USD 54 billion from 1995 through 2003, reaching USD 55 billion in 2004. Increasingly these inflows have taken the form, not of greenfield investment, but of mergers and acquisitions, the number of which rose from 107 in 2002 to 214 in 2003.

The FDI receipts of other Asian countries held up well through 1996, and their subsequent slump was presumably a consequence of the financial crisis of 1997–98. But flows of FDI to developing countries then declined by 26 per cent between 1999 and 2003, while those to China rose sharply (Palmade and Anayiotas, 2004). It was not possible to attribute these disturbing trends to the passing effects of the 1997–98 crisis. They thus created worries that China was siphoning off FDI to countries in East Asia and Latin America that had previously been among the dominant developing-country destinations for foreign investment (IMF, 2004). Although FDI in developing countries picked up in 2003, it did so unevenly. Thus, while flows to developing countries in Africa and Asia rose, they continued falling in Latin America and the Caribbean, perhaps reflecting 'the relocation of production from some Latin American countries to lower-cost locations such as China' (United Nations, 2004, p. 39).

Thus, the central issue, in the words of Wong and Adams (2002), 'is whether China is absorbing a predominantly large share of FDI and crowding out FDI to the rest of Asia'. The same question can also be asked of FDI flows to other parts of the world. But, as these same authors caution, 'viewed from a longer term perspective, FDI inflows to China and to the other part of Asia could well be complementary rather than competitive'. This is the issue we address in the remainder of this chapter.

3.   DATA AND METHODOLOGY

The data for our study are drawn mainly from 'Source OECD'. The OECD provides data for FDI flows, disaggregated by destination, for 29 OECD source countries. It breaks down outflows from these countries, by destination, distinguishing 60 OECD and non-OECD recipients. To broaden our coverage of FDI flows in Asia, we also added data on FDI inflows from national sources for Bangladesh, Pakistan and Vietnam.

We focus on the period from 1988 to 2003. The OECD provides FDI in source-country currency. We convert it into millions of US dollars and then deflate it by the US CPI for urban consumers. Real GDP and GDP per capita in constant 1995 US dollars are obtained from the World Bank's *World Development Indicators*. Other country-specific variables, such as land area and language, are from Rose (2003), as is the distance variable.

The framework for our analysis is the gravity model, where the log of FDI is related to measures of the economic size of the source and destination countries and the distance between them. We consider bilateral flows between all 29 source and 63 destination countries. We regress the log of FDI by country *i* in country *j* (say, of Japan in Mexico) on their log GDPs, their log per capita GDPs, the distance between them, and the other now-standard gravity model arguments (combined land area, land lockedness, number of islands, common language, common colonizer, whether the countries in question were ever in a colonial relationship). Our innovation is to include a measure of China's FDI receipts from the same source country (in the present example, Japan). We model separately China's own FDI receipts and the FDI receipts of other countries using this same framework.

We also include for both the source and destination country the index of political risk of the International Country Risk Guide (ICRG), on the grounds that the riskiness of the political, economic and financial environment is relevant to the foreign investment decision.

It is important to recognize the endogeneity of Chinese FDI in an equation designed to explain FDI flows between other country pairs. Unobserved factors that increase Japanese FDI in Mexico will also in general increase Japanese FDI in China, creating a correlation between the error term and the key explanatory variable. The standard treatment for this problem is instrumental variables, the difficulty being the paucity of plausible and powerful instruments.

Fortunately, in the present context the gravity model suggests an instrument that is both exogenous and strongly correlated with Chinese FDI, namely the distance between China and the country that is the source of the foreign investment.

A problem is that this instrumental variable does not vary over time. This would mean that we are using the cross-section variation in our instrument to identify the exogenous component of Chinese FDI but using the result to address a time-series question. The gravity model suggests including China's GDP as a time-varying variable in the first-stage regression. In addition, we build on the literature on FDI and institutional quality by including the ICRG index of political risk in China as an additional time-varying instrumental variable for Chinese FDI. Alternatively we substituted the Heritage Foundation's index of economic freedom and obtained the same results. Finally, we introduce time-fixed effects in the first and second stages. This entails dropping China's GDP and political risk from the list of instrumental variables since both are linear functions of the time dummies. Reassuringly, our results for the second stage are very similar across all these specifications of the first stage. In what follows we use the time dummies in our baseline specification.

4.   BASIC RESULTS

Table 11.1 shows the second stage estimates. We provide ordinary least squares (OLS) estimates in order to show how much difference is made by the instrumental variables.

The basic gravity variables enter as expected. Larger countries send and receive more FDI. Higher labour costs in the originating country and lower labour costs in the destination country (as captured by per capita GDP) are associated with larger FDI flows. Distance between the sending and receiving countries has a negative impact, while common language, common land border, common colonizer, past colonial relationship, access to sea lanes, and the existence of a currency union all have a positive impact. Our time-varying measure of institutional quality enters positively for both the sending and receiving countries.

The key coefficient for present purposes is that on Chinese FDI. In the instrumental-variables regressions, the coefficient on this variable is negative but not significantly different from zero at the 95 per cent confidence level. Since FDI is expressed in logs, the coefficient can be interpreted as an elasticity; thus a 10 per cent increase in China's FDI receipts will reduce other countries' FDI receipts by 0.1 per cent. Clearly, this effect is very small, but we show below that regional disaggregation leads to much larger effects. Observe how much difference instrumentation makes; in the OLS estimates provided only for comparison, the coefficient on Chinese FDI is instead strongly positive. This is the direction of bias we would expect, since FDI in China and FDI in other countries tend to be affected by the same trends in globalization and shifts in investor sentiment.

The question is whether FDI in China has the same impact on FDI in all regions – that is, whether the weak negative coefficient on Chinese FDI is in fact conflating different effects in different parts of the world. In Table 11.2 we therefore distinguish FDI flows to Asia, Latin America, Central

Table 11.1   Second-stage estimates of China's FDI receipts on other countries' FDI inflows

	IV Coef.	IV St Err.	OLS Coef.	OLS St Err.
China's FDI inflow (log)	−0.01	0.04	0.25	0.02
GDP of outflow country (log)	1.43	0.08	0.98	0.04
GDP per capita of outflow country (log)	1.58	0.11	1.25	0.09
GDP of inflow country (log)	1.11	0.04	1.05	0.03
GDP per capita of inflow country (log)	−0.23	0.05	−0.17	0.05
Product of land areas (log)	−0.07	0.02	−0.01	0.02
Distance (log)	−0.96	0.05	−0.98	0.04
Common language dummy	1.13	0.12	0.94	0.11
Number of land locked (0/1/2)	−0.41	0.09	−0.34	0.08
Number of islands (0/1/2)	−0.59	0.08	−0.48	0.08
Land border dummy	0.34	0.14	0.39	0.17
Common colonizer post-1945	7.02	0.67	6.68	1.67
Pairs ever in colonial relation	1.86	0.17	1.97	0.17
Strict currency union	4.29	0.34	4.50	1.02
Political risk for outflow country	0.08	0.01	0.07	0.01
Political risk for inflow country	0.05	0.00	0.04	0.00
Constant	−80.1	2.86	−64.1	1.6
Number of observations	7642		7642	
R-squared	0.55		0.56	

Note: Time-fixed effects are included though not reported.

Source: Authors' calculation.

and Eastern Europe, and the OECD, where we exclude from the OECD Mexico and South Korea (we include them instead with Latin America and Asia) as well as Japan (which we also include with the Asian grouping). It appears that Chinese FDI inflows are complementary with the FDI inflows of other Asian countries. This was also the finding of Chantasasawat et al. (2004), using a different methodology. We find essentially the same thing for Central and Eastern Europe and no impact on the FDI receipts of Latin America.[2] There is little evidence here, in other words, that China's FDI creates problems for other developing economies by limiting their own access to FDI.

By implication, the weak negative coefficient obtained for the full sample is driven by the only remaining country grouping, the OECD. This result appears to be robust; it is not driven by the observations for any one OECD economy. An interpretation is that in some cases, notably those

Table 11.2 Effect of China's FDI receipts on other countries' FDI inflows, by region

	Asia		Latin America		Central and Eastern Europe		OECD	
	Coef.	St Err.	Coef.	St Err.	Coef.	St Err.	Coef.	St Err.
China's FDI inflow	0.74	0.10	-0.10	0.17	0.21	0.10	-0.13	0.06
GDP of outflow country	0.33	0.17	1.96	0.35	1.06	0.22	1.31	0.11
GDP per capita of outflow country	0.74	0.25	1.68	0.35	0.64	0.26	2.23	0.16
GDP of inflow country	0.07	0.08	1.02	0.15	1.67	0.18	1.34	0.04
GDP per capita of inflow country	0.10	0.11	2.40	0.46	-1.08	0.24	-0.77	0.16
Product of land areas	0.14	0.05	-0.48	0.12	0.02	0.12	0.15	0.04
Distance	-0.33	0.19	-2.99	0.75	-1.35	0.16	-1.41	0.09
Common language dummy	0.28	0.22	-3.13	1.80			1.51	0.17
Number of land locked (0/1/2)	0.02	0.26	-1.79	0.38	1.19	0.17	-0.79	0.13
Number of islands (0/1/2)	0.35	0.14	-1.44	0.47	-1.52	0.42	-0.29	0.13
Land border dummy			-2.74	1.02	0.97	0.29	-1.02	0.18
Common colonizer post-1945			6.87	1.77	2.29	0.73		
Pairs ever in colonial relation	2.14	0.22	0.17	0.69	2.12	0.75	0.96	0.25
Strict currency union								
Political risk for outflow country	0.07	0.02	0.06	0.02	0.08	0.02	0.07	0.01
Political risk for inflow country	0.06	0.01	-0.02	0.02	0.10	0.02	0.08	0.01
Constant	-27.8	5.12	-79.0	16.1	-75.9	8.13	-87.8	4.21
Number of observations	1454		941		1025		3353	
R-squared	0.63		0.61		0.57		0.62	

Note: Time-fixed effects are included though not reported. OECD columns do not include Japan, Mexico, and South Korea as inflow countries. (Japan and South Korea are instead included with Asia, Mexico with Latin America.)

Source: Authors' calculation.

involving OECD countries, competition for FDI is driven not merely by relative costs of production but also by market-size considerations. Automobile producers, for example, when considering in which countries to undertake FDI, take into account the advantages of producing close to the final market both for tariff-jumping reasons and in order to be able to better tailor their product mix to local demand. Motor-vehicle producers', desire to get into China in order to tap that country's growing demand for their products, which has been much discussed since the early 1990s, is a case in point.

5. A CLOSER LOOK AT JAPANESE FDI

The preceding results suggest that China's emergence may be particularly important for the direction of FDI flows in the case of Japan. The rapid growth of Japanese FDI in China is consistent with this presumption: the share of the country's FDI destined for China rose from 5 per cent in 1989 to fully 49 per cent in 2003. In this section we therefore examine Japan's FDI flows in more detail.

Table 11.3 disaggregates Japanese foreign investment over the period 1989–2003 into eight manufacturing industries and nine non-manufacturing sectors. For each region, we report the simple correlation between Japan's sector-specific FDI in China and its sector-specific FDI in other countries.

The results are consistent with those obtained from our gravity-model analysis. There is a positive correlation between Japanese FDI flows to China and Japanese FDI flows to other Asia whether we consider manufacturing, non-manufacturing or total FDI. This is the same complementarity that we observed using the gravity model above.

For Latin America, we obtain the same weak negative correlation as in the gravity-model analysis. Again, this is evident for manufacturing, non-manufacturing and total FDI alike. In Central and Eastern Europe, where we obtained a positive coefficient in the gravity-model analysis, we again see positive correlations for manufacturing, non-manufacturing, and total Japanese FDI. The positive correlation for manufacturing seems heavily driven by electrical machinery/electronics and motor vehicles/transport equipment. We suspect that this correlation is spurious, as argued above.[3] The positive correlation for non-manufacturing investment is primarily driven by minerals and mining and by real estate. (In the case of mining it is important to observe that our data for Eastern Europe include Russia as an inflow country.) Again, we suspect that this is correlation, not causation, as argued above.

Table 11.3   Correlation between Japan's FDI outflow to China and other regions, by sector

	Asia	Latin America	Central and Eastern Europe	OECD
Manufacturing Total	0.32	−0.05	0.10	−0.23
Food	−0.40	0.00	−0.28	−0.20
Textile	0.30	0.37	−0.03	0.08
Lumber & Pulp	0.14	0.12	−0.18	−0.04
Chemical	−0.29	−0.25	−0.06	0.42
Metal	0.42	0.40	0.23	−0.31
Machinery	0.16	−0.11	0.11	−0.15
Electrical	0.51	−0.11	0.49	−0.32
Transport	0.30	−0.08	0.51	−0.22
Non-Manufacturing Total	0.20	−0.34	0.32	−0.02
Farming & Forestry	0.56	0.16	−0.14	0.23
Fishery	0.36	0.06	0.46	−0.08
Mining	0.18	−0.13	0.91	0.57
Construction	−0.15	0.39	−0.12	−0.22
Trade	−0.47	0.00	0.39	−0.05
Finance & Insurance	−0.27	0.20	−0.07	−0.01
Service	0.50	0.49	0.22	0.58
Transportation	0.63	0.32	0.36	−0.24
Real Estate	0.20	0.51	0.86	0.04
Total	0.18	−0.22	0.07	−0.33

Note: The sample period is 1989–2003. FDI is expressed in real US dollar terms. OECD columns do not include Mexico and South Korea.

Source: Authors' calculation.

The last column of Table 11.3 considers the correlation between Japanese FDI in China and Japanese FDI in OECD countries. Our surprising result was the finding of significant diversion of Japanese FDI away from OECD destinations as Japanese FDI in China expanded. The same correlation is evident here in the sectoral results. There is a negative correlation between Japanese FDI in China and Japanese FDI in the OECD for manufacturing, non-manufacturing, and the total alike, although it is small in the case of non-manufacturing sectors. The correlation is negative for six of the eight manufacturing industries; the exceptions are textiles and chemicals. The effects are more heterogeneous in the case of non-manufacturing sectors – not surprisingly given the existence of only a very small negative correlation for non-manufacturing industries overall.

6. CONCLUSIONS

There has been considerable recent discussion of the possibility that China's emergence as a destination for investment has diverted FDI receipts from other countries, Asian countries in particular. In this chapter we analysed this possibility using both aggregated and disaggregated data. The aggregate analysis employing bilateral FDI flows from OECD sources to OECD and non-OECD destinations does not indicate FDI diversion from other Asian countries. If anything, there is some evidence that developments making China a more attractive destination for FDI also make other Asian countries more attractive destinations for FDI, as would be the case if China and these other economies are part of the same global production networks.

At the same time there is some evidence of FDI diversion from OECD recipients. We interpret this in terms of FDI motivated by the desire to produce close to the market where the final sale takes place. For whatever reason – limits on their ability to raise finance for investment in multiple markets or limits on their ability to control operations in diverse locations – firms more inclined to invest in China for this reason are corresponding less inclined to invest in the OECD.

As we found in our previous paper on trade, blanket statements concerning China's impact are not particularly supportable. The country's emergence is a mixed blessing requiring a nuanced analysis.

NOTES

1. University of California, Berkeley and the International Monetary Fund, respectively. This chapter was prepared when Hui Tong was at the Bank of England. None of the views expressed here are necessarily those of the Bank of England or the International Monetary Fund. Reprinted, with abridgement and updates, from *Journal of the Japanese and International Economies*, doi:10.1016/j.jjie.2006.07.001, B. Eichengreen, H. Tong, 'Is China's FDI coming at the expense of other countries?', Copyright (2006), with permission from Elsevier.
2. It turns out that the positive coefficient on China's FDI in the equations for Central and Eastern Europe is driven by the observations for Hungary. (The other members of this region for which we have observations are Bulgaria, the Czech Republic, Poland, the Slovak Republic, Romania, Russia, Slovenia and Ukraine.) More precisely, this effect is driven by the observations for 1993–95, when Hungary engaged in a burst of privatization transactions and China was simultaneously opening to foreign flows. In other words, there may be reason to worry that this particular correlation is spurious.
3. The correlation reflects the fact that Japanese firms were separately increasing their capacity in these manufacturing industries in both China and Eastern Europe in the late 1990s and the early part of the present decade, not that Eastern Europe and China were part of an integrated supply chain.

REFERENCES

Chantasasawat, Busakorn, K.C. Fung, Hitomi Iizaka and Alan Siu (2004), *Foreign Direct Investment in China and East Asia*, unpublished manuscript, National University of Singapore, UC Santa Cruz and University of Hong Kong, November.

Eichengreen, Barry, Yeongseop Rhee and Hui Tong (2004), 'The impact of China on the exports of other Asian countries', *NBER Working Paper* No. 10768, September.

IMF (2004), 'China's emergence and its impact on the global economy', *World Economic Outlook*, April.

McKibbin, Warwick and Wing T. Woo (2003), 'The consequences of China's WTO accession for its neighbors', *Asian Economic Papers*, **2** (2), 1–38.

Palmade, Vincent and Andrea Anayiotas (2004), 'FDI trends: looking beyond the current gloom in developing countries', Public Policy for the Private Sector, Note No. 273, September, Washington, DC: World Bank.

Rose, Andrew (2003), *Notes on Other Things the WTO Might Be Doing (Besides Liberalizing Trade)*, unpublished manuscript, University of California, Berkeley.

United Nations (2004), *World Investment Report 2004*, Geneva and New York: United Nations Conference on Trade and Development.

United Nations (2006), *World Investment Report 2006*, Geneva and New York: United Nations Conference on Trade and Development.

Wong, Yu Ching and Charles Adams (2002), *Trends in Global and Regional Foreign Direct Investment Flows*, unpublished manuscript, IMF, August.

World Bank (2006), *Global Development Finance 2006*, Washington, DC: World Bank.

12. FDI in services: recent developments and prospects in Europe

Arjan Lejour[1]

INTRODUCTION

Foreign direct investment flows are on the rise again. After the peak of FDI inflows of USD 1400 billion in 2000, the size of FDI flows declined in response to the worsening economic climate. Now FDI is increasing again and reached USD 916 billion in 2005 from less than USD 600 billion in 2003.[2] The remarkably high FDI growth rates in 2004 and 2005 are an indicator of the confidence in prolonged economic growth worldwide.[3]

The increase of FDI flows outpaces that of trade flows: FDI flows increased by about 25 per cent per year in the 1980s and 1990s, while trade flows increased annually by about 10 per cent. Sales of foreign affiliates increased by 10 per cent to 15 per cent each year, while GDP increased at most by 5 per cent per year.[4]

With a large share of FDI flows destined for services, their share in the FDI stock is becoming comparable to that in value added. The FDI growth rates for services sectors are higher than for manufacturing, and the ceiling has not been reached yet. Against this backdrop this chapter starts with the discussion of some recent developments in FDI for services in section 2. Section 3 focuses on developments in the new EU member states including the candidate members Croatia and Turkey, in particular in services. Section 4 discusses some prospects for FDI in services within Europe, including the role of the Services Directive and transparency in attracting FDI, in particular for the countries in Central and (South-)East Europe.

FDI IN SERVICES

The recent rise in FDI is not new, nor is the underlying pattern. The services sectors are the main recipients of FDI. This trend is continuing, and

Table 12.1   Value of cross-border M&As worldwide (USD billion, 2005)

Sector/industry	Sales	Purchases
Primary	115	106
Manufacturing	204	149
Services	397	462
Electricity, gas, water	38	26
Trade and distribution	29	15
Transport, storage and communication	98	66
Finance and banking	94	290
Business services	93	49
Rest services	45	16
Total	716	716

Note: Numbers may not add up because of rounding.

Source: UNCTAD (2006).

the share of manufacturing is decreasing. Even the share of the primary sectors increased by 4 percentage points between 2004 and 2005 at the expense of manufacturing. That said, FDI in the primary sectors is unlikely to continue to grow, at least not at the cost of services. From a longer time perspective the share of primary sectors is steadily decreasing in the world economy. The recent need for natural resources due to the big industrial expansion in China and India is the main course for extra investment in primary sectors. In particular, China invests actively in natural resources in regions such as Africa.

Measured by the size of mergers and acquisitions (M&A), the share of services increased from 30 per cent in 1987 to nearly 60 per cent in 2005 with a peak of more than 70 per cent in 2000 (this represents the hype of telecommunications). This pattern is also reflected by the numbers of M&As (UNCTAD, 2006). Table 12.1 presents the value of sales and purchases in 2005. The total of USD 716 billion is less than the total amount of FDI, valued at USD 916 billion, because the latter number also includes greenfield investment.

The purchase and sales values per sector are not equal because producers in one sector may invest in other sectors. For example a car manufacturer's investment in a distribution network abroad is a purchase of services made by a manufacturing firm. Within services, most M&As occur in *transport, storage and communication, finance and banking* and *business services.* On the sales side these three sectors are equally important, but on the purchase side the share of *finance and banking* stands out. The importance of

Table 12.2   Direct investment stocks in services in the reporting economy (2003)

	In USD billion	In % of EU-25
Austria	32.5	0.9
Luxembourg	27.4	0.8
Finland	24.6	0.7
France	326.8	9.5
Germany	466.4	13.5
Greece	10.8	0.3
Ireland	98.5	2.9
Italy	78.0	2.3
Netherlands	221.9	6.4
Portugal	37.9	1.1
United Kingdom	484.1	14.0
Remaining EU-15	1568.1	45.5
EU-15	3377.0	97.9
Czech Republic	17.0	0.5
Hungary	15.6	0.5
Poland	32.5	0.9
Slovakia	4.9	0.1
Remaining new members	1.2	0.0
EU-25	3448.1	100.0
United States	626.6	

Note: EU-25 estimated on basis of the EU's foreign direct investment yearbook 2006.
The remaining EU-15 countries are Belgium, Denmark, Spain and Sweden.

Source: Eurostat (2006).

inward FDI in services varies across countries. Table 12.2 provides an overview of service FDI stocks in the EU countries.

Four facts are noteworthy.[5] First, the total stock of FDI in EU service industries is about five times higher than the stock in US service industries. Second, Germany, the remaining EU-15 (mainly Belgium) and the UK together attract two-thirds of all FDI flowing to EU service industries, while FDI flows to the Italian and Spanish services industries are surprisingly small. Third, Table 12.2 shows a very high share of service FDI stocks for Belgium, which, according to other data sources reflects large FDI flows for financial intermediation services. Fourth, despite the rise and importance of FDI for the new EU member states, their share in the European FDI stock in services remains modest.

There is a striking difference between the structures of FDI stock in the EU and in the US, with the share of manufacturing-related FDI being

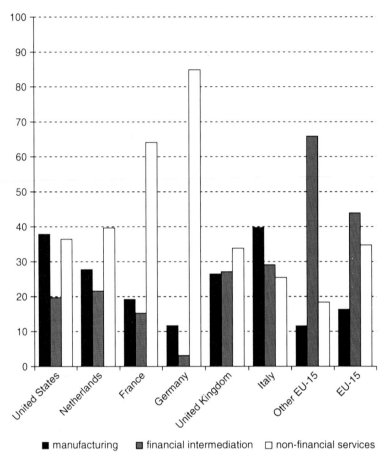

Source: Eurostat (2006).

*Figure 12.1   Structure of total FDI stock of the recipient economy
by main economic sector (2003)*

much higher in the US. Figure 12.1 shows the structure of total FDI inflows
by main economic sector.[6] With the exception of Italy, service FDI dominates in the European countries, accounting for about 75 per cent of the
FDI stock in some EU countries at the time of writing. This is slightly
higher than the share of services in the European economy.

The activities by foreign service multinationals tend to be spread quite
unevenly over domestic service industries in the EU. Kox et al. (2004) illustrate this using the concept of 'FDI inflow intensities', that is the share of a
particular sector in total service FDI inflows in relation to the sector's share

Table 12.3 FDI inflow intensity: sectoral share in total service FDI inflows divided by the sector's share in total domestic service production, selected countries (1998–2000[a])

	Germany	France	UK	Spain[c]	Netherlands	USA[b]
Trade, distribution	0.1	−0.4[e]	0.5	0.3	0.5	1.3
Business services and real estate	1.9	1.5	0.4	1.9	0.2[d]	0.4
Tourism and other services	0.0	0.1	0.2	0.1	0.2	1.0
Communication	1.2	0.8	6.4	4.3	3.0	−1.3
Transport services	0.0	0.2	0.0	0.1	0.1	0.6
Financial intermediation	1.1	4.5	2.6	0.7	7.9	4.1
Insurance (incl. auxiliary services)	−0.1	0.5	1.0	0.0	1.2	3.0
Unweighted average	0.6	1.0	1.6	1.1	1.9	1.3

Notes:
a) Service sector shares in total domestic service production are for 1999, except for Germany (1998).
b) USA FDI inflow data refer to 1998.
c) For Spain, production data for *business services and real estate*, and for *tourism and other services* refer to 1998, while data on *communication, financial intermediation*, and *insurance* refer to 1997.
d) Excluding FDI inflows in financial holding companies.
e) The negative value reflects a net FDI outflow (disinvestment).

Source: Kox et al. (2004).

in total domestic service production. This indicator would be 1 if the share of FDI inflows attracted by a service sector corresponds with its share in domestic production. Table 12.3 indicates that service sectors like *trade and distribution, tourism* and *transport* account for a much smaller share of FDI inflows than corresponds with their share in domestic service production.

Unlike the USA, all EU countries in the table attract remarkably little FDI in the *trade and distribution* services and *transport services*. The predominantly consumer-oriented *tourism and other services* are underrepresented in FDI flows. In the UK, the Netherlands and Spain, *business services and real estate* attracts a relatively low share of direct investment compared to the sector's size; the opposite holds for France and Germany. *Communication* is relatively popular with foreign investors, which may well be due to deregulation that took place in the late 1990s, combined with the auctions for mobile phone licences. Except in the Netherlands, the banking sector (*financial intermediation*) attracts more FDI than one would expect on the basis of the sector's relative size. The strong national disparities in the structure of FDI inflows are much larger than are justified by national differences in the domestic size of specific service industries. Golub (2003) and Golub and Nicoletti (2004) find that regulation factors, including tax regimes, are important determinants of intra-European FDI flows in services. Apart from policy factors, this FDI inflow pattern may also reflect network factors, scale effects and sector-specific transaction costs.

FDI TOWARDS CENTRAL AND EAST EUROPE

In 2005 FDI towards many Central and Eastern European countries (CEECs) remained steady or even declined compared to 2004. Examples are Romania and Bulgaria. This is surprising because their accession to the EU in 2007 is expected to initiate large investment flows. It is possible that foreign investors already anticipated EU accession years ago or that FDI is hampered by factors such as the tax regime, regulatory obstacles, lack of transparency and political and economic stability. In this book, Resmini (2006) presents a more in-depth analysis of the determinants of FDI (not sector-specific) in CEECs from the beginning of the 1990s until 2006, while section 4 of this chapter discusses the prospects for FDI with respect to these determinants for this region.

The Czech Republic, Turkey and Poland are the main recipients of FDI in 2005 in the country listing of Table 12.4. Poland and Turkey, while being the largest economies, do not receive much FDI as a percentage of gross fixed capital formation. The numbers for Bulgaria and Romania are comparable to those of the Czech Republic. As a share of GDP the FDI stocks in Bulgaria and Romania are slightly smaller than the average. However, larger economies are less open to trade and investment than small countries.

Compared to the values of FDI stocks in Demekas et al. (2005) for 2003, FDI stocks are substantially higher for most countries. Sometimes the increase is 50 per cent, to a large extent realized in 2004.

The openness of countries towards foreign investment can be summarized by the transnationality index developed by UNCTAD (2006). The index is an average of four indicators: FDI stocks as share of GDP and FDI flows as share of gross fixed capital formation (see also Table 12.4) as well as the foreign employment and foreign sales ratios. Figure 12.2 presents the index for nearly all CEECs. The numbers for Macedonia and Estonia are extremely high, partly reflecting the smallness of these countries. This contrasts with low numbers for Albania, Bosnia and Herzegovina, Serbia and Montenegro, and Turkey, and reflects mainly the latter group's national policies towards FDI. For Turkey the size of the economy also matters, but Lejour et al. (2004) among others argue that

Table 12.4   FDI stocks and flows towards Central and Eastern Europe (2005)

Country	FDI stocks (USD billion)	FDI flows (USD billion)	FDI flows (% of gross fixed capital formation)	Stocks (% of GDP)
Albania	1.6	0.3	13.8	20.1
Bosnia	2.1	0.3	16	21.9
Bulgaria	9.2	2.2	35.1	34.3
Croatia	12.5	1.7	15.4	33.3
Macedonia	1.9	0.1	9.7	37.5
Romania	23.8	6.4	28.1	24.2
Serbia	5.5	1.5	35.8	20.7
Turkey	42.2	9.7	13.6	11.6
Czech Republic	59.5	11	34	48.1
Estonia	12.3	2.9	79.1	93.6
Hungary	61.2	6.7	26.5	55.9
Latvia	4.8	0.6	13.9	28.7
Lithuania	6.5	1	17.7	25.1
Poland	93.3	7.7	14.6	31.1
Slovakia	15.3	1.9	15.7	32.8
Slovenia	8.1	0.5	5.9	23.7

Source: UNCTAD (2006).

unstable macroeconomic policies and a less favourable institutional environment have significantly hampered FDI flows to Turkey.

To which sectors are foreign investments destined? It is not easy to answer this question due to the limited availability of data. The published UNCTAD data only give regional aggregates. In 2005 FDI flows to South-Eastern European countries (SEECs) and the CIS (Commonwealth of Independent States) remained at a level of USD 40 billion.[7] FDI flows to major recipient countries like Romania, Bulgaria and Russian federation declined in 2005. Compared to the numbers 5 or 10 years ago this is still substantial, but for these emerging economies the lack of FDI growth in 2005 is worrisome. FDI in SEECs is USD 12 billion: a slowdown from USD 13 billion in 2004 after a consecutive rise from 2002. FDI comes mostly from developed countries, in particular the EU, and focuses on *transport, storage and communications* and *finance and banking*. The share of services is below the average of 50 per cent. This region focuses more on manufacturing (in particular metals). Table 12.5 presents the sectoral distribution for SEECs and the CIS region.

In Central and Eastern Europe FDI is more directed towards services; about 60 per cent of the total FDI stock is in services. In the primary sector

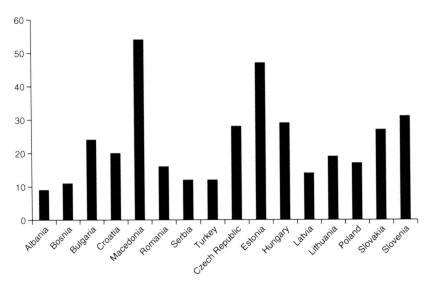

Source: UNCTAD (2006).

Figure 12.2   Openness measured by transnationality index, 2005

FDI is not important in the CEECs, and is probably not in the SEECs either; the latter's relatively high numbers are, however, inflated by FDI in natural resources in Russia and other CIS countries.

PROSPECTS FOR FDI IN SERVICES

FDI growth has been abundant since the 1980s. FDI in services grew even faster, but the ceiling has not been reached yet. In spite of these developments, European producers complain about the fragmentation of the services markets in Europe (European Commission, 2002). They experience bottlenecks in serving foreign markets either by exporting or establishing foreign affiliates. The Services Directive proposed by the European Commission aims to integrate national services markets by reducing these barriers. Several studies indicate that bilateral trade and FDI in services could be boosted substantially. Kox and Lejour (2006) approach the issue by quantifying the market-entry costs of country-specific regulations, accounting for differences in product-market regulations between each EU country pair.[8] The degree of bilateral policy heterogeneity between countries is used as a proxy for sunken export costs; it may differ between each pair of countries. Applied in gravity equations for bilateral services trade in

Table 12.5   Sectoral distribution FDI stocks and flows

Sectors	Central and Eastern Europe	CIS and South-East Europe	
	FDI stocks, 2001	FDI stocks, 2004	FDI flows, average 2002–2004
Primary	1.2	20.7	4.9
Manufacturing	36.6	20.5	6.6
Services	58.3	34.3	7.2
Electricity, gas, water	3.6	1.2	0
Trade	15.9	7.2	2.6
Transport, storage and communication	11.0	12.0	0.8
Finance	16.7	6.7	1.0
Business services	8.6	4.5	1.6
Rest services	0.6	3.2	1.2
Total	101.9	82.0	19.4[1]
Unallocated	5.9	6.7	0.7

Note: 1. The average value of FDI inflows in CIS and SEECs of nearly USD 20 billion for the period 2002–2004 is less than the USD 40 billion in 2004. We know that the value was USD 24 billion in 2003. This suggests that FDI was nearly absent or even negative in 2002. This is not necessarily the case because the limited quality of FDI data in general could imply that the totals of sectoral FDI flows (as in this table) do not match the country totals (mentioned in the text).

Source: UNCTAD (2006) for the FDI data for CIS and SEECs. Van Leeuwen and Lejour (2006) for FDI stock data for CEECs.

the EU, regulatory heterogeneity in policy areas like competition and trade regulation appears to have a robustly negative trade impact. At detailed levels Kox and Lejour subsequently estimate to what extent the Commission's Services Directive would affect bilateral policy heterogeneity. The results are combined to simulate the effects of the Services Directive:

- trade in commercial services (excluding transport and travel) could increase by 30 to 62 per cent;
- intra-EU FDI in services could increase by 18 to 36 per cent.

Table 12.6 presents the underlying cause of the increase in FDI. In particular, less heterogeneity in *barriers to competition* and a lower level of *FDI restrictions* contribute to more FDI.

Table 12.6   Impact of EU directive on intra-EU FDI stocks (% change based on 1999 data)

Effects	Minimum variant	Central variant	Maximum variant
Total effect on bilateral FDI stocks in the EU-17	18	26	36
Due to less heterogeneity in *Barriers to competition*	7	12	18
Due to less heterogeneity in *State control*	0	1	2
Due to lower level of FDI restrictions in destination countries	11	13	16

Source: Kox and Lejour (2006).

The Services Directive does not eliminate all heterogeneity in *barriers to competition* and *state control*. Also some FDI restrictions in destination countries will remain in place. If all this heterogeneity in regulation were eliminated, services FDI could increase by about 130 per cent in Europe on average, and inward FDI stocks in CEECs could increase by more than 200 per cent. These stunning numbers are of course out-of-sample predictions, but they underpin the relevance of regulation and differences in regulation as a barrier for FDI.

In order to estimate the macroeconomic importance of the Services Directive, De Bruijn et al. (2006) fed the estimated trade impacts (not the FDI effects) into a large applied general equilibrium model, WorldScan. They conclude that average European consumption could increase by between 0.5 and 1.2 per cent. If the effects of more FDI (derived from Lejour et al., 2007) are added as well, consumption could increase by 0.5 to 1.5 per cent. The limited openness of commercial services for trade and foreign investment explains why these macroeconomic effects are relatively modest. However, expressed in terms of the 2004 European GDP, the measures would add EUR 35 to 95 billion. This still ignores the productivity and innovation impacts of more trade and FDI. These results take account of scale effects and of forward and backward linkages in the economy, but ignore the effects of more competition on productivity and innovation in the long term.

Copenhagen Economics (2005) also analyses the EU proposals with an applied general-equilibrium model. Their model also accounts for FDI effects. According to their simulation results, overall consumption in the EU would increase by 0.6 per cent due to the Services Directive. This is somewhat smaller than the results reported by the CPB Netherlands Bureau for Economic Policy Analysis.

These results are the outcomes for Europe as a whole. For the CEECs the effects could be larger. Kox and Lejour (2006) estimate that FDI stocks could increase by 53 per cent in Poland, by 42 per cent in the Czech Republic and by 45 per cent in Hungary, compared to 26 per cent in the EU on average in the central variant in Table 12.6. The main reasons for these relatively large increases are the stringent rules these countries impose towards FDI and the relatively big differences between their regulatory rules and those of the other European countries. The level of FDI restrictions and the heterogeneity in regulatory policies are thus larger than for the average European country. The effects on consumption and GDP are correspondingly larger for the new member states. De Bruijn et al. (2006) estimate that consumption in the Czech Republic and Hungary could increase by 1.5 per cent to 3.5 per cent. For Poland the effects are more modest and correspond to the EU average. The reason is that Poland is less open, so the trade effects have less impact on the total economy.

The indexes on the intensity and heterogeneity of regulation are based on OECD regulation data, which do not contain data for other CEECs.[9] We know, however, that these indexes are positively correlated to other country indexes on the market economy and institutions. Examples are the Heritage indicator for Economic Freedom, the Kaufmann indicators of the World Bank, and the transparency index of Transparency International. We use the correlation of the last index to gauge the impact for other CEECs.

Figure 12.3 presents the transparency index for most CEECs. The index represents the degree of corruption perceived by professionals, academics and risk analysts derived from surveys and is constructed by Transparency International. The assessment is between 0 and 10. In 2006 Haiti scored lowest with an index of 1.8, and Finland, Iceland and New Zealand the highest with 9.6. For Estonia and Slovenia the index exceeds 6, comparable to some old EU member states. The other CEECs score lower, but Hungary, the Czech Republic and Poland score higher than most other CEECs. Because the transparency index correlates positively with the heterogeneity index of Kox and Lejour (2006), it is likely that the heterogeneity in regulation between the other CEECs and the old member states is higher than between the three OECD countries from Central and Eastern Europe and the old EU member states (excluding Slovakia). The corresponding increases in FDI in services due to the implementation of the Services Directive could be substantially higher. In some countries the FDI stock in services could even double.

Not only could the implementation of the Services Directive and the full elimination of FDI restrictions increase FDI, the improvement of economic

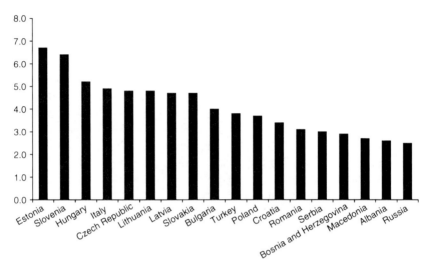

Source: Transparency index of Transparency International (2006).

Figure 12.3   Transparency index for Central and Eastern European countries

institutions is also important. Unclear institutional environments, bureau-cracy, vague rules and lack of observing rules, hamper investment in general and foreign investment in particular. The lack of FDI in Turkey is often ascribed to these factors (see, among others, Lejour et al., 2004).

OECD (2006) also concludes that FDI flows to the Balkans remain below potential. The results in Table 12.4 already point in that direction. A recent IMF study (Demekas et al., 2005) concludes that the gap between actual and potential FDI in 2003 ranges from 50 per cent in Serbia to 82 per cent in Bosnia and Herzegovina. Potential FDI is measured by assum-ing best practices on foreign exchange and trade liberalization, infrastruc-ture reform, unit labour cost, tariff level, and corporate tax burden across CEECs and SEECs in 2003. For most CEECs the gap is much smaller, sug-gesting that SEECs could do more on market-reforming policies than CEECs. The OECD is pleading for regulatory reform and enforcement of anti-corruption measures in South-Eastern Europe. Enforcement is a major issue here, as is the improvement of tax administration. The anti-corruption indicator in Figure 12.3 also indicates that the Balkan states have much to gain. The level of the transparency index for Finland is of course beyond reach in the coming decade for SEECs, but a substantial improvement in the direction of the CEECs is hopefully an achievable goal.

CONCLUSIONS

After a hiccup at the beginning of the new millennium due to the bad economic climate in most OECD countries, FDI is on the rise again. FDI has reached a level of more than USD 900 billion, and the larger part of this amount is destined towards services sectors. Europe is the key destination for FDI, and FDI is prominent in service sectors like *transport, storage and communication, finance and banking* and *business services*. Also in the CEECs most of the FDI goes to services. In spite of the rapid rise in FDI in the 1990s, the potential for FDI is still large, in particular in CEECs and SEECs. FDI in the EU is still hampered by differences in regulation and FDI restrictions. Implementation of the Service Directive could increase FDI by 20 to 35 per cent, and a complete elimination of all differences in regulation could double the FDI stock. These numbers are EU averages. For CEECs the effects could be twice as large, because they face more stringent FDI restrictions and more differences in regulation than other EU member states. For SEECs the benefits could be even greater. On average, institutional settings in SEECs are less market-friendly than those in CEECs, possibly as a matter of time because the reform processes in these countries started off later. These countries have much to gain in terms of attracting more FDI if regulatory reform, anti-corruption measures and enforcement are reinforced. IMF calculations show a gain of 50 per cent to 80 per cent for individual countries, excluding measures like the Services Directive in streamlining or reducing differences in regulation with other countries.

The landscape of European FDI is indeed changing. FDI becomes more and more important for serving foreign markets, relatively more FDI is directed towards services sectors, and more FDI will be destined to CEECs. By implementing policies on regulatory reform, anti-corruption and the Services Directive, there is much scope to continue these trends.

NOTES

1. Arjan Lejour, CPB Netherlands Bureau for Economic Policy Analysis, www.cpb.nl, e-mail a.m.lejour@cpb.nl. I want to thank Nico van Leeuwen for assistance with the data.
2. Source: UNCTAD (2006).
3. These numbers also illustrate the volatility of (foreign) direct investment flows. Moreover, FDI numbers are significantly affected by some individual transactions (mergers or acquisitions), in particular at the sector level. For instance in 2005 Shell Trade and Transport (UK) merged with Royal Dutch Petroleum (the Netherlands), a transaction of USD 74 billion. This transaction is responsible for a large part of the large increase in FDI flows in 2005. Note that Dutch FDI outflows were valued at USD 114 billion and UK inflows at USD 165 billion.

4.　Sources: Markusen (2002), and UNCTAD (2004).
5.　The relevance of these facts does not change much over time. Kox et al. (2004) also mention these facts based on OECD data on FDI inflows for the period 1998 to 2000.
6.　The bars in Figure 12.2 do not add up to 100 per cent, because the primary sector is not shown here.
7.　FDI outflows have increased, albeit at a much lower level. Nearly 90 per cent of the FDI outflow comes from Russia. Source: UNCTAD (2006).
8.　Using country data on some 200 different items in product-market regulations from the OECD International Regulation database. The indicator is decomposed into five different areas of product-market regulation.
9.　A recent OECD database on regulation does contain data for Slovakia (Conway et al., 2005).

REFERENCES

Conway, P., V. Janod and G. Nicoletti (2005), 'Product market regulation in OECD countries: 1998 to 2003', *OECD Economics Department Working Papers*, No. 419, Paris.
Copenhagen Economics (2005), 'Economic assessment of the barriers to the internal market for services: final report', report commissioned for the European Commission, http://www.copenhageneconomics.com/upload/pdf/copenhagen-economics-65.pdf.
De Bruijn, R., H. Kox and A.M. Lejour (2006), 'The trade-induced effects of the Services Directive and the country of origin principle', *CPB document* 108.
Demekas, D.G., B. Horváth, E. Ribakova and Y. Wu (2005), 'Foreign direct investment in Southeastern Europe: how (and how much) can policies help?', *IMF Working Paper* WP/05/110.
European Commission (2002), Report from the Commission to the Council and the European Parliament on the State of the Internal Market for Services, Brussels.
European Commission (2004), Proposal for a Directive of the European Parliament and of the Council on Services in the Internal Market, SEC (2004) 21, Brussels.
Eurostat (2006), 'Economy and finance, Balance of payments – International transactions, EU direct investment positions, breakdown by country and economic activity', Luxembourg.
Golub, S. (2003), 'Measures of restrictions on inward foreign direct investment for OECD countries', *OECD Economics Department Working Papers* No. 357, Paris: OECD.
Golub, S. and G. Nicoletti (2004), 'The influence of policies on foreign direct investment', mimeograph, Paris: OECD.
Kox, H.L.M., A.M. Lejour and R. Montizaan (2004), 'Intra-EU trade and investment in service sectors, and regulation patterns', CPB Memorandum 102.
Kox, H.L.M. and A.M. Lejour (2006), 'The effects of the services directive on intra-EU Trade and FDI', *Revue Economique*, **57** (4), 747–69.
Lejour, A.M., R.A. de Mooij and C.H. Capel (2004), 'Assessing the economic implications of Turkish accession to the EU', CPB Document 56.
Lejour, A.M., H. Rojas-Romagosa and G. Verweij (2007), 'Opening up services markets within Europe: modelling foreign establishments', forthcoming as *CPB Discussion Paper*.
Markusen, J. (2002), *Multinational Firms and the Theory of International Trade*, Cambridge, MA: MIT Press.

OECD (2006), *OECD Investment Compact's Investment Reform Index Report 2006* (for South-East Europe), Paris: OECD.

Resmini, L. (2006), 'The determinants of FDI in Central, Eastern and South-Eastern Europe: lessons from the past and prospects for the future', see chapter 14 of this volume.

Transparency International (2006), *Transparency Index*.

UNCTAD (2004), *World Investment Report* 2004, Geneva: United Nations.

UNCTAD (2006), *World Investment Report* 2009, Geneva: United Nations.

Van Leeuwen, N.I.M. and A.M. Lejour (2006), 'Bilateral FDI stock data by sector', CPB Memorandum 164.

13. Outward FDI from new European Union member states

Marjan Svetličič and Andreja Jaklič[1]

INTRODUCTION

The integration of transition economies into the world economy is typically accelerated by the deregulation, privatization and liberalization processes that accompany transition, with inward internationalization initially exceeding outward internationalization in terms of speed and volume. Despite its rapid development at the end of the 1990s, outward investment by transition economies has, with few exceptions,[2] long been ignored by the literature, partly due to its marginal share in world or even EU outward FDI. However, growth rates clearly indicate that the new EU member states (NMS) are internationalizing fast (even when compared to emerging economies), which brings important implications for development. Apart from Russia, the new EU members are the main outward investors among transition economies, but large differences remain across countries, many of which have yet to fully exploit the potential of internationalization.[3] Differences in internationalization performance arise from a variety of factors: domestic market size, initial openness and development level, speed of reforms, privatization, deregulation, liberalization and integration process; and these factors have also determined the inward FDI levels, competition levels in the domestic market, and the scope and variety of industries involved in internationalization.

While developments since the mid-1990s have confirmed evolutionary internationalization patterns and traditional theoretical models, developments were accelerated by the globalization process and by some players frequently overjumping stages; moreover the creation of multinational corporations (MNCs) by transition economies introduced many new patterns, innovative strategies and adaptations of smaller players (born globals, regional small- and medium-sized companies (SMEs)). Though MNCs from transition economies rarely compete 'face to face' with MNCs from developed economies,[4] many of them have become important global players in selected niches or indispensable parts of global value chains in several industries.

190

The objective of this chapter is to give a brief overview of the development of outward FDI in NMS, particularly those from transition economies, and their major characteristics and implications by summarizing and updating some previous research.[5] After evaluating the relative importance, patterns and geographical allocation of outward FDI from NMS, we evaluate the performance and effects of outward FDI, and conclude with policy recommendations.

THE IMPORTANCE AND PATTERN OF OUTWARD FDI FROM NMS

In the pre-transition period and even at the start of transition in 1990 NMS were almost non-existent on the FDI map, and they still contributed modestly to global trends at the time of writing. With inward FDI remaining much more important than outward FDI as predicted by theory,[6] the NMS' net investment position is still moving downwards[7] while that of incumbent EU members is moving up (Figure 13.1). However, NMS growth rates are very high and in some NMS even exceed inward FDI growth, which indicates the 'investment development path' (IDP) (Dunning, 1993).[8] Outward FDI flows, though oscillating, result in constantly growing stocks that also increase as a share of GDP (Table 13.1). The outward FDI stock of NMS grew 21-fold in the 1990–2004 period, and it grew more than three-fold since 2000, yet the share of NMS in the outward FDI stock of the EU-25 increased from 0.15 per cent in 1990 to 0.35 per cent in 2004 (Table 13.2,

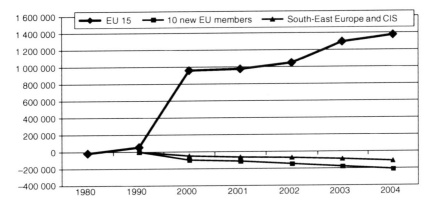

Source: Calculations based on UNCTAD (2006).

Figure 13.1 Net investment position (outward minus inward FDI stocks, USD million)

Table 13.1   Outward FDI stocks as a % of GDP and of gross fixed capital formation (GFCF)

	OFDI stocks as a % of GDP						OFDI stocks as a % of GFCF					
	2000	2001	2002	2003	2004	2005	2000	2001	2002	2003	2004	2005
Cyprus	6.4	8.9	12.7	16.0	17.4	18.2	11.0	15.9	24.7	24.3	49.8	31.0
Czech Republic	1.3	1.9	2.0	2.5	2.9	3.4	0.3	1.0	1.1	0.9	3.5	2.7
Estonia	5.0	7.9	10.4	12.4	12.5	15.0	4.8	13.5	7.1	5.9	8.4	16.7
Hungary	2.7	3.0	3.3	4.3	4.5	6.0	5.5	3.0	1.9	8.9	4.9	5.3
Latvia	3.4	0.6	0.8	1.0	1.7	1.8	0.2	5.5	3.0	1.9	2.7	3.0
Lithuania	0.3	0.4	0.4	0.7	1.9	2.8	0.2	0.3	0.6	0.9	5.4	5.8
Malta	5.7	7.2	7.2	7.6	6.7	15.8	2.8	2.6	−1.1	56.6	n.a.	−2.2
Poland	0.6	0.6	0.8	0.9	1.1	1.6	0.0	−0.2	0.6	0.8	1.8	2.7
Slovakia	1.6	2.1	2.0	1.9	1.5	1.2	0.4	0.6	0.1	0.3	−1.4	1.3
Slovenia	4.0	5.1	6.8	7.1	7.5	10.6	1.3	3.1	3.1	7.2	7.0	6.7

Source: UNCTAD (2006).

Table 13.2   Growth rates of outward FDI stock (in %)

	2001	2002	2003	2004	2005
EU-15	6.5	14.4	27.2	9.7	5.4
10 new EU members	27.3	36.6	47.6	32.0	44.5
South-Eastern Europe and CIS	55.9	69.2	31.4	12.8	43.2
Cyprus	44.5	57.9	60.7	30.7	13.2
Czech Republic	53.9	29.7	55.0	34.0	38.5
Estonia	70.5	53.0	51.0	36.9	40.8
Hungary	21.6	39.2	63.3	26.4	47.7
Latvia	−81.8	45.5	65.6	113.2	30.1
Lithuania	63.3	24.3	101.1	253.4	67.4
Malta	28.6	6.8	26.5	2.5	137.6
Poland	13.6	26.0	27.3	43.5	75.5
Slovakia	37.1	8.9	29.2	−1.5	3.2
Slovenia	30.7	48.0	31.4	25.5	49.8

Source: Calculations based on UNCTAD (2006).

Table 13.A1). Higher growth rates of outward FDI from NMS appear to reflect the stronger impact of external globalization factors (as in emerging countries but not for 'old' EU or OECD internationalization vanguards), and they also reflect small-domestic-market push factors. That is, apart from Poland (whose outward FDI dynamics lag behind that of other NMS), all NMS are small countries. Moreover, internal push factors including changes to the system, liberalization and foreign competition all of a sudden opened doors to previously forbidden outward FDI. In the case of the old EU or OECD foreign investors, developments had been much more gradual.

The investment dynamics in almost all countries intensified after 2000, especially from 2002 to 2005, particularly in the least developed states, Poland, Lithuania and Latvia, which started from very low levels. With the exception of Latvia and Slovakia, the importance of outward FDI in GDP is growing substantially, particularly in non-transition NMS, Cyprus and Malta but also in Estonia, Slovenia and Hungary (Table 13.1).

The lag of NMS against old EU members is nowhere greater than with gross fixed capital formation (GFCF), even though outward FDI from NMS (except for Malta) is contributing more and more to GFCF. In 2004, the average outward FDI share of GFCF was 3 per cent for NMS, compared with 26 per cent for the EU-15, which indicates its low relevance in total investment activity and suggests that outward FDI is unlikely to constrain domestic capital formation significantly. The underlying issue of this indicator is substitution (crowding-out) and/or complementarities of outward FDI to local (home country) investment; empirical tests have so far found no evidence that outward FDI would crowd out local investment. It is far more likely that outward FDI will complement and reinforce local investment (Globerman and Shapiro, 2006, p. 37). Moreover, Jaklič (2001) and Jaklič and Svetličič (2003) found positive and significant correlation between outward FDI and investment in a parent firm for some NMS. Thus, growing domestic gross capital formation, and productivity gains and restructuring are likely to drive up GDP as NMS' share of outward FDI in GFCF increases.

The potential restructuring role of outward FDI from NMS also largely depends on its geographical allocation. After all, the location of outward FDI reflects given firm-specific advantages and it influences the further development of the investing firms and home country effects. The domination of outward FDI in countries at similar or lower development levels would appear to indicate the relatively weaker competitive position of investing firms and limit the latter's development potential. Following the argument that early FDI stages are normally dominated by market-seeking investments (as confirmed for NMS by Jaklič and Svetličič, 2003, pp. 113–29) the NMS would be expected to have established most of their outward FDI of NMS in their major partner countries, that is in the EU. Yet this is not the case. The geographical spread of outward investment shows a strong regional concentration in countries at lower or similar development levels, with a similar history, tradition, economic structure and institutional system (socialist countries) or with strong national minorities. More distant emerging markets (like China, India or Latin America) have gained importance only recently. Our survey[9] revealed that most (and especially first) foreign affiliations were established in neighbouring countries, which were mostly other transition economies (over 54 per cent); for example Estonian banks in neighbouring Baltic countries, Czech investments in Slovakia, and Slovenian investments in the successor states of former Yugoslavia. Previous export experience and historical and cultural proximity are the main reasons for Central European economies being the dominant investment hosts for NMS. These location-specific factors are complemented by the ownership-specific advantages of the investing firms (strongly home-country-location-based), which reinforce such a regional concentration of outward FDI. The main locational advantages of target markets are thus: (i) similar tastes and markets; (ii) knowing and understanding the consumer, existing distribution channels, ability to adjust and communicate; (iii) established business ties, networks; (iv) less foreign competition, (while MNCs from developed economies serve a narrow top market segment, regional MNCs originating from transition economies are more capable of adjusting technology, organization and management style and cover more or broader market segments); (v) knowledge of informal institutions and better ability to overcome institutional barriers than competitors from developed economies; and (vi) poor enforcement of contracts and intellectual property rights protection, which may be an invitation to invest abroad to protect market position or prevent imitation by local firms; (vii) for more advanced transition economies, expertise in privatization due to similarities in privatization processes even if involving different models.

Though MNCs from NMS may be more successful in exploiting locational advantages in transition economies, their firm-specific advantages are weaker than those of MNCs from developed economies, which forces them to employ specific internationalization strategies. Most successful MNCs from NMS have chosen one or a combination of the following strategies: (i) becoming a domestic/regional market leader, and entering neighbouring markets after gaining a strong position and economies of scale in the domestic market; (ii) exploiting a first-mover advantage in other transition economies; (iii) developing a niche strategy, specialized product, intermediary product specialization; (iv) becoming a supplier to a global company; (v) follow the leader and/or the customer.

Some strategies were also fully applicable in developed markets, though the number of affiliations established in EU countries was much lower (21 per cent of all foreign affiliations according to our survey). Unlike the case of Austria, Portugal and Spain, the 2004 enlargement round basically consolidated trade relations with the EU for the NMS rather than changing the concentration of investment in other transition economies, of which many are potential future EU members,[10] or rather than rerouting investment flows – those changes were basically pre-integration (investment creation) effects that had already occurred after accession agreements were concluded.[11] The firm-specific advantages of most NMS firms are not strong enough to overcome their latecomer positions in advanced markets. Asset-augmenting outward FDI to complement local skills with those available in the EU is poorly developed at the present stage of outward FDI. Some firms with high firm-specific advantages (strong technological know-how, innovation capacity and managerial knowledge; mostly IT or services firms) have opted to change their erstwhile transition economy image and moved their headquarters to developed countries (or even knowledge centres).

Transition- and globalization-specific factors can be expected to speed up the investment development path (IDP) and the creation of MNCs by NMS. Speeding-up factors also include policies to enhance the restructuring of local industries, as they may work in the same direction, and firm-specific advantages that fill a gap in the host policy environment of other transition economies. Bilateral IDPs are therefore more advanced (Gorynia et al., 2006). The most important explanatory variable for differences between transition and non-transition countries, or more generally between highly- and medium-developed countries, may be the different weight attributed to the ownership advantages of firms and the location advantages of countries. In spite of the strong idiosyncratic nature of such investment,[12] it seems, at least, that small NMS share characteristics which make their potential IDPs similar (small markets, similar economic structure, same timing and character of reforms, governance, similar foreign trade structure . . .). The fast growth of outward FDI but further decline of the net investment position would imply that NMS will remain at this stage for some time to come, although with outward FDI strongly exceeding inward FDI growth on average.

PERFORMANCE AND EFFECTS OF OUTWARD FDI

Most transition economy studies have so far examined only the performance and effects of inward FDI. Several 'early-1990s studies' found positive host country effects and emphasized positive allocation effects and foreign affiliates' superior performance compared with domestic firms in terms of productivity, export orientation and profitability.[13] Deeper insights into foreign ownership as one of the major determinants of performance differences provided new findings. Later studies that also considered market structure (competition effect), corporate heterogeneity and spillover effects (and pointed to the methodological weaknesses of earlier studies) provided less conclusive results (Blomström and Kokko, 1998; Lipsey, 2002; Javorcik, 2004; Damijan et al., 2003; Damijan and Rojec, 2004). Studies which included more complete data (including inward and outward investors) and considered corporate heterogeneity emphasized multinationality per se as a major determinant of superior performance (Bellak, 2004a, 2004b) and heterogeneity, or found domestic multinational firms (parent firms) to be more successful than foreign affiliates (Castellani and Zanfei, 2005; Jaklič, 2004). Comprehensive and comparative studies on this issue are still to be done, yet specific country studies show similar results and suggest that 'national MNCs' are also of vital importance for every national economy, or even more important than foreign MNCs headquartered in the country. They are a crucial element for integration into the world economy (international trade and production) and consequently influence the level of knowledge and information exchange as well as access to production factors, which in turn determines the level of welfare. Parent firms that create the growth and development strategy normally possess, and have access to, the best sources to create competitive advantages (tangible and intangible knowledge, innovation/R&D potential, capital and talent) and maintain their advantage with international sourcing and integration into the international environment.

The most important impacts of outward FDI from the transition economies' point of view are restructuring, growth and development in general, while effects on trade and competitiveness, domestic production and employment are cited most often. Estimates of the macroeconomic impact of outward FDI are limited, particularly due to short time series and the still modest value of such flows. Therefore, the effects of outward FDI are evaluated mostly at the firm level based on firms' own perceptions (evaluations).

Our survey on five NMS demonstrated that our sample companies have been surprisingly successful with their outward FDI projects on average, given the early stage of internationalization; investors have mostly realized their original aims. Very few investing firms have failed and very few have achieved more than expected. The most important effect of outward FDI for investing firms has been maintaining and gaining additional market shares, which pushed up export growth. A direct presence in foreign markets has helped investing companies respond to customer needs more rapidly. Investors have improved their image and enhanced and broadened their marketing, management and organizational skills. The majority of sample companies introduced new products, adaptations or a wider range of products while improving their quality. Many investors improved innovation capacity and increased investments in R&D (average increase in R&D expenditures to sales ratio was 2.5 per cent in two years), although the investing firms had already had above-average R&D expenditures before. International competition thus motivated the sample companies to strengthen their firm-specific advantages. Companies have restructured their production programmes (production volume mostly increased) and even their organization as a result of investing abroad. Investing abroad has improved a range of products and feedback with customers, and in this way has provided access to new knowledge clusters. According to our survey the majority of firms did not cut staff due to investment abroad, but rather succeeded in retaining jobs which would have been lost otherwise. Very few companies started to relocate production abroad because of rising wages at home; no export substitution has been found so far (Jaklič and Svetličič, 2003, pp. 49–59). The positive home country employment effect was also confirmed by selected econometric country studies, for example in Slovenia (Jaklič et al., 2005) and Estonia (Varblane et al., 2006).

These effects were not found to be limited to large investors that contribute capital value of outward stocks, but were significant also in SMEs, which constitute the majority of investing firms (in terms of numbers).[14] Though SMEs face many limitations in terms of capabilities (especially financial constraints) they also have some advantages (like flexibility and networking potential), and studies show more similarities than differences in internationalization patterns (Svetličič et al., 2007).

Outward FDI thus enables firms to exploit the advantages of globalization and to draw on factor endowments abroad. All these changes influence the industrial structure of the home economy closer to optimal allocation of resources due to the international division of labour under globalization pressures. Companies investing abroad on average show better performance indicators than non-investing firms (revenues, export, labour and total factor productivity), and these indicators also improve more quickly (Svetličič and Jaklič, 2003, pp. 71–5, Jaklič et al., 2005).[15]

CONCLUSIONS

While outward FDI by NMS basically follows traditional internationalization patterns, their IDP stages are much shorter, and the specific weight of drivers, types of firm-specific advantages and consequently types of FDI and regional orientation differ somewhat.

The strong impact of globalization and changes in the economic system accelerated the process and (especially small) NMS face fast growth in outward internationalizations despite modest policy stimulation. Transition, general liberalization and privatization and more globalized environments certainly outperformed integration-specific factors, although EU association agreements and later membership certainly created a stimulating infrastructure and climate for FDI. New multinationals from NMS are hardly on a par with MNCs from developed economies, yet may become competitors in some niches and in some services, but less so in manufacturing or in the area of resource-seeking outward FDI, where emerging economy multinationals are becoming quite strong. Though large firms are the most important investors in terms of volume, SMEs in NMS account for most direct investors abroad in terms of numbers.

The type of firm-specific advantage and path (systemic) dependency decisively determine the regional allocation of NMS investment abroad. Although the trade relations of NMS are mostly concentrated in the EU, their external funds mostly flow to neighbouring countries and other transition markets (that had the same – socialist – system), of which many are potential or current EU candidates. Concentration in less developed markets is high and continual, yet the home country effects are positive and important. The effects of outward FDI on parent companies largely reflect the initial motives for investment, which also explain the high degree of expectations realized. As a reflection of the prevailing market-seeking-motivated investment, firms particularly stressed the trade and competitiveness effects. Stable or even rising market shares that boost exports were by far the most important. The effects on improving strategic assets, like a better international image, customer responsiveness, knowledge spillovers and higher quality, increased product variety and efficiency that were motivated by strategic-asset-seeking and efficiency-seeking aims, follow as the second most important group of impacts.

A low investment presence in EU members might imply that such investment can, apart from market creation, only very modestly impact restructuring processes in old EU states, yet the development effects resulting from NMS' and potential future members' direct presence on foreign markets are significant. The internationalization of NMS companies has enhanced the restructuring and transformation of the investing companies and hence stimulated the transition process. Investing abroad might be treated as a catching-up tool since it helps narrow the gap in productivity, efficiency and knowledge (above all, in marketing, organization and management). For many firms from small countries or for those that reached the upper limit of market concentration allowed in the home economy, investing abroad has become the most promising or only way to grow.

Direct investment abroad in most cases seems sustainable and is not a whim, provided that the resulting profits are used creatively to strengthen one's own capabilities and not only to defend achieved market positions. Above-average R&D expenditures promise that the prevailing home country location-driven advantages thus far will gradually be replaced by firm-specific advantage-driven internationalization.

The policy of promoting outward FDI is not likely to succeed unless accompanied by changes in the underlying governance of private and public sector activities, and unless outward FDI contributes to higher income levels in the home country more generally, to include those who are not owners of investing firms. Nevertheless, it seems that a certain orchestrating of outward FDI is needed in the early stages of development, for most firms' new processes in NMS. From the policy point of view, a really important barrier to internationalization is the lack of knowledge and experience of management. This is an area where firms and respective home governments can do much in order to promote internationalization. Education systems are not yet sufficiently equipped to educate 'ready-made' global managers. Training is still functionally oriented; there remains a lack of holistic knowledge about internationalization and outward FDI.

NOTES

1. Professor and assistant professor at the Faculty of Social Sciences, University of Ljubljana. E-mails: marjansvetlicic@siol.net, andreja.jaklic@fdv.uni-lj.si.
2. See, for instance, McMillan, 1987; Hamilton, 1986; Jaklič and Svetličič, 2003, and Svetličič and Rojec, 2003.
3. The World Investment Report regularly presents large differences in estimations on potential and actual performance FDI indexes (UNCTAD, 2003–2006).
4. There is not a single enterprise from the NMS among the world's top 50 financial or 100 non-financial MNCs (UNCTAD, 2006).
5. Up-to-date macro data will be evaluated, while most analyses concentrate on just 5 transition economy NMS (based on questionnaires conducted in 2001) given a lack of data on Latvia, Lithuania and Slovakia.
6. See, for example, evolutionary models like Uppsala school or Dunning's investment development path.
7. Still, the net investment position of NMS is much higher than that of other former communist countries (apart from Russia).
8. Dynamic models of internationalization such as the Uppsala model and investment development path (IDP) predict that outward FDI is a function of the development level of the country whose net investment position depends on the GDP per capita. An updated IDP version (Dunning and Narula, 1998) claims that, although the general trend still holds, the stages and amplitudes are shrinking due to country-specific factors such as the quality of the country's institutions, its economic structure, its openness to international trade and government policy towards FDI (see Dunning et al., 2006, p. 7). The link between inward/outward FDI is, however, not causal, as emphasized by Lipsey (2002). There is more of a co-evolution involved (Globerman and Shapiro, 2006, p. 10). NMS are on average still between the second and third stage (Bellak and Svetličič, 2003; Globerman and Shapiro, 2006).
9. A sample of 180 outward investors from the Czech Republic, Estonia, Hungary, Poland and Slovenia were evaluated in 2001 on the basis of a fully structured questionnaire.

10. Such geographical concentration has also been influenced by indirect investors (inward investors in NMS) that use NMS as a springboard to less developed markets (Jaklič and Svetličič, 2003, pp. 64–70).
11. The theoretically expected increase of intra-EU flows has not occurred (yet), though we face time limitations for sophisticated evaluation. There was no longer any reason for system-escape type or tariff factories within EU markets. Therefore, some of such investment created before EU membership has been abandoned, including trade-facilitating affiliations. Enlargement has, at the same time, stronger investment diversion effects since most of outward FDI is in fact directed to other transition economies that are (still) not EU members. The effects have therefore been mixed. The new EU borders have in a way destimulated intra-FDI flows to countries with previous free-trade arrangements and stimulated them from another perspective (tariff factories). With the changing and enhancing of firm-specific advantages, more outward FDI in the EU may be expected as the asset-augmenting type of outward FDI, as is already happening in the case of emerging economies' outward FDI. More outward FDI in the EU is expected, particularly in the service sector as a consequence of the liberalization of services in the EU and the competitive advantages of firms from NMS in some service activities (construction, engineering and design) (Damijan and Rojec, 2004).
12. Reasons may be different, as in the case of Austria and Slovenia. In Slovenia the reasons are mostly transition- and history-specific while in Austria they are EU integration- and enlargement-specific (see Bellak and Svetličič, 2003, p. 26).
13. See, among others, evaluating effects on transition economies, Hunya, 2000; Rojec, 2000, for Slovenia; Djankov and Hoekman, 1998, for the Czech Republic. Similar results were found for developed countries.
14. As in other countries, major investors abroad from five NMS are larger firms but not in terms of the number of investors. Smaller ones ranged from 10 per cent in Hungary to 79 per cent of all investors in Slovenia. The role of SMEs in outward investing is strongest in the smallest countries, Estonia and Slovenia. Specialized SMEs in these national markets are often too limited in scale to survive, and international expansion is a means of their survival.
15. A study for Slovenia demonstrates that premiums (in sales, profits, productivity) are highest for investors who started to invest between 1998 and 2000, demonstrating that at least a 2-year time lag is needed for assessing the results of such an investment. Even more important is a dynamic evaluation demonstrating that premiums on employment, productivity, salaries per worker and capital per worker have decreased for non-investing exporters. This analysis of 634 new investors (80 per cent started after 2000, with a 3-year time lag based on a matching technique singling out 122 investors) revealed that firms significantly increased their sales in the second year (all firms including SMEs) due to investing abroad (Jaklič et al., 2005, pp. 38 and 67).

REFERENCES

Bellak, C. (2004a), 'How domestic and foreign firms differ and why does it matter?', *Journal of Economic Surveys*, **18** (4), 483–514.

Bellak, C. (2004b), 'How performance gaps between domestic and foreign firms matter for economic policy', *Transnational Corporations*, **13** (2), August, 29–55.

Bellak, C. and M. Svetličič (2003), 'Investment-development path of small economies: comparative evaluation of Austria and Slovenia', in M. Svetličič and M. Rojec (eds), *Facilitating Transition by Internationalization: Outward Direct Investment from Central European Economies in Transition*, (Series: Transition and Development), Aldershot, UK, Burlington, USA: Ashgate, pp. 17–28.

Blomström, M. and A. Kokko (1998), 'Multinational corporations and spillovers', *Journal of Economic Surveys*, **12** (3), 247–77.

Castellani, D. and A. Zanfei (2005), *Multinational Firms and Productivity Spillovers: The Role of Firms Heterogenity*, Paper presented at EIBA conference, Oslo, 2005.

Damijan, J.P. and M. Rojec (2004), 'Foreign direct investment and the catching-up process in new EU member states: is there a flying geese pattern?' *WIIW Research Reports*, 310, October, Vienna: The Vienna Institute for International Economic Studies.

Damijan, J.P., M. Knell, B. Majcen and M. Rojec (2003), 'Technology transfer through FDI in top-10 transition countries: how important are direct effect, horizontal and vertical spillover?', *William Davidson Institute Working Paper* 549.

Djankov, S. and B. Hoekman (1998), 'Avenues of technology transfer: foreign investment and productivity change in the Czech Republic', *CEPR Discussion Paper* 1883.

Dunning, J.H. (1993), *Multinational Enterprises and the Global Economy*, Wokingham: Addison Wesley Publishing Company.

Dunning, J.H. and R. Narula (1998), *Foreign Direct Investment and Governments, Catalysts for Economic Restructuring*, London and New York: Routledge.

Dunning, J., C. Kim and D. Park (2006), *Old Wine in New Bottles: A Comparison of Emerging Market TNCs and Developed Country TNCs*, paper presented at the International Conference on 'The Rise of Transnational Corporations from Emerging Markets: Threat or Opportunity?', Columbia University, NY, October.

Globerman, S. and D. Shapiro (2006), *Outward FDI and the Economic Performance of Emerging Markets*, paper presented at the International Conference on 'The Rise of Transnational Corporations from Emerging Markets: Threat or Opportunity?', Columbia University, NY, October.

Gorynia, M., J. Novak and R. Wolniak (2006), *The Investment Development Path of Poland Revisited: A Geography Analysis*, 32 EIBA Annual Conference, University of Friburg, Switzerland, December.

Hamilton, J. (1986), *Red Multinationals or Red Herrings? The Activities of Enterprises from Socialist Countries in the West*, London: Frances Pinter.

Hunya, G. (2000), *Integration through Foreign Direct Investment: Making Central European Industries Competitive*, Cheltenham, UK and Northampton, MA: Edward Elgar.

Jaklič, A. (2001), *Outward Internationalisation by Direct Investment – the Case of Slovenia*, Phare ACE project P97–8073–R CIR, Ljubljana.

Jaklič, A. (2004), *What is behind the Ability to Create MNEs in Transition Economies? Examining the Case of Slovenia*, EIBA 2004, Ljubljana.

Jaklič, A. and M. Svetličič (2003), *Enhanced Transition Through Outward Internationalization: Outward FDI by Slovenian Firms* (Series: Transition and Development), Aldershot, UK and Burlington, USA: Ashgate.

Jaklič, A., A. Burger and M. Rojec (2005), Dinamika in makroekonomske posledice izhodne internacionalizacije v Sloveniji [The dynamics and macroeconomics effects of outward FDI], CMO–FDV, University of Ljubljana, mimeo.

Javorcik, Beata Smarzynska (2004), 'Does foreign direct investment increase the productivity of domestic firms? In search of spillovers through backward linkages', *American Economic Review*, **94** (3), 605–27.

Lipsey, Robert E. (2002), 'Home and host country effects of FDI', *NBER Working Paper* 9293.

McMillan, C. H. (1987), *Multinationals from the Second World*, London: Macmillan Press.

Rojec, M. (2000), 'Restructuring and efficiency upgrading with FDI', in G. Hunya (ed.), *Integration Through Foreign Direct Investment*, Cheltenham, UK and Northampton, USA: Edward Elgar in association with The Vienna Institute for International Economic Studies (wiiw), pp. 130–49.

Svetličič, M. and A. Jaklič (2003), 'Outward FDI by transition economies: basic features, trends and development implications', in M. Svetličič and M. Rojec (eds), *Facilitating Transition by Internationalization. Outward Direct Investment from Central European Economies in Transition*, (Series: Transition and Development), Aldershot, UK and Burlington, USA: Ashgate, pp. 49–78.

Svetličič, M. and M. Rojec (2003), *Facilitating Transition by Internationalization. Outward Direct Investment from Central European Economies in Transition*, (Series: Transition and Development), Aldershot, UK and Burlington, USA: Ashgate.

Svetličič, M., A. Jaklič and A. Burger (2007), 'Internationalisation of small and medium-sized enterprises from selected Central European economies', *East European Economies*, forthcoming.

UNCTAD, statistical data base (www.unctad.org).

United Nations Conference on Trade and Development (UNCTAD) (2006), 'World Investment Report 2005', UNCTAD, Division on Transnational Corporations and Investment, Geneva.

Varblane, U., P. Vahter and J. Masso (2006), *The Impact of Outward FDI on the Home Country Employment in the Low Cost Transition Economy*, paper presented at the 32nd EIBA Annual Conference, University of Fribourg, Switzerland, December.

Table 13.A1   FDI flows and stocks by individual NMS, EU-10 and EU-15 (USD million)

ECONOMY	CATEGORY	1990	2000	2001	2002	2003	2004
Cyprus	FDI inflows	126.6	854.9	944.4	1057.4	1010.8	1146.2
	FDI inward stock	–	2910.4	3854.9	4912.3	6986.2	8132.4
	FDI outflows	4.6	172.1	249.6	461.3	523.9	629.7
	FDI outward stock	8.5	560.4	809.9	1278.9	2054.6	2684.3
Czech Republic	FDI inflows	1444*	4986.3	5641.4	8482.7	2101.4	4463.3
	FDI inward stock	19.6*	21643.7	27092.2	38669.2	45286.7	56414.5
	FDI outflows	–	42.9	165.4	206.5	206	546.2
	FDI outward stock	–	737.8	1135.6	1473	2283.5	3060.6
Estonia	FDI inflows	–	386.9	542.4	284.3	890.6	926
	FDI inward stock	–	2644.7	3160	4226.4	6510.5	9529.6
	FDI outflows	–	63.4	199.7	131.8	148.1	257.4
	FDI outward stock	–	259.1	441.8	676	1020.8	1397.5
Hungary	FDI inflows	623.4	2764.1	3936	2993.5	2161.8	4166.9
	FDI inward stock	569	22869.9	27406.9	36223.9	48320.4	60328.3
	FDI outflows	16.1	620.5	368.1	278.1	1646.5	537.6
	FDI outward stock	196.8	1279.9	1556.1	2166.5	3537.2	4472.4
Latvia	FDI inflows	–	412.6	132.1	253.7	300	646.9
	FDI inward stock	–	2083.8	2328	2751	3282	4493
	FDI outflows	–	12.3	18.9	3.7	36.2	109
	FDI outward stock	–	241.4	44	64	106	226
Lithuania	FDI inflows	–	378.9	445.8	732.0	179.2	773.1
	FDI inward stock	–	2334.3	2665.5	3981.3	4959.8	6388.9
	FDI outflows	–	3.7	7.1	17.6	37.2	262.6
	FDI outward stock	–	29.3	47.9	59.5	119.7	422.8

Table 13.A1   (continued)

ECONOMY	CATEGORY	1990	2000	2001	2002	2003	2004
Malta	FDI inflows	45.8	622.1	258.9	−426.3	294.4	420.9
	FDI inward stock	465.3	2385.5	2560.9	2440.6	3136.3	3557.2
	FDI outflows	–	25.9	21.8	−9.5	19.5	8.8
	FDI outward stock	–	203.1	261.2	278.9	352.7	361.5
Poland	FDI inflows	89	9343	5714	4131	4123	6159
	FDI inward stock	109	34227	41247	48320	55268	61427
	FDI outflows	5.4	16	−90	230	196	806
	FDI outward stock	408	1018	1156	1457	1855	2661
Slovakia	FDI inflows	–	1925.4	1584.1	4093.8	668.8	1122.4
	FDI inward stock	–	3732.9	4836.2	8529.8	11863.6	14500.7
	FDI outflows	–	20.9	34.9	4.92	22	−155.5
	FDI outwardstock	–	325.2	445.7	485.5	627.3	617.9
Slovenia	FDI inflows	–	135.9	370	1686.1	337.0	516.1
	FDI inward stock	–	2893.7	2601.9	4108.9	4445.9	4962.1
	FDI outflows	–	65.3	144.5	153.2	465.9	497.9
	FDI outward stock	–	767.9	1003.9	1485.9	1951.9	2449.8
10 new EU members	FDI inflows	1049.8	21810.1	19569.2	23288.2	12067	20340.8
	FDI inward stock	2450.9	97725.9	117753.5	154163.4	190059.4	229733.6
	FDI outflows	45.6	1043.2	1120.1	1477.6	3301.3	3499.8
	FDI outward stock	870.9	5422.1	6902.2	9425.2	13908.6	18353.9
EU-15	FDI inflows	96709.2	674484.8	363051.1	397144.8	326611.3	196098.7
	FDI inward stock	751255.6	2077108	2261471	2657380	3416864	3794201
	FDI outflows	130701	812370.2	432807.3	383071.6	369098.9	276330
	FDI outward stock	804980.5	3040879	3238648	3705674	4712965	5171384

Note: * data for Czechoslovakia.

Source: UNCTAD (2006), own calculations.

PART III

How to attract sustainable investment:
theory and practice

14. The determinants of FDI in Central, Eastern and South-Eastern Europe: lessons from the past and prospects for the future

Laura Resmini

1. INTRODUCTION

The marked rise of FDI flows to Central, Eastern and South-Eastern European countries since the early 1990s has prompted substantial empirical research into the underlying factors, for at least two reasons. First, FDI has become an important part of the domestic economy. In 1990, FDI stocks averaged just 0.9 per cent of GDP, ranging from virtually zero in several countries to 3.8 per cent in Slovenia. By 2005, FDI stocks averaged 36 per cent of GDP, ranging from about 20 per cent in Albania to 93 per cent in Estonia. Second, foreign investments played and still play a crucial role in the recipients' transition from centrally planned to market economies, providing substantial financial capital, technological know-how and managerial expertise. Yet the patterns of absolute and relative FDI inflows have been quite erratic, with Central and Eastern European countries (CEECs) receiving the bulk of FDI, and Southern and Eastern European countries (SEECs) still lagging behind.[1] Therefore, an in-depth analysis of the factors determining FDI inflows is needed not only to understand these differences but also to predict future patterns of FDI into the area and provide policy makers with guidelines on how to improve FDI inflows.

This chapter provides a critical review of the literature on the determinants of FDI in European transition countries, focusing on the *external factors* that are likely to affect the location and the magnitude of foreign investments. The contribution of the chapter is to evaluate what we can say with relative confidence about FDI behaviour in transition countries, and what we cannot say because of the lack of evidence.

To guide the analysis, the chapter starts with a summary of the major trends in foreign investments in Central, Eastern and South-Eastern

European countries since the fall of the Berlin Wall. A brief discussion of the main theories on FDI determinants will precede the analysis of the empirical literature on such determinants in Central, Eastern and South-Eastern European countries. This critical review aims both at understanding general trends, and at highlighting the issues that still need extra analysis, such as similarities and differences across economic sectors and the geographical location of foreign firms within the considered countries. This analysis can serve both as a guide for a better comprehension of future patterns of FDI into the region, and as a starting point for future research areas.

2. MAJOR TRENDS AND STYLIZED FACTS OF FDI IN TRANSITION COUNTRIES

The opening up and the transition to market economy of Central, Eastern and South-Eastern European countries have been accompanied by a surge of FDI flows into these countries, both in absolute levels and relative to other less developed regions (Table 14.1).

The bulk of FDI flows to the area has gone to CEECs, notably Poland, Hungary and the Czech Republic, three of the largest CEE economies and in fact the earliest members of the Central European Free Trade Area (CEFTA). FDI inflows to SEECs, which lag behind flows to CEECs, have been highly concentrated in Romania, Bulgaria and Croatia since the end of the 1990s, when progress with political and social stabilization and economic and political reforms started to exert their beneficial effects. By 2005, these countries were collecting about 83 per cent of total FDI inflows to the Balkan area.

Inter-country comparisons require some scaling to account for differences in country size. In so doing, top receivers become rather small countries, such as Estonia, Croatia and Macedonia, whose rank changes substantially with the scaling factor (population or GDP; see Table 14.2). Overall, the data confirm the lag of SEECs.

FDI has flown quite unevenly to the different sectors of the European transition economies. According to the few existing official data (UNCTAD, 2003),[2] little FDI has flown to primary industries, given modest natural resource endowments, land restrictions and environmental legacy problems and their potential liabilities under EU standards. FDI in manufacturing was higher than in services until the privatization of banks, telecommunications and utilities opened the door to foreign investors. In 2000, FDI stocks in the service sector represented more than one-half of the capital invested in the Czech Republic, the Baltic States, Hungary, Poland

Table 14.1   Inward FDI flows by host region and economy, 1990–2005 (USD millions)

	1990–95[1]	1995–00[1]	2001	2002	2003	2004	2005
Central and Eastern Europe	5936	14973	18366	22608	11307	27111	32312
Czech Republic	947	3387	5641	8483	2101	4974	10991
Estonia	165	315	542	284	919	1049	2853
Hungary	3135	3664	3936	2994	2137	4654	6699
Latvia	117	367	132	254	292	699	632
Lithuania	36	395	446	732	179	773	1009
Poland	1385	6007	5714	4131	4589	12873	7724
Slovakia	164	653	1584	4094	756	1261	1908
Slovenia	93	186	370	1636	333	827	496
South-Eastern Europe	404	2660	4240	3877	8457	13283	12445
Albania	50	73	207	135	178	332	260
Bosnia and Herzegovina	0	65	119	265	381	606	298
Bulgaria	56	510	813	905	2097	3443	2223
Croatia	91	774	1338	1213	2133	1262	1695
Macedonia, TFYR	7	64	442	78	95	157	100
Romania	162	1001	1157	1144	2213	6517	6388
Serbia and Montenegro	82	172	165	137	1360	966	1481
Yugoslavia (former)	93	–	–	–	–	–	–
World	224275	740665	832248	617732	557869	710755	916277
Developed economies	149324	538294	599272	441238	358539	396145	542312
Developing economies	72840	193471	221447	163583	175138	275032	334285

Note: 1. Averages over the period.

Source: UNCTAD (2006).

*Table 14.2   FDI indicators in Eastern Europe, re-ranked by population
and GDP*

FDI stocks/population (USD)			
Country	1995	Country	2005
Hungary	1094	Estonia	9126
Slovenia	949	Hungary	6069
Czech Republic	712	Czech Republic	5831
Estonia	455	Slovenia	4036
Average	**285**	Slovakia	2845
Latvia	245	Croatia	2816
Poland	203	**Average**	**2805**
Slovakia	151	Poland	2445
Croatia	100	Latvia	2080
Lithuania	95	Lithuania	1892
Macedonia, TFYR	81	Bulgaria	1185
Albania	62	Romania	1101
Bulgaria	53	Macedonia, TFYR	924
Romania	36	Serbia and Montenegro	665
Serbia and Montenegro	31	Albania	537
Bosnia and Herzegovina	2	Bosnia and Herzegovina	529

FDI stocks/GDP annual flows (percentages)			
Country	1995	Country	2005
Hungary	25.31	Estonia	93.64
Estonia	15.45	Hungary	55.92
Czech Republic	13.30	Czech Republic	48.10
Latvia	12.59	Macedonia, TFYR	37.47
Slovenia	9.42	**Average**	**35.40**
Albania	8.11	Bulgaria	34.33
Average	**7.61**	Croatia	33.33
Poland	5.77	Slovakia	32.77
Lithuania	5.51	Poland	31.05
Slovakia	4.18	Latvia	28.73
Macedonia, TFYR	3.57	Lithuania	25.11
Bulgaria	3.40	Romania	24.16
Croatia	2.54	Slovenia	23.70
Romania	2.31	Bosnia and Herzegovina	21.93
Serbia and Montenegro	2.21	Serbia and Montenegro	20.71
Bosnia and Herzegovina	0.45	Albania	20.12

Source: UNCTAD (2006).

and Slovenia. A more in-depth analysis of the distribution of FDI across manufacturing sectors (Nicolini and Resmini, 2004) indicates that about two-thirds of foreign affiliates in Bulgaria, Czech Republic, Hungary, Poland and Romania operate in traditional labour-intensive sectors.[3]

Not surprisingly, most FDI comes from the old EU-15 member states. The importance of the EU investors can be explained by geographical proximity, historical factors, the need to be present in highly promising markets and the integration process as well. In 2000, the share of EU in total FDI inward stocks into transition countries ranged from 60 per cent in Latvia to 89 per cent in the Czech Republic (UNCTAD, 2003).

3. THEORETICAL BACKGROUND

The analysis of main trends in FDI in transition countries highlights a strong geographical concentration in the more advanced countries in both CEECs and SEECs, and an even stronger specialization in manufacturing (typically, medium-low and low technologies). In order to understand these differences and formulate policies to attract FDI, it is necessary to identify the conditions under which foreign investment is profitable because of the inherent costs for foreign firms to enter new markets and produce abroad. In this respect, the economic theory suggests that FDI takes place when three sets of determining factors co-exist (Markusen, 1995; Dunning, 1977):

1. The presence of *ownership-specific advantages*, which include all tangible and intangible assets that give the firms cost advantages and market power sufficient to cover the costs of producing abroad;
2. The presence of *locational advantages* in the host countries, which make it more profitable to produce abroad rather than serving foreign markets through exports;
3. The presence of superior commercial benefits in an intra-firm rather than arm's-length relationship between investor and recipient (*internalization advantages*).[4]

Unlike ownership and internalization advantages, which are firm-specific characteristics determining whether FDI occurs or not, locational advantages are external to firms and affect the magnitude of FDI flows. Therefore, in the rest of the chapter the focus is on this type of advantage, which, within the conditions for FDI to occur, is the only advantage that host countries' governments can control for.

Locational advantages do not necessarily arise spontaneously; sometimes they need to be created or nurtured through appropriate open policies[5] that allow FDI to enter a country, and other economic policies that become crucial to ensure an appropriate inflow of FDI. These policies can be broadly divided into macro-organizational policies (such as privatization policies, R&D and human resource development policies, competition policies, labour market policies, infrastructural policies, innovation policies, policies aimed at developing linkages between foreign and domestic firms or building up technological capabilities) and macroeconomic policies, such as stabilization policies, fiscal policies and exchange rate policies (UNCTAD, 1998). Although these policies may individually explain FDI,[6] it is quite impossible to assess their separate contributions since they are strongly interrelated. All together, they represent a country's investment climate, whose friendliness is a pre-condition for attracting FDI and allowing economic factors to assert themselves as locational advantages.

The academic literature on the economic determinants of FDI does not represent a coherent framework of analysis. Among the different strands helping to identify these determinants, the *classical theory of comparative advantages* argues that relative factor endowments and initial conditions attract FDI to some countries rather than others (Kravis and Lipsey, 1982; Aliber, 1970; Bhagwati, 1987; Veugelers, 1991). Therefore, the only way the host country can affect FDI is by changing its own economic fundamentals. Developments in the *new trade theory* led to the proximity-concentration framework, which explains FDI as a trade-off between trade costs and economies of scale (Markusen, 1984; Helpman, 1984; Brainard, 1993 and 1997), while *traditional and new location theories* emphasize the importance of trade integration and (self-reinforcing) agglomeration effects as main drivers of FDI (Markusen and Venables, 1995; Baldwin and Ottaviano, 1997). A growing body of literature argues that the *quality of institutions* is another important determinant for FDI activity, particularly in less developed countries. In fact, poor quality of institutions and corruption increase the cost of doing business; also, poor institutions usually lead to poor public goods, such as infrastructures (Wei, 2000; Antras, 2003; Antras and Helpman, 2004). Finally, in the absence of property rights protection, a firm will prefer to engage in FDI rather than in arm's-length contracts with local suppliers.

Whether and to what extent these economic characteristics affect FDI flows depend on the motives of foreign investors.[7] In this respect, three types of FDI are traditionally considered. First, *market-seeking* or *horizontal FDI* occurs when firms set up production facilities abroad in order to serve local and regional markets. Given its objective, market size and growth of the host economy are key drivers. Access impediments such as trade barriers and high transportation costs also encourage this type of FDI (Shatz and Venables, 2000; Brainard, 1993). Second, FDI in search of low-cost inputs is called *vertical* or *efficiency-seeking*, since it implies slicing the vertical chain of production and relocating part of it to a low-cost location. In general, vertical FDI is stimulated by international differences in input prices. Since vertical FDI is usually export-oriented, frequently to the multinational's home market, low trade and transportation costs and proximity to the home market are also important drivers. Third, *resource-* or *asset-seeking FDI* occurs when firms invest abroad to acquire resources not available in the home country, such as natural resources and raw materials, or specific advantages that help them maintain their competitiveness. Host countries' relative factor endowments, including an advanced research and technology base, as well as privatization policies, stimulate this kind of investment (Buigues and Jacquemin, 1994).

The next section discusses the experience of transition countries within this theoretical framework.

4.   THE DETERMINANTS OF FDI IN TRANSITION COUNTRIES: A REVIEW OF THE EMPIRICAL LITERATURE

Although Central, Eastern and South-Eastern European countries represent interesting laboratories to study FDI, the empirical evidence on the determinants of FDI inflows is rather sparse given the short transition process and the initial lack of reliable statistics. This explains why early studies rely on survey data to examine the overall behaviour of multinational firms in the CEECs (Lankes and Venables, 1996; Genco et al., 1993; Sheehy, 1994), while recent studies apply more or less sophisticated econometric techniques to analyse FDI determinants.[8]

The few studies on FDI determinants that do exist – less than 30 – typically focus on the 1990 decade and on newly acceded EU countries of Central and Eastern Europe. Only three works, at least to my knowledge, consider either the other Balkan countries or the CIS (Brada et al., 2006; Campos and Kinoshita, 2003; Merlevede and Schoors, 2004).[9] With few exceptions, data refer to annual inflows or inward FDI stocks at country level. Finer geographical and/or sectoral disaggregations are barely used, given the lack of consistent and reliable official data. Very often, FDI data refer to the manufacturing sector, given its importance in the economy of transition countries and its involvement in large- and small-scale privatization.

Table 14.3 summarizes the main determinants of FDI, as they emerge from the analysis of the literature based on aggregate data at country level. Two interesting facts emerge. First, FDI inflows have been driven by a small set of economic and political variables. Second, policy variables seem to

Table 14.3   The determinants of FDI: general trends

Determinants	CEECs[1]	SEECs	CIS
Market size, growth and potential	+	+	+
Factor costs (labour)	−/+/n.s.		−/n.s.
Factor endowment	n.s.		+
Education	+/n.s.		−
Agglomeration among FDI	+		n.s.
Infrastructures	n.s.		+
Economic reforms	+		+
Trade openness	+/n.s.		+
Integration process with the EU	+		
Privatization	+		−
Conflict and policy instability		−	
Incentives (corporate taxes)	−/n.s.		
Quality of the institutions	+		+

Notes:
1. Bulgaria and Romania included.
n.s. = not significant.

Source: Author's compilation.

have been more important than economic variables, since the literature agrees on their potential effects on FDI inflows or inward stocks.

Among the economic characteristics, market size would appear to be the most robust determinant of FDI. Proxied by real GDP or GDP per capita, market growth rates or market potential indexes, it is highly significant in virtually all the analysed studies (Merlevede and Schoors, 2004; Bevan and Estrin, 2000; Campos and Kinoshita, 2003; Janicki and Wunnava, 2004; Carstensen and Toubal, 2003; Clausing and Dorobantu, 2005). The larger the potential or actual market that foreign firms are able to serve by producing in a host country, the larger the FDI inflows that this country can attract. As expected, factor endowment is extremely important for the CIS (Campos and Kinoshita, 2003; Merlevede and Schoors, 2004),[10] while agglomeration among FDI and infrastructure appear able to affect FDI, but only on a geographical basis. Finally, factor costs exert contrasting effects on FDI flows, not only because of geographical issues. This lack of consistent evidence can, in fact, be explained either by differences in methodologies and measurement techniques, or by unobserved characteristics at country, sector and firm level.[11]

The impact of the policy variables is clearer than that of the economic variables and, with the exception of national privatization processes, appears unconditioned by geographical issues. Overall, the existing evidence suggests that the investment climate, broadly defined, exerts an important role on FDI inflows, which have been encouraged by improved economic reforms (Bevan and Estrin, 2000; Campos and Kinoshita, 2003; Jensen, 2002; Janicki and Wunnava, 2004; Carstensen and Toubal, 2003; Merlevede and Schoors, 2004; Holland and Pain, 1998; Woodwark et al., 2000); more open trade policies (Carstensen and Toubal, 2003; Campos and Kinoshita, 2003; Janicki and Wunnava, 2004; Lansbury et al., 1996);[12] the integration process with the EU (Bevan and Estrin, 2000; Clausing and Dorobantu, 2005; Holland and Pain, 1998); and privatizations tailored to foreign investors (Carstensen and Toubal, 2003; Merlevede and Schoors, 2004; Holland and Pain, 1998). In the case of the Balkan countries, conflict and policy instability have substantially reduced FDI flows below what one would expect for comparable Western European countries (Brada et al., 2006), while the impact of corporate taxes on FDI flows is uncertain (Carstensen and Toubal, 2003; Clausing and Dorobantu, 2005; Woodwark et al., 2000). This is not surprising since corporate taxes, as any other type of incentives, can play only a supporting role. If a host country does not possess some basic economic determinants or its investment climate is unsatisfactory, no promotional efforts or incentives will help attract significant FDI.

5. THE SECTORAL AND GEOGRAPHICAL ISSUES

While the previous results would explain why FDI flowed into CEECs after the 1990s, and country differences, they do not explain either sectoral specialization in low-tech manufacturing sectors or geographical concentration both within and across countries (see section 2). To answer these questions, we need to understand whether and to what extent the impact of the above-mentioned forces changes across economic activities.

The few existing studies[13] suggest that the determinants of FDI may vary a lot across sectors and sometimes over time (see Table 14.4), with very few exceptions. Market size, growth and/or potential are the most important FDI determinants, regardless of the sector of activity, but they are the only variable able to affect FDI in the service sector (Altomonte and Guagliano, 2003). In contrast, FDI flows to manufacturing industries are affected by several factors, with important distinctions between low- and high-tech sectors.[14] While the empirical evidence shows that, probably due to legacy inefficiencies, both high-tech and low-tech foreign investors reacted negatively to industry tradition – usually proxied by manufacturing sector jobs – in the early 1990s (Resmini, 2000), this was no longer true in the late 1990s. Countries with a

Table 14.4   The determinants of FDI by economic activity

Determinants	Services	Manufacturing	High tech	Low tech
Market size, growth and potential	+	+	+	+
Factor costs (labour)		−	−(*)	−
Education(***)		+		
Agglomeration among FDI(***)		+	+	+
Industry tradition		−/+	−(*)	−/+
Infrastructures(***)		+	+	+
Concentration of domestic firms(***)		+	+	+
Economic reforms	n.s.	+/−	+/−	n.s./−
Trade costs/openness(**)		n.s.	−	+
Corporate taxes(***)		−		
Other incentives(***)		n.s.	n.s.	n.s.

Notes:
(*) Significant in the early 1990s only. (**) Estimated for the early 1990s only.
(***) Estimated for the late 1990s only.
n.s. = not significant.

Source: Author's compilation.

well developed manufacturing sector have been able to attract FDI, though, in traditional labour-intensive sectors only (Pusterla and Resmini, 2007).[15] Another interesting difference concerns trade openness, which seems able to affect FDI positively in low-tech manufacturing industries and negatively in high-tech manufacturing industries. This result may indicate different motivations for FDI, with the prevalence of vertical FDI in traditional manufacturing sectors and horizontal FDI in technologically advanced manufacturing sectors, which, however, became sensitive to labour costs in the late 1990s. Finally, the literature indicates that the impact of the process of economic reforms on FDI became negative in the late 1990s regardless of the manufacturing sectors. This, however, does not mean that foreign investors are less risk averse than in the past, but simply that higher risks are now compensated by higher profits, given improvements in the market conditions, especially on the demand side (Pusterla and Resmini, 2007).

So far patterns of FDI have been analysed at a country level. However, the determinants of FDI cannot be fully understood without analysing the patterns of geographical location within the host countries. Using firm-level databases on FDI in a sample of CEECs, recent studies indicate that location patterns of FDI have become more dispersed across countries

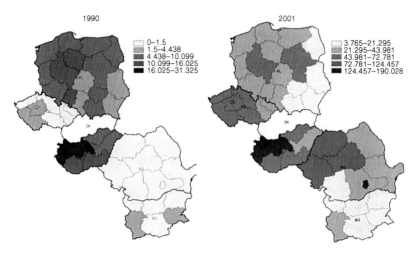

Source: Pusterla and Resmini (2007).

Figure 14.1   The location pattern of multinational firms in Eastern Europe (1990 and 2001)

and over time (Pusterla and Resmini, 2007; Resmini, 2007; European Commission, 2005). Despite that, patterns of agglomeration emerge within the host countries (see Figure 14.1). Therefore, one might conclude that regional characteristics may sometimes be more important than national ones in attracting FDI. In order to identify these characteristics, it is necessary to understand how foreign firms choose their location within host countries. According to the literature, this choice cannot be separated from the choice of how to produce, basically because space and its economic characteristics, related either to a specific point (labour and land costs, and market density) or to the overcoming of the space itself, that is transport costs, may affect the process of profit maximization (McCann, 2002). Therefore, regional characteristics able to affect firms' profits, both on the demand and the supply side, can be considered as micro-determinants of FDI. In this framework, market potential and accessibility, rather than market size, become the relevant variables, while labour costs remain attractive only if wage and productivity differentials are sufficiently marked within the host countries. Finally, clusters and agglomerations of both indigenous and foreign firms now exert a clear impact on foreign firms, as they are by definition easier to measure at regional rather than national levels (Pusterla and Resmini, 2007).

At this point the question arises as to whether multinational enterprises specifically look for adequate regions when seeking a new location or whether they choose the country first. Pusterla and Resmini (2007) indicate that regions rather than countries compete for FDI and that decision processes vary across manufacturing sectors. In particular, low-tech foreign firms compare the locational advantages of EU regions with EU candidate country regions, while high-tech foreign firms choose their ultimate location among three separate groups of similar regions: the capital regions, regions bordering the EU and other regions.[16]

6.   LESSONS FROM THE PAST: POLICY ISSUES

 The past experience of CEECs has important lessons and policy implications. First, the regional concentration of FDI reflecting positive externalities has a cumulative effect, causing poorer regions to be caught in a vicious cycle of underdevelopment and little FDI. Thus it takes public regional development policies to prevent further imbalances.

Second, judging from the limited data available, the sectoral composition of FDI flows would appear to be biased towards labour-intensive sectors. Although this bias may reflect the host and origin country specialization, it might affect the long-run sustainability of existing FDI inflows as the wage gap between old and new EU member states will tend to close, possibly prompting foreign-owned companies to relocate further east or to other emerging countries. Yet cost advantages are important drivers for efficiency-seeking FDI only, and the empirical evidence discussed above demonstrated that demand factors are more robust than supply factors as determinants of FDI. This, in turn, implies that CEECs have attracted more market-seeking than efficiency-seeking investors. Therefore, the risk of footloose FDI would appear to be limited.

Third, high-tech foreign firms are rather scarce in Central, Eastern and especially South-Eastern European countries. However, it is this type of FDI that is most likely to exert positive effects on the host country's economy and development, in particular through technology transfers. Therefore, it becomes urgent for policy makers to understand how to improve host countries' attractiveness for high-tech foreign investors. In this respect, agglomeration economies seem to be a powerful driver of FDI. Already established foreign firms may attract both foreign and indigenous firms operating in complementary sectors, creating a virtuous, self-sustaining cycle of development. These results underline the importance of attracting a critical mass of FDI in high-tech sectors.

Fourth, the importance of the reform process clearly indicates the road that laggard South-Eastern European countries have to take in order to attract consistent FDI inflows and catch up with the more advanced

CEECs. Particular attention should be paid to social and political stability, as well as to EU integration.

Finally, incentives and FDI promotion policies do not seem to be able to significantly affect FDI inflows. In order to become effective, policy interventions should not only be tailored to the manufacturing sector foreign investors belong to, but should also take into account that competition for FDI occurs at regional rather than at national levels. Before implementing any policy measure aimed at attracting FDI, policy makers should find an answer to the following questions: which kind of FDI is a region able to attract, given its characteristics? Are there other regions with similar characteristics? Which country do they belong to?

7. THE FUTURE PATTERN OF FDI: A NEW PROSPECT

Despite this long list of acknowledged facts on FDI determinants and their implications for policy makers, some issues remain that deserve further analysis.

First, it is important to understand how present FDI patterns will evolve over time. Given that transition and privatization have been largely completed in most CEECs, now EU members, further economic reforms should affect FDI inflows less strongly than in the past. Consequently, it is reasonable to wonder whether and to what extent agglomeration economies and further gains in local purchasing power will be able to compensate the lower attractiveness of the policy determinants.

Second, with the tendency to focus on Central Europe in discussions on FDI, South-Eastern European countries fear they may fall permanently behind in the FDI tournament, as they are poorly positioned with regard to the factors outlined above that tend to attract FDI. Domestic markets are weak, given still very low standards of living, while economic difficulties and poor quality institutions tend to increase the perceived risks. Moreover, the initial gap in inward FDI with the more advanced countries might keep on growing given the cumulative nature of FDI. Therefore, more effort should be devoted to understanding convergence processes between laggard and advanced countries in terms of FDI. From a theoretical point of view, this implies understanding the optimum amount of FDI that has to be attracted in order to ignite a virtuous cycle of development through foreign investments.

Third, studies on FDI determinants in the service sector are still lacking, especially with regard to those service activities that countries or regions can compete to attract. Very recently it has been observed that multinational enterprises tend to consolidate service activities in one location and standardize their services across the world, in order to improve efficiency and productivity. This trend has been creating new opportunities for FDI, especially in countries with a skilled and relatively inexpensive labour force. Since Central, Eastern and South-Eastern European countries are relatively well endowed in this regard, they would appear to be a good location for Western European enterprises to consolidate their service functions. Therefore, in order to attract a sustainable inflow of such competitive-enhancing FDI it is necessary to improve those locational advantages which fit best the motivations for this particular kind of FDI. In other words, understanding FDI behaviour in the service sectors is crucial for a better comprehension of the future dynamics of FDI.

Finally, it is also important to understand FDI outflows, which have grown rapidly in the mid-1980s and are continuing to gain momentum in developing and transition countries (UNCTAD, 2006). Although outward FDI volumes are still very small, especially when compared with inward FDI,[17] this might indicate that something is changing in the investment development path of these countries and that they are achieving that minimum level of development at which ownership advantages arise among domestic firms (Dunning and Narula, 1996; Dunning, 1998). Therefore, it would be interesting to understand at which point of the investment development path CEECs are, and whether and to what extent structural changes in the composition of FDI flows, both inward and outward, have been occurring. This analysis, together with a better comprehension of the home and host countries' determining factors, and the nature of emerging comparative advantages for CEECs' multinational companies, will help the competitive position of CEECs in a continuing liberalizing world to be understood.

8.   SUMMARY REMARKS AND CONCLUSIONS

This chapter has analysed the factors that have encouraged and impeded FDI flows into Central, Eastern and South-Eastern Europe. Guided by the economic theory, the pattern of FDI and the results of the empirical research highlighted several areas of agreement among scholars regarding the geography of foreign investments into the region. Both demand-side – such as market size, market growth and market potential – and supply-side factors – such as labour costs, skilled labour force, localization externalities and previously established foreign firms – proved to be important drivers for FDI flows. The impressive economic and institutional reform process to open market economies and EU integration played an even bigger role in attracting FDI, while implementation delays, together with social conflicts and political instability, have kept the volume of FDI in South-Eastern Europe substantially below its potential.

The relative scarcity of empirical studies on FDI determinants specifically for Eastern Europe reflects a lack of detailed sectoral data and incomplete and inconsistent time series data, both at country but even more so at regional levels. Consequently, the scope and the need for further research are evident. In particular, it would be useful to know whether and to what extent Central and Eastern European countries will continue to attract an increasing share of investment flows, given that most of the location advantages that have characterized the transition phase have exhausted their attractiveness. Another area where more of both theoretical and empirical analysis is needed is regarding the determinants of FDI in the service sectors and, in particular, in the newly developed mobile export oriented services. Finally, it would be worth considering in detail the development of Eastern European country multinationals. Eastern European countries play only a minor role in outward FDI, but their share is rising. Their future development will confirm what we know about the determinants of FDI in transition countries, or suggest new questions about the location and the behaviour of multinational enterprises.

NOTES

1. From a geo-political point of view, CEECs include the Baltic Republics, Hungary, Czech and Slovak Republics, Poland and Slovenia, while SEECs include Albania, Bosnia and Herzegovina, Bulgaria, Croatia, Macedonia, Romania and Serbia and Montenegro. Despite that, researchers usually also include Bulgaria and Romania among CEECs.
2. Although information on FDI flows and stocks by industry is a major issue, not only for analytical purposes, but also for formulating effective FDI policies, only a few countries report complete and detailed breakdowns. Data on FDI by economic activity refer to Bulgaria, Croatia, the Czech Republic, the Baltic Republics, Hungary, Poland, Slovakia and Slovenia.
3. Figures used in the above-mentioned study and in similar ones (Pusterla and Resmini, 2007; Resmini, 2000) come from original databases, collecting information at firm level on foreign firms operating in CEECs since the beginning of the transition phase. These databases provide information on the location of foreign firms within the host countries (NUTS II and III levels), the activity of the foreign affiliates (NACE Rev. 1 at four digits), the date of incorporation, the country of origin and the name of the parent firms, and other qualitative and quantitative information on foreign affiliates. See the above-mentioned studies for an in-depth description of these databases. Of course, FDI statistics derived from these databases are not fully comparable with official statistics derived from balance of payments data.
4. Early conceptualization of this notion also includes Williamson's work on transaction costs (1975, 1985) and Rugman (1980). More recently, hold-up issues and agency theory have also been applied to provide a more formal framework to understand why a firm

chooses to set up production plants abroad. See Barba Navaretti and Venables (2004) for a survey on these issues.

5.   Open policies may be either passive (FDI may enter and operate at the same conditions as domestic firms) or pro-active, aiming at attracting competitiveness-enhancing FDI. This kind of policy includes promotional efforts, business facilitating measures, and financial and fiscal incentives. Thus, passive open policies exert their effect on the entry decision only, while pro-active policies can either affect the sectoral composition and the geographical distribution of FDI, or encourage specific contributions to the local economy and mitigate possible undesired effects emanating from FDI.

6.   Blonigen (2005) provides a good survey on the impact of some of the individual policies quoted above on FDI flows (exchange rate, taxes, trade policies and institutions).

7.   Needless to say, there are also factors that are likely to affect all types of FDI, such as agglomeration effects, the business environment, and incentives. See Lim (2001) for an extensive analysis of the expected impact of the most important FDI determinants.

8.   They include traditional OLS regression analysis (Jensen, 2002), cross-sectional analysis (Janicki and Wunnava, 2004), panel data analysis (Resmini, 2000; Campos and Kinoshita, 2003; Carstensen and Toubal, 2003; Clausing and Dorobantu, 2005; Bevan and Estrin, 2000; Holland and Pain, 1998; Lansbury et al., 1996), discrete choice models (Pusterla and Resmini, 2007; European Commission, 2005; Altomonte and Guagliano, 2003) as well as spatial econometric techniques (Baltagi et al., 2005).

9.   The above-mentioned studies explore the FDI determinants on a comparative basis. Other interesting studies focusing on FDI from a single-country perspective include Bekes (2004) for Hungary, and Walkenhorst (2004) for Poland.

10.   Brada et al. (2006) do not find any significant effect for the natural resource endowment, proxied by land size. However, in their analysis, they do not distinguish CIS from non-CIS countries, as the above-mentioned studies do.

11.   Labour costs are negative, but not significant in Merlevede and Schoors (2004) and Clausing and Dorobantu (2005). The former, however, demonstrate that labour costs turn out to be significant when interacted with time variables. Therefore, the authors conclude that the importance of factor cost competitiveness has increased over time. The latter, instead, argue that the lack of significance mainly reflects spurious correlation between the average compensation rate (their proxy for labour costs), and GDP per capita (proxy for local purchasing power). Campos and Kinoshita (2003) find mixed evidence of the impact of factor costs on FDI flows, while Janicki and Wunnava (2004) find a positive and significant sign for the labour cost variables. This result is explained by the fact that wages always reflect productivity.

12.   In Clausing and Dorobantu (2005) the openness variable is positive but not always significant, while Jensen (2002) and Bevan and Estrin (2000) find a negative but not significant impact on FDI. This lack of robustness may be explained either by differences in FDI motivations or by the fact that most CEECs opened their borders to trade and FDI very promptly, thus making this variable irrelevant to the choice of which host country to invest in.

13.   Resmini (2000), Altomonte and Guagliano (2003), Pusterla and Resmini (2007) and European Commission (2005). All of them refer to CEECs.

14.   Although the classification of the manufacturing sectors is not homogeneous across studies, it is fairly similar because it is based on the technological content of different productions. In fact, Resmini (2000) and Altomonte and Guagliano (2003) classified manufacturing sectors using Pavitt's taxonomy of four homogeneous groups of sectors (traditional, high-tech, scale-intensive and specialized producer sectors), while Pusterla and Resmini (2007) and Nicolini and Resmini (2004) rely on a different four-sector classification developed by OECD (high, medium high, medium-low and low-tech manufacturing sectors), which partially overlaps with Pavitt's framework.

15.   In interpreting results across studies, readers should keep in mind that different methodologies have been applied. Therefore, changes in signs of the same variable may indicate that the variable was not correctly specified and that results are not robust, even when the time periods differ.

16. Similar location choice studies demonstrate that national boundaries have lost impor-
    tance in the EU integration process. See Disdier and Mayer (2003) and Basile et al.
    (2003).
17. According to UNCTAD (2006), average FDI outflows do not exceed USD 1 billion.

REFERENCES

Aliber, R.Z. (1970), 'A theory of direct foreign investment', in C.P. Kindleberger
    (ed.), *The International Corporation*, Cambridge, MA: MIT Press.
Altomonte, C. and C. Guagliano (2003), 'Comparative study of FDI in Central and
    Eastern Europe and the Mediterranean', *Economic Systems*, **27** (2), 223–46.
Antras, P. (2003), 'Firms, contracts, and trade structure', *Quarterly Journal of
    Economics*, **118** (4), 1375–418.
Antras, P. and E. Helpman (2004), 'Global sourcing', *Journal of Political Economy*,
    112 (3), 552–80.
Baldwin, R. and G. Ottaviano (1997), 'Multiproduct multinationals and reciprocal
    FDI dumping', mimeo, Graduate Institute of International Studies, Geneva.
Baltagi, B., P. Egger and M. Pfaffermayr (2005), 'Estimating regional trade agree-
    ment effects on FDI in an interdependent world', mimeo.
Barba Navaretti, G. and A. Venables (2004), *Multinational Firms in the World
    Economy*, Princeton, US and Oxford, UK: Princeton University Press.
Basile, R., D. Castellani and A. Zanfei (2003), 'Location choices of multinational
    firms in Europe: the role of national boundaries and EU policy', *Working Paper*
    No. 78, University of Urbino, Faculty of Economics.
Bekes, G. (2004), 'Location of manufacturing FDI in Hungary: how important are
    business to business relationships?', mimeo.
Bevan, A. and S. Estrin (2000), 'The determinants of foreign direct investment in
    transition economies', *WDI Working Paper* No. 342.
Bhagwati, J. (1987), 'VERs, Quid Pro Quo DFI and VIEs: Political economy theo-
    retic analysis', *International Economic Journal*, **1** (1), 1–14.
Blonigen, B. (2005), 'A review of the empirical literature on FDI determinants',
    NBER Working Paper No. 11299.
Brada, J., A. Kutan and T. Yigit (2006), 'The effects of transition and political insta-
    bility on foreign direct investment inflows', *Economics of Transition*, **14** (4),
    649–80.
Brainard, S. (1993), 'A simple theory of multinational corporations and trade with
    a trade-off between proximity and concentration', *NBER Working Paper*
    No. 4269.
Brainard, S. (1997), 'An empirical assessment of the proximity–concentration
    trade-off between multinational sales and trade', *American Economic Review*, **87**
    (4), 520–44.
Buigues, P. and A. Jacquemin (1994), 'Foreign direct investment and exports to the
    European community', in D.J. Encarnation and M. Mason (eds), *Does Ownership
    Matter? Japanese Multinationals in Europe*, Oxford: Oxford University Press.
Campos, N. and Y. Kinoshita (2003), 'Why does FDI go where it goes? New evi-
    dence from the transition economies', *IMF Working Paper* No. 03/228.
Carstensen, K. and F. Toubal (2003), 'Foreign direct investment in Central and
    Eastern European countries: a dynamic panel analysis', mimeo.

Clausing, K.A. and C.L. Dorobantu (2005), 'Re-entering Europe: does European Union candidacy boost foreign direct investment?', *Economics of Transition*, **13** (1), 77–103.

Disdier, A.C. and T. Mayer (2003), 'How different is Eastern Europe? Structure and determinants of location choices by French firms in Eastern and Western Europe', *Journal of Comparative Economics*, **32** (2), 280–96.

Dunning, J. (1977), 'Trade, location of economic activity and the multinational enterprise: a search for an eclectic approach', in B. Ohlin, P. Hesselborn and P. Wijkman (eds), *The International Allocation of Economic Activity*, London: Macmillan, pp. 395–418.

Dunning, J. (1998), 'Location and the multinational enterprise: a neglected factor?', *Journal of International Business Studies*, **29** (1), 45–66.

Dunning, J. and R. Narula (1996), 'The investment development path revisited: some emerging issues', in J. Dunning and R. Narula (eds), *Foreign Direct Investment and Governments: Catalysts for Economic Restructuring*, London: Routledge.

European Commission (2005), 'The location of multinationals across EU regions', in *The EU Economy 2005 Review*, pp. 237–49.

Genco, P., S. Taurelli and C. Viezzoli (1993), 'Private investment in Central and Eastern Europe', *EBRD Working Paper* No. 7.

Helpman, H. (1984), 'A simple theory of international trade with multinational corporations', *Journal of Political Economy*, **92** (3), 451–71.

Holland, D. and N. Pain (1998), 'The diffusion of innovation in Central and Eastern Europe: a study of the determinants and impact of foreign direct investment', *NIESR Discussion Paper* No. 137.

Janicki, H. and P. Wunnava (2004), 'Determinants of foreign direct investment: empirical evidence from EU accession candidates', *Applied Economics*, **36** (5), 505–9.

Jensen, N. (2002), 'Economic reform, state capture, and international investment in transition economies', *Journal of International Development*, **14** (7), 973–7.

Kravis, I.B. and R.E. Lipsey (1982), 'The location of overseas production and production from export by US multinational firms', *Journal of International Economics*, **12** (3–4), 201–23.

Lankes, H.P. and A.J. Venables (1996), 'Foreign direct investment in economic transition: the changing pattern of investments', *Economics of Transition*, **4** (2), 331–47.

Lansbury, M., N. Pain and K. Smidkova (1996), 'Foreign direct investment in Central Europe since 1990: an econometric study', *National Institute Economic Review*, **156** (1), May, 104–14.

Lim, E. (2001), 'Determinants of, and the relation between, foreign direct invest and growth: a summary of recent literature', *IMF Working Paper* No. 01/175.

Markusen, J. (1984), 'Multinational, multi-plant economies and the gains from trade', *Journal of International Economics*, **16** (3–4), 205–26.

Markusen, J. (1995), 'The boundaries of multinational enterprises and the theory of international trade', *Journal of Economic Perspectives*, **9** (2), 169–89.

Markusen, J. and A. Venables (1995), 'The theory of endowments, intra-industry and multinational trade', *CEPR Discussion Paper* No. 1341.

McCann, P. (2002), 'Classical and neoclassical location production models', in P. McCann (ed.), *Industrial Location Economics*, Cheltenham, UK and Brookfield, US: Edward Elgar.

Merlevede, B. and K. Schoors (2004), 'Determinants of foreign direct investment in transition economies', mimeo.

Nicolini, M. and L. Resmini (2004), 'Agglomeration and FDI in Eastern Europe: facts and figures', *EURECO Working Paper*.

Pusterla, F. and L. Resmini (2007), 'Where do foreign firms locate? An empirical investigation', *The Annals of Regional Science*, forthcoming.

Resmini, L. (2000), 'The determinants of foreign direct investment in the CEECs. New evidence from sectoral patterns', *Economics of Transition*, **8** (3), 665–89.

Resmini, L. (2007), 'The location of multinational enterprises in Central and Eastern European countries', in C. Krieger-Boden, E. Morgenroth and G. Petrakos (eds), *The Impact of European Integration on Regional Structural Change and Cohesion*, London: Routledge, forthcoming.

Rugman, A. (1980), 'Internalization as a general theory of foreign direct investment: a re-appraisal of the literature', *Weltwirtschaftliches Archiv*, **116** (2), 365–79.

Shatz, H. and A. Venables (2000), 'The geography of international investment', *Policy Research Working Paper* No. 2338, The World Bank, Washington, DC.

Sheehy, J. (1994), 'Foreign direct investment in the CEECs', *European Economy*, **6**, pp. 131–48.

UNCTAD (1998), *World Investment Report, Trends and Determinants*, New York and Geneva: United Nations.

UNCTAD (2003), *World Investment Directory*, VIII, 'Central and Eastern Europe', Geneva and New York: United Nations.

UNCTAD (2006), *World Investment Report. FDI from Developing and Transition Economies: Implications for Development*, New York and Geneva: United Nations.

Veugelers, R. (1991), 'Locational determinants and ranking of host countries: an empirical assessment', *Kyklos*, **44** (3), 363–82.

Walkenhorst, P. (2004), 'Economic transition and the sectoral patterns of foreign direct investment', *Emerging Markets, Finance and Trade*, **40** (2), 5–26.

Wei, Shang-Jin (2000), 'Local corruption and global capital flows', *Brookings Papers on Economic Activity*, No. 2, pp. 303–53.

Williamson, O.E. (1975), *Markets and Hierarchies: Analyses and Antitrust Implications*, New York: The Free Press.

Williamson, O.E. (1985), *The Economic Institutions of Capitalism*, New York: The Free Press.

Woodwark, D., R. Rolfe, P. Guimaraes and T. Doupnik (2000), 'Taxation and the location of foreign direct investment in Central Europe', in K. Fatemi (ed.), *The New World Order: Internationalism and the Multinational Corporations*, Pergamon Press, pp. 192–203.

15. How to make FDI in Central and Eastern European countries sustainable

Christian Bellak and Markus Leibrecht[1]

'(T)here is no ideal universal strategy on FDI.' (Sanjaya Lall, 2000)

INTRODUCTION

Advanced Central and Eastern European countries (CEECs) have attracted a considerable amount of foreign direct investment (FDI) by multinational enterprises (MNEs) since the mid-1990s. The FDI inward stock of the 10 CEECs which became members of the European Union (EU) on 1 January 2007 amounted to USD 293.9 billion in 2005, while it was USD 317.9 billion in China (UNCTAD database, 28 December 2006). Since the early transition years – when low labour costs were the CEEC's main comparative advantage, besides being new markets close to the EU – the environment for FDI attraction has changed considerably.

During the first phase of transition, single CEECs secured themselves a certain slice of the FDI cake, which was driven by demand and supply factors as well as by international regulations such as tariffs and quotas, and via the help of investment incentives. The question arises whether these early FDI projects are now threatened and prone to relocation as competition for FDI has intensified with the emergence of new competitor locations further east, such as Ukraine or Belarus. After all, in the more recent period of transition, the CEECs experienced an erosion of some of their main location factors, the first of which being an increase in labour costs. The rising labour costs affect vertical FDI, which may be diverted to cheaper locations, but also horizontal FDI, where plant-level economies of scale and low transport costs prevail and where production may therefore be concentrated in low-cost locations, too.

Moreover, as transition-specific FDI attraction policies like the privatization of state-owned firms have largely come to an end, greenfield FDI needs to be attracted, which is generally more difficult.

Clearly, the loss of some initial FDI stocks is inevitable. But which role can policy play in this process of structural change in the more advanced CEECs? After all, a key rationale of providing incentives for FDI was the expectation that FDI substitutes for the lack of domestic capital and thus will contribute to long-run growth. This chapter therefore deals with the question of how to make FDI (existing or new, horizontal or vertical) in the more advanced CEECs sustainable. We focus on useful policy strategies but do not discuss single policy measures, except for illustrative purposes. The chapter concludes that – provided some preconditions like a sound institutional environment are fulfilled – interventionist government policies have a role to play. These need to be designed according to the changing nature of the value-added stages located by foreign MNEs in a particular location (fragmentation). Like the industrialized countries, the more advanced CEECs can no longer compete on low-cost production, and thus follow a high-wage, high-tech catching-up strategy as outlined, for example, by Rodrick (1996).

The chapter is organized as follows: section 2 explains how market failure justifies government intervention to attract FDI or to make it more sustainable. Section 3 provides a definition of sustainable FDI and briefly outlines why targeting policies towards different value-added stages of firms is crucial. Section 4 discusses various channels through which government policies may impact on the sustainability of FDI. Section 5 concludes.

WHY IS GOVERNMENT POLICY TOWARDS FDI NECESSARY?

Government policies may be divided into regulatory and interventionist policies. *Regulatory policy* includes the provision of public goods like an investor-friendly institutional environment (for example property rights or dispute settlement procedures). Regulatory policy can be considered as a precondition to attracting FDI and making it sustainable. This government role is widely undisputed, and most of the more advanced CEECs established appropriate institutional frameworks years ago. For example, Kobrin (2005, using data from an UNCTAD database on FDI policies) finds that the 19 CEECs included carried out 228 FDI policy changes falling in one of eight FDI liberalization categories during 1992 and 2001. By far the most changes have come into effect in the categories concerning promotional measures, sectoral liberalization, operational conditions and protection of property rights. Together with these FDI-specific changes, the EU accession process and finally EU membership for 10 CEECs led to a number of changes in the institutional environment not directly concerned with FDI.

In contrast, economic justification of *interventionist* government policies towards FDI is disputed. Public economists usually base their analysis on the efficiency and equity results of private markets (for example Stiglitz, 2000). Specifically, government intervention is justified if market failures and/or undesirable distributional results arise. In this respect four impacts of FDI on the host economy are usually considered important (see, for instance, Ekholm, 2002): (i) rents accruing to the host country (for example lower unemployment); (ii) competition effects at the industry level; (iii) effects on host country firms (for instance positive inter-company spillover effects); and (iv) according to Baldwin (2005), the impact on growth and restructuring. Thus, with respect to FDI, governments may intervene in the market process due to market failure that is specific to MNE production (see, for example, Blomström, 2002, p. 8) by providing monetary incentives or by providing location factors where the markets do not provide such factors (see, for example, Hanson, 2001; Blalock and Gertler, 2005; and Pack and Saggi, 2006 on industrial policy with respect to FDI). In addition, governments may also intervene if market forces lead to an undesirable regional distribution of FDI and hence to an undesirable regional distribution of jobs, income and wealth.

Interventionist policies can be further separated into *re-active* and *pro-active* policies (for instance, Rothstein, 2005). *Re-active* policies include measures to strengthen the existing locational advantage, for instance R&D incentives to encourage product or process innovations; measures to support the exploitation of advantages abroad, like export subsidies or guarantees; incentives to foreign MNEs to locate in a certain region, characterized by an ageing cluster of activities; training of employees; creation of new education facilities and so on. *Pro-active* policies comprise measures to generate new locational advantages, by promoting infant industries, targeting new sectors and industries, attracting resources to new fields, encouraging companies to adapt production processes in the light of new findings and so on.

So far, the discussion has been implicitly based on the assumption of a welfare maximizing social planner, who intervenes and fully corrects for market failures. Yet empirical evidence shows that government action – even when following general guidelines like the ones presented below – is not always successful. Moreover, governments intervene even in the absence of market failure, or fail to act in the event of market failure (for example Stiglitz, 2000). Generally speaking, the desirability of government action is linked to the 'ability of governments' (UNCTAD, 1999, p. 325). Thus, the possibility of government failure needs to be considered. There are at least four reasons for government failure (for example Stiglitz, 2000): (i) governments have limited information; (ii) governments have limited control over private market responses (limited policy instruments); (iii) legislature has limited control over bureaucracy; and (iv) governments are influenced by special interest groups ('capturing'). For example, special interests might successfully lobby for strong FDI controls (such as ownership restrictions, approval measures), causing re-active government policy to fail. Or governments might, given limited information, grant incentives for FDI in R&D in regions with insufficient skill endowment, causing pro-active government policy to fail. In both instances, FDI would have no positive external effects on the host economy – which is why any evaluation of policies towards FDI needs to include possible government failure. Independently of the single measures taken, interventionist policies towards FDI should be built on a strong *regulatory* framework in order to avoid government failure, like overspending on incentives.

DEFINITION OF SUSTAINABLE FDI AND FRAGMENTATION OF PRODUCTION ACTIVITIES

No clear-cut definition of sustainable FDI has been put forward in the literature so far. In this chapter we consider an investment as sustainable if it stays in a certain location in the long term, either because the location strategy of the MNE for the exploitation of its ownership advantages changes, or the location policy of the government changes, or both. Hence, a precondition for FDI to be sustainable is that locational needs of MNEs are matched by the public services provided. Sustainable FDI can thus be thought of as the opposite of footloose FDI. As we are concerned with a policy question, we will consider strategies of MNEs as a means to adjust to structural change here, only in so far as they are relevant to policy.

In order to be able to craft a strategy to make FDI more sustainable, governments first need to understand why firms locate where they do. In other words, they need to understand the determinants of firm location and of geographical and industrial concentration and fragmentation (for example, Defever, 2006; Feenstra, 1998). MNEs are located in a given place mainly for four possible reasons, namely historical accident, proximity to other firms, proximity to markets, and efficiency (Meyer-Stamer, 2004). These explanations point to firm-specific (first two items) and location-specific factors (third and fourth item). Factors within both groups may change over time.

A stylized fact of MNEs' location decision is the fragmentation of production (see, for instance, Buckley and Ghauri, 2004). Venables (1999, p. 935) states that '(t)he term "fragmentation" has been coined to describe the phenomenon by which reductions in trade barriers and the costs of moving goods and information make it possible to break up an integrated production process, moving separate elements of the process to lower cost locations'. The key concept here is the value chain of the MNE, which has been defined by Kogut (1985, p. 15) as 'the process by which technology is combined with material and labour inputs, and then processed inputs are assembled, marketed and distributed. A single firm may consist of only one link in this process, or it may be extensively vertically integrated . . .'. Buckley and Ghauri (2004) note that an important aspect of the globalization strategies of MNEs is that 'the increasingly sophisticated decision making of managers in MNEs is slicing the activities of firms more finely [. . .] in finding optimum locations for each closely defined activity'. The relative importance of each location factor varies, depending on which of their closely defined activities MNEs locate in the host country (for example Bellak, 2005). For example, customers (a large market) are a relevant location factor for banks investing in the CEECs if the purpose of the FDI is to gain or expand market share. Or, a combination of low labour cost and skilled personnel may be relevant if the direct investor is relocating its own accounting services to the CEECs.

In essence, FDI will be the more sustainable, the better the location factors of a host country match the value-added stages of foreign MNEs. In this respect, CEECs have experienced not only a change in location factors, as described in the introduction, since the mid-1990s, but today CEECs also see MNEs locate other activities in the CEECs than in the early period of transition. For example, the Vienna Institute for International Economic Studies (wiiw) concluded in an assessment of the current competitiveness of the CEECs that

> a distinguishing feature of the new members [NMS, authors] is their strong performance in terms of human capital and business infrastructure. . . . NMS have moved rapidly in changing the composition of industrial production and exports in the direction of a strong representation of medium-high tech industries. NMS are not particularly competitive in labour-intensive, low skill industries. (Landesmann and Woerz, 2006, p. ii)

The next section asks which type of policy is necessary to match location factors and value-stages.

POLICY CHANNELS TO MAKE FDI SUSTAINABLE

It should have become clear from the above discussion that *pro-active* policies determine the sustainability of FDI mainly via the selection of certain new sectors and industries. *Re-active* policies may influence the sustainability through a number of channels which governments may try to influence. These channels are based on different strands of theories which are concerned with explaining the industrial and sectoral concentration of production. The theories are the traditional (comparative advantage) and new trade theory (economies of scale) as well as the new economic geography (agglomeration forces; for an overview, see, for example, Traistaru et al. (2003) on CEECs; and Shatz and Venables, 2000, on FDI). The following channels have been shown to be relevant for FDI in the CEECs, although the empirical evidence is slowly emerging:

1. Comparative advantage: Does FDI in CEECs follow comparative advantages? For 1998, Woerz (2004) finds a significant correlation between export specialization and FDI for Lithuania, Latvia, Poland, Slovenia and Hungary. In 2002 this holds true also for Slovakia and Estonia but no longer for the Czech Republic and Croatia. The conclusion from this pattern is that the CEECs attracted FDI mainly because they offered location advantages in the form of an educated labour force, lower wages than in the home countries, growing domestic markets).

2. Economies of scale: How much FDI is directed into scale-intensive industries in CEECs and explained by demand patterns in CEECs? Woerz and Hildebrandt (2004) do not find significant effects of scale economies on the concentration of industries in the CEECs. But Traistaru et al. (2003, p. 446) find that scale-intensive industries locate close to the capital region and in EU border regions.

3. Agglomeration forces: Is FDI attracted by agglomeration forces which explain sectoral and regional concentration in the CEECs? Altomonte and Resmini (2000) find positive agglomeration effects between domestic and foreign firms for Poland. Brülhart and Koenig (2005) reveal relatively higher employment growth in regions proximate to the large markets of incumbent EU members in five CEECs (the Czech Republic, Hungary, Poland, Slovenia, Slovakia) in the second half of the 1990s. However, Disdier and Mayer (2004) have shown that agglomeration effects are less strong in CEECs than in EU countries. They emphasize the quality of the institutional framework as a decisive location factor. See also Chapter 14 by Laura Resmini in this volume.

Yet not every location factor is susceptible to government intervention in the same way. According to Baldwin (2005), three groups of factors which can be influenced to different degrees by policy interventions must be distinguished. Note that these factors are again derived from the three strands

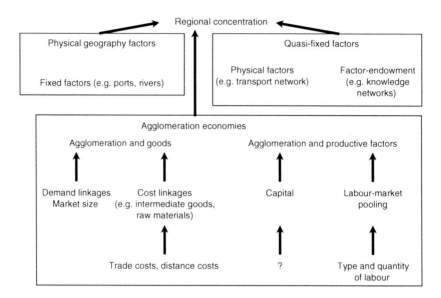

Note: The ? indicates uncertainty of the capital-related determinants of agglomeration.

Source: Based on Baldwin (2005).

Figure 15.1   Location factors

of theories discussed above, with the traditional and new trade theory factors being represented in the two upper boxes and the new economic geography factors included in the lower box of Figure 15.1. While physical geography factors are largely set and quasi-fixed factors can be changed only in the long term, it is factors influencing agglomeration economies which are most susceptive to policy intervention.

One must not, of course, forget the congestion-based dispersion forces, which also determine the location of production, such as land prices, housing rents or natural resources.

Since *reactive* government policies to make FDI sustainable can impact through each of these channels in the CEECs, we briefly discuss some policies here.

1.   Policies may either *reinforce* existing comparative advantages or provide incentives to *develop* such advantages. Reinforcing measures may comprise measures to stimulate entrepreneurship in certain industries or to exploit comparative advantages abroad, as mentioned above. The downside of these policies is that they may create the danger of a lock-in, especially if competitors move into new areas. In this case, FDI

may not be sustainable in the long run. Measures which improve the *created* location factors include education, efforts to build up a national system of innovation or investments in tangible and intangible (information and communication) infrastructure, and so on. Attention should be given to the so-called co-location of value-added stages, because they may sometimes create contradictory locational needs which must be addressed if FDI is to be made sustainable. In this respect, producer-related services may be important, since high quality services make other value-added stages location-bound, like, for example, production and R&D. In addition, measures to speed up relocation of labour-intensive activities to lower cost locations may feed back positively on the remaining activities and may free resources at home.

2. The existence of scale economies on the plant level suggests the importance of trade costs and thus the provision of a developed transport and other logistic infrastructure in order to avoid congestion. In terms of FDI attraction, it may be useful to target specific sectors or industries that are less footloose than, for instance, the textile sector, which realizes economies of scale as well.

3. Policy makers may also utilize the *self-reinforcing nature* of agglomeration advantages. This makes not only existing FDI more sticky but may also attract more FDI in turn and thus serves to both attract FDI and make it sustainable. The lead firm concept has frequently proven useful in this respect, as, for instance, was demonstrated in a detailed study by Rothstein (2005). A lead firm may comprise very different value-added stages itself. It can be a final good producer who then requires upstream firms as suppliers as well as downstream firms, or it can be an intermediate good supplier who again requires suppliers of parts and components, a developed logistics centre, certain raw materials or specific types of skill and so on. Since a lead firm may have an important impact on the location of other firms of the same or related industries, it may be important for regional sustainability.

Most of these policies apply to horizontal as well as vertical FDI; they may have a regional or a sectoral focus or they may be applied on a national level.

CONCLUSIONS FOR THE CEECs

This chapter discussed how FDI can be made sustainable by government intervention. It has been argued that sustainability of FDI requires a match between location factors and value-added activities. The policy challenge therefore is to restore coherence between location factors and value-added activities of MNEs after one or both of these factors have changed. Proactive and re-active policies are needed to achieve sustainability of FDI: the former are geared to attract FDI and therefore affect the sustainability via sectoral targeting, the latter aim at making FDI more sustainable through three distinct policy channels. In this respect, emphasis should be put on providing specific bundles of location factors as public goods, that is the locational qualities for closely defined value-added activities of the MNE.

In light of the above discussion, one may ask whether the FDI attraction policies currently applied in the CEECs will indeed make FDI more sustainable. While space constraints do not allow us to thoroughly assess this important question, we would like to emphasize that the advanced CEECs currently appear to pursue a policy mix to attract FDI by providing general location factors like the abolition of obstacles (tariff reduction, capital flow liberalization, reduction of ownership restrictions and so on), creating incentives (for example at the regional level, for R&D activities) and improving the investment climate through infrastructure investment, deeper integration into the EU, and so on.

NOTE

1. Both authors: Department of Economics, Vienna University of Economics and Business Administration, Augasse 2-6, 1090 Vienna, Austria. Contact author: christian.bellak@wu-wien.ac.at

REFERENCES

Altomonte, C. and L. Resmini (2000), 'The geography of transition: regional industrial patterns in Poland', *IEP-Bocconi Working Paper No. 9*, Bocconi University.

Baldwin, R.E. (2005), 'Industry location: the causes', *Swedish Economic Policy Review*, **12** (1), 9–27.

Bellak, C. (2005), 'Adjustment strategies of multinational enterprises to changing international competitiveness', *International Journal of the Economics of Business*, **12** (1), 139–62.

Blalock, G. and P. Gertler (2005), 'Foreign direct investment and externalities: The case for public intervention', in T. Moran, E. Graham and M. Blomström (eds), *Does Foreign Direct Investment Promote Development?*, Washington, DC: Institute for International Economics, pp. 73–106.

Blomström, M. (2002), *The Economics of International Investment Incentives*, Stockholm School of Economics, NBER and CEPR, Paper presented at the ECLAC / World Bank Seminar on Globalization, March.

Brülhart, M. and P. Koenig (2005), *New Economic Geography Meets Comecon: Regional Wages and Industry Location in Central Europe*, mimeo, web download 22 December, 2006.

Buckley, P.J. and P. Ghauri (2004), 'Globalisation, economic geography and the strategy of multinational enterprises', *Journal of International Business Studies*, **35** (2), 81–98.

Defever, F. (2006), 'Functional fragmentation and the location of multinational firms in the enlarged Europe', *Regional Science and Urban Economics*, **36** (4), 658–77.

Disdier, A.-C. and Th. Mayer (2004), 'How different is Eastern Europe? Structures and determinants of location choices by French firms in Eastern and Western Europe', *Journal of Comparative Economics*, **32** (2), 280–96.

Ekholm, K. (2002), Comment on Michael P. Devereux and Rachel Griffith: 'The impact of corporate taxation on the location of capital: A review', *Swedish Economic Policy Review*, **9**, 103–5.

Feenstra, R.C. (1998), 'Integration of trade and disintegration of production in the global economy', *Journal of Economic Perspectives*, **12** (4), 31–50.

Hanson, G.H. (2001), 'Should countries promote foreign direct investment?', United Nations Conference on Trade and Development, *G-24 Discussion Paper Series*, No. 9.

Kobrin, S. (2005), 'The determinants of liberalization of FDI policy in developing countries: a cross-sectional analysis, 1992–2001', *Transnational Corporations*, **14** (1), April, 67–104.

Kogut, B. (1985), 'Designing global strategies: comparative and competitive value-added chains', *Sloan Management Review*, **26** (4), 15–28.

Lall, S. (2000), 'FDI and development: policy and research issues in the emerging context', *Queen Elizabeth House Working Paper Series* 43, web download (10 December 2006).

Landesmann, M. and J. Woerz (2006), 'CEECs' competitiveness in the global context', *WIIW Research Reports*, No. 327, May, Vienna.

Meyer-Stamer, J. (2004), 'Paradoxes and ironies of locational policy in the new global economy', in H. Schmitz (ed.), *Local Enterprises in the Global Economy*, Aldershot, UK and Brookfield, US: Edward Elgar, pp. 326–48.

OECD (1995), *Taxation and Foreign Direct Investment: The Experience of the Economies in Transition*, Paris.

Pack, H. and K. Saggi (2006), 'Is there a case for industrial policy? A critical survey', *The World Bank Research Observer*, **21** (2), 267–97.

Rodrick, D. (1996), 'Coordination failures and government policy: A model with applications to East Asia and Eastern Europe', *Journal of International Economics*, **40** (1–2), 1–22.

Rothstein, J.S. (2005), 'Economic development policymaking down the global commodity chain: attracting an auto industry to Silao, Mexico', *Social Forces*, **84** (1), 49–69.

Shatz, H.J. and A.J. Venables (2000), 'The geography of international investment', in G.L. Clark, M.P. Feldman and M.S. Gertler (eds), *The Oxford Handbook of Economic Geography*, Oxford: Oxford University Press, pp. 125–45.

Stiglitz, J.E. (2000), *Economics of the Public Sector*, 3rd edn, New York: W.W. Norton & Company.

Traistaru, I., P. Nijkamp and L. Resmini (2003), 'The emerging economic geography in EU accession countries: concluding remarks and policy implications', in

I. Traistaru, P. Nijkamp and L. Resmini (eds), *The Emerging Geography in EU Accession Countries*, Aldershot: Ashgate, pp. 442–9.

UNCTAD (1999), *World Investment Report: Foreign Direct Investment and the Challenge of Development*, Geneva: UNCTAD.

Venables, A. (1999), 'Fragmentation and multinational production', *European Economic Review*, **43** (4-6), 935–45.

Woerz, J. (2004), 'Does FDI follow comparative advantage?', *WIIW Monthly Report*, No. 8–9, Vienna, pp. 1–12.

Woerz, J. and A. Hildebrandt (2004), 'Determinants of industrial location patterns in CEECs', *WIIW Working Papers*, No. 32, Vienna.

16. Does FDI help development? The good, the bad, the surprising and the mistaken. Policy issues for developed countries, developing countries and multilateral lending institutions

Theodore H. Moran[1]

1. INTRODUCTION

Foreign direct investment comes in three – perhaps four – distinct forms: FDI in manufacturing and assembly; FDI in extractive industries (oil, gas and mining); FDI in infrastructure (power generation, electrical utilities, water and sewerage, toll roads, airports, telecommunications); and FDI in services (usually included within the category of FDI in manufacturing and assembly). It is not commonly recognized that each form of FDI can have positive and/or negative aspects for the host country.

This chapter will focus on the relationship between manufacturing FDI and development, including the challenges of attracting FDI flows. It will provide a short summary of the policy issues posed by FDI in extractive industries and FDI in infrastructure. It concludes with the policy implications for developed countries, for developing countries and for multilateral lending institutions.

2. THE RELATIONSHIP BETWEEN MANUFACTURING FDI AND HOST COUNTRY DEVELOPMENT: GOOD NEWS, BAD NEWS AND SURPRISING NEWS

2.1 Bad News and Good News

Research over the past two decades shows that manufacturing FDI takes two distinct forms. The major distinction is between FDI that is oriented toward domestic markets (often protected domestic markets) and FDI that is oriented toward export markets (in particular destined to be an integral part of the parent multinational corporation's (MNC) global supply chain). This distinction emerged in the 1970s and 1980s when some countries (most notably Singapore, followed by Malaysia and Hong Kong in Southeast Asia) began to use the plants of foreign investors as the industrial base for export-led growth, whereas many countries in Latin America, the Middle East, South Asia and Africa tried to formulate development strategies using FDI for import substitution.

As part of the disillusionment with efforts at import substitution, the evidence from FDI that was used by host authorities within protected host markets began to show quite dismal results in the 1980s and 1990s. The hope had been that foreign investors would build modern auto assembly plants, chemical and petrochemical plants, electronics assembly plants to produce products for the protected local market, train workers and managers in how to accomplish this efficiently, establish backward linkages into the domestic economy, and thus form the basis for infant industry growth to competitive maturity.

A prominent feature of the import-substitution-via-FDI strategy was to impose what were called 'performance requirements' on the foreign investors as a condition of their being granted access to the domestic economy. The most frequent performance requirements were domestic content requirements (for example 30 per cent of an automobile or a computer produced for the local market had to consist of local components), joint venture requirements (mandatory local partners with majority or minority ownership), and other technology sharing requirements (access to parent patents and trade secrets).

Foreign investors responded to this import substitution 'opportunity' by building subscale plants with the capacity to meet local needs, and by importing 'kits' of semi-knocked-down autos or computers to be assembled locally while incorporating simple, low-tech local parts. Even in large protected markets (like India, Brazil, Mexico, China), there was a multiplication of less-than-world-scale plants. Domestic content requirements generated production of indigenous components, but the host country companies were also relegated to building plants that failed to capture all economies of scale. Joint venture (JV) requirements led the parent multinationals to use older technology within the JV plants, precisely to prevent 'leakage' to partners who might become rivals, a phenomenon that was repeated when there were technology-sharing mandates. Auto assembly plants averaged 10 000–20 000 vehicles per year, whereas full scale plants in the USA, EU or Japan averaged 200 000. Computer assembly plants built a few tens of thousands of PCs, without the benefit of high precision assembly lines and quality control procedures (in Mexico, before the liber-alization of the informatics regime, the local Hewlett Packard JV or Compaq JV hand-soldered assemblies together). Local suppliers did not have orders large enough to support the equipment or technology that were standard in world-class auto parts or computer parts fabricators.

The outcome was that FDI-led infant industry development produced infants, but the adults did not have the wherewithal to grow to fully com-petitive adulthood. Indigenous workers and managers did not gain the dynamic learning that would propel them to the frontier in international industry. It should be noted that for the MNCs themselves, participation in protected developing country markets could be highly profitable. Chrysler reported that its boutique plants in Mexico, before the country's export-promotion auto strategy, were a 'cash cow' among its most highly profitable affiliates. Hewlett Packard (see above) sold three-year-old computers for 140–180 per cent of world market prices. The burden of the FDI-for-import-substitution strategy did not simply fall on host country consumers. It was also borne by host country firms that were hindered in their own struggles to become competitive – Pemex in Mexico and Petrobras in Brazil complained that they could not do advanced seismic computations using domestically-produced computers; Embraer was a major foe of the country's informatics policy, arguing that it could not engage in sophisti-cated CAD-CAM design operations.

The alternative strategy – using FDI in manufacturing and assembly – to bolster export-led growth also held surprises – pleasant surprises, rather than disappointments. The initial success story focused on FDI in elec-tronics in Southeast Asia and featured US, European, and (later) Japanese multinationals searching for low-cost assembly sites for consumer goods. But the evidence from the late-1980s showed a much more potent relation-ship between foreign parent MNCs and local affiliates in Singapore or Penang than merely shopping around for cheap inputs. As plants in the developing world were integrated into the global strategy of the parent to compete in international markets, they were invariably built to full scale and incorporated the most advanced production technology and quality control procedures known to the corporation. Moreover, they were upgraded on a near real-time basis to keep them at the frontier of the indus-try. In this setting, the parent multinational insisted upon wholly-owned or majority-owned affiliates and freedom from domestic content requirements so that the corporation could source from wherever fitted its needs best.

The evidence of the 1990s and early 2000s showed a pattern that was much more intimate than a search for inexpensive parts. The international parent exercises what has come to be characterized with the phrase 'parental supervision' over all stages and supply relationships.[2] In the electronics industry, FDI plants in Singapore, Hong Kong, Malaysia and Thailand were given design and development functions for increasingly sophisticated subassemblies and functions.

In the automotive industry, after the creation of NAFTA, the North American auto industry has integrated component development and assembly with latest developments transmitted to plants in Mexico and Canada within hours of initial execution in the United States. Multinational auto firm exports of vehicles and parts from Mexico grew from very small numbers in the 1970s to USD 32 billion in 2004, employing one out of every eight workers in the Mexican manufacturing sector at USD 1.76 – USD 11.42 per hour, rates that are second in the country after the petroleum sector. Foreign-owned assembly and parts plants in Mexico win world-highest quality and efficiency scores from independent rating services. Relying on production sites in Mexico (and Brazil), the major US auto companies have used these affiliates to slow the erosion in market share they have suffered vis-à-vis Japanese and European producers, leading Japanese and European MNCs to match the new pattern of sourcing from Latin American plants (the redesign of Ford's best-selling F-150 truck in 2004–05 depended upon low-cost, high-quality steel from an affiliate in Monterrey and high-performance engines from the Ford plant in Ontario). The same process is now taking place within the EU and Eastern Europe, with engines, chassis, and other platform components capable of absorbing engineering adjustments continuously.

2.2   Surprising News

The 'surprising news' comes from discoveries about FDI and the creation of backward linkages.

Many development strategists had feared that using FDI for export-led growth would leave the host countries taking part only in the most simple assembly operations, with little value added and no backward linkages. But the data, over time, have indicated otherwise. Whereas multinational corporations are very hesitant to transfer technology in a horizontal direction, for fear of creating rivals, the same is not true in a vertical direction. Longitudinal studies in Southeast Asia and Latin America showed foreign MNCs shopping around for indigenous parts suppliers, supplying them with advice, drawings, design specifications, equipment requirements and quality control procedures in order to create a viable component base. Backward linkages, using technology and management know-how transferred vertically from foreigner to local firms, have thickened over time. In contrast to the import-substitution model, these local firms have had large enough orders from the export-oriented foreign buyers to enable them to reach full economies of scale and to incorporate world-class production and management techniques. The spillovers of technology and production know-how have not been limited to the industries where the MNCs participated – the Malaysian machine tool industry, for example, was created by managers (and workers) first employed in US, European and Japanese telecom and computer companies.[3] These Malaysian-owned-and-managed machine tool companies are now multinationals that compete with machine tool companies from the developed world, Korea and Taiwan.

World Bank survey data from Eastern Europe show a similar pattern. A survey of 119 majority-owned foreign affiliates operating in the Czech Republic in 2003 indicates that 90 per cent purchased inputs from at least one Czech firm, while the median multinational purchased inputs from ten Czech suppliers and the top quartile of multinationals purchased inputs from at least 30.[4] The sectors in this FDI survey include fabricated metals, publishing and printing, rubber, machinery, apparel, electrical machinery, food products, textiles, non-metallic mineral products, furniture, pulp and paper, wood products, chemicals, radio, TV and communications equipment, leather, basic metals, medical equipment, motor vehicles and other transport equipment.

This powerful drive to develop backward linkages is a finding that has proven counter-intuitive to many development strategists. The imposition of domestic content and joint venture requirements upon multinational corporations leads to less domestic content and less technology transfer than leaving multinational corporations free to structure their operations as best suits their interests. It should be noted that this is an empirical observation, not an ideological proposition. Evidence from the past two decades has shown that the most powerful mechanism for backward linkages from foreign multinationals to local firms has been the phenomenon of 'contract manufacturing' of the latter for the former. As part of this process, many local firms become certified as Original Equipment Manufacturers (OEM), qualifying them to supply the MNC parent anywhere in the world.

3.   MEASURING THE IMPACT OF FDI ON DEVELOPMENT

The impacts from these two different kinds of FDI are substantially larger – positive and negative – than conventional estimates envision.

FDI in manufacturing and assembly can help a country do what comparative advantage enables it to do more efficiently. Thus, FDI in wine or wool can help a country compete more effectively in international markets for processed goods and beverages or textiles. Mauritius became an 'African success story' via textile FDI. Ukraine could become the true 'breadbasket' for the EU via FDI by Heinz, Unilever and Gerber and (hypothetical!) agricultural liberalization on the part of the European Union member states.

More important, FDI in manufacturing and assembly can underpin 'dynamic comparative advantage' in which FDI allows the host economy to shift from one production frontier to another more advanced production frontier. What is the comparative advantage of Costa Rica? Thirty years ago the answer, with a bit of FDI, was coffee and bananas. Fifteen years ago, with a bit more FDI, the answer was textiles and footwear. Today, with much more sophisticated FDI – and, most importantly, an increasingly better trained and skilled and motivated workforce – the answer is semiconductors and other electronics, medical products, pharmaceuticals, call centres and management services, with exports exceeding USD 5 billion per year in 2005.

The same mechanism of dynamic comparative advantage via trade-and-investment liberalization can be seen in the recent economic history of Slovakia.

Thus comparative advantage, with the spread of FDI, is not static and determined by geography and inherent endowment of resources. Rather, contemporary comparative advantage is dynamic, and results from an interaction of FDI, trade, skills, infrastructure, communications and competitive/open market opportunities.[5]

4.   MISTAKEN MEASUREMENTS OF THE IMPACT OF FDI ON DEVELOPMENT

This split into potentially quite positive and potentially quite negative impacts also explains a major mistake that has infected economic – especially econometric – analysis of how FDI affects the host economy.

Failure to differentiate between export-oriented FDI and import-substitution FDI, or between foreign investors free to source from wherever they wish and foreign investors operating with domestic content requirements, or between foreign investors obliged to operate as minority shareholders and foreign investors with whole- or majority-ownership, accounts for the inability of earlier studies – such as the oft-cited works of Aitken and Harrison – to make sense of how FDI impacts a host economy. The data on industrial plants in Aitken and Harrison's Venezuelan study (1999) come from 1976 to 1989, a period during which Venezuela followed a heavy-handed import substitution development strategy with multiple controls on foreign investment.[6]

In this setting, Aitken and Harrison concluded that the net effect of foreign investor participation in the Venezuelan economy was quite small, with positive effects from firms with foreign ownership only slightly out-weighing negative effects on domestic firms. These findings are interesting, not because they fail to show a strongly beneficial impact from foreign direct investment on the host economy, but because they reveal outcomes that appear to be beneficial at all.

5. ATTRACTING FDI TO DEVELOPING COUNTRIES

The divergent nature of manufacturing FDI has important implications for host country efforts to attract FDI (to engage in 'investment promotion'). This is an important area where developed-country assistance can play a crucial role. There are three distinct strategies to attract foreign direct investment.[7]

First, throughout the 1970s and 1980s, the principal method of dealing with foreign investors was to set up an investment screening agency. As long as most developing countries viewed FDI as part of an import substitution strategy, the main duty of an investment screening agency was to preside over the entry to the protected domestic market and wait for MNCs to show up, looking to earn rents free from competition. As a condition of entry, then, the agency would impose performance requirements upon the multinational, usually in the form of domestic content, joint venture or other technology-sharing requirements.

Second, as appreciation of the importance of outward-oriented FDI has grown, it has become clear that the primary job of an investment promo-tion agency is – in the words of the Foreign Investment Advisory Service (FIAS) of the World Bank Group – to 'market the country', that is, to demonstrate to potential investors why they should choose this particular host rather than others.[8] This requires the investment promotion agency (IPA) to be pro-active, seeking out investors and providing them with up-to-date information and FDI regulations, with links to important min-istries and current investors ('satisfied customers').

A study done for FIAS discovered that IPAs that could act as a one-stop-shop facilitator for multinational investors, enabling them to obtain all information and permits at the same time, generated USD 4 in investment for every US dollar spent on promotion.[9] One problem, however, is that most ministries do not want to give up turf to the IPA (Ministries of Treasury, Immigration, Environment, Trade, Land Permits, and so on). A practical solution to this is to have the various ministries second an expert to the IPA to act as ministry representative on the IPA staff. A second problem is that IPA personnel skilled enough to be effective have to be compensated with a salary higher than normal civil service standards. A third problem is that IPA managers are often sought out as employees by the multinationals that come in, to act as trouble-shooters at salaries much higher than they are paid in the government.

The third kind of Investment Promotion Agency is seldom written about, but is familiar to all multinational investors that try to set up operations in developing countries. This is the IPA whose board is composed of indigenous businesses whose major interest is barring competition from entering the host country market. In effect these IPAs are investment-prevention agencies, unless the foreign applicant is willing to partner or team up with the companies represented on the board. This conflict-of-interest structure is quite hard to reform or abolish.

6. POLICY IMPLICATIONS FOR DEVELOPING COUNTRIES, FOR DEVELOPED COUNTRIES AND FOR MULTILATERAL LENDING INSTITUTIONS LIKE THE EBRD

The preceding two sections sketched out policy implications for FDI in extractive industries and infrastructure. What are the implications of the analysis of FDI in manufacturing and assembly for policies of developing countries, developed countries and multilateral lending institutions?

6.1 Policy Implications for Developing Countries

The contrast in performance between foreign plants integrated into the supply networks of the parent, and foreign plants prevented by domestic content requirements and mandatory joint venture requirements from being so integrated, is clear from the evidence presented earlier. This understanding about the detrimental impact of 'performance requirements' needs to spread from the world of development strategists to the world of trade negotiators. At the Hong Kong Ministerial Conference in December 2005, developing country representatives insisted upon modifying the terms of the TRIMs (Trade Related Investment Measures) Agreement that had banned the imposition of domestic content requirements. Developing countries have now been empowered to demand that foreign investors meet old and new kinds of performance requirements for no less than seven more years and possibly until 2020.[10] As seen above, governments that actually pursue this strategy are sorely misguided about how foreign direct investment can best contribute to host country growth and welfare.

6.2 Policy Implications for Developed Countries

Based on the evidence presented earlier, the conclusion is clear that official political risk insurers – like the Overseas Private Investment Corporation in the United States or the Export Credits Guarantee Department (ECGD) in the United Kingdom – should not provide coverage indiscriminately, ignoring the positive or negative consequences of the investment of the developing host economy. The evidence introduced here indicates that FDI in manufacturing and assembly subtracts from host country output when it involved projects oriented toward small, protected local markets.

Here many developed countries would receive a poor grade. In 2005, a survey of 19 developed countries with political risk guarantee agencies showed that 18 (including those in the United Kingdom, Canada, France, Germany, Italy and Japan) do not disqualify projects that depend upon protection to survive.[11]

6.3 Policy Implications for Multilateral Lending Institutions

More damaging, the community of developed countries has been negligent by failing to exert pressure upon multilateral guarantee agencies where they have a strong voice – such as the International Finance Corporation (IFC) and the Multilateral Investment Guarantee Agency (MIGA) of the World Bank Group, the Inter-American Development Bank and the Asian Development Bank – to initiate such a screening process for projects they support.

NOTES

1. Marcus Wallenberg Professor of International Business and Finance, School of Foreign Service, Georgetown University.
2. Moran (2001).
3. Rasiah (1994).
4. Javorcik and Spatareanu (2005).
5. Grossman and Helpman (1991), chapter 7; Aghion and Howitt (1998). For an imaginative attempt to model these gains, see Markusen (2005).
6. Aitken and Harrison (1999), p. 69.
7. The World Bank's 'Doing business in 2004: understanding regulation' provides a systematic review of the principal efforts to assess a country's business environment, including Business Environment Risk Intelligence (BERI), Euromoney Institutional Investor (EII), International Country Risk Guide (ICRG), Country Risk Review (CRR), the Heritage Foundation, World Markets Research Center and A.T. Kearney, Washington,

DC: a co-publication of the World Bank, the International Finance Corporation and Oxford University Press, chapter 1.
8.   Morriset and Andrews-Johnson (2003); Wells and Wint (2000).
9.   Wells and Wint (2000).
10. World Trade Organization (2005).
11. Roodman (2005).

REFERENCES

Aghion, Philippe and Peter Howitt (1998), *Endogenous Growth Theory*, Cambridge, MA: MIT Press.

Aitken, Brian J. and Ann E. Harrison (1999), 'Do domestic firms benefit from direct foreign investment? Evidence from Venezuela', *American Economic Review*, **89** (3), June, 605–18.

Grossman, Gene M. and Elhanan Helpman (1991), *Innovation and Growth in the Global Economy*, Cambridge, MA: MIT Press.

Javorcik, Beata Smarzynska and Mariana Spatareanu (2005), 'Disentangling FDI spillover effects: what do firm perceptions tell us', in Theodore H. Moran, Edward M. Graham and Magnus Blomström (eds), *Does Foreign Direct Investment Promote Development?* Washington, DC: Center for Global Development and Institute for International Economics.

Markusen, James (2005), 'Modeling the offshoring of white-collar services: from comparative advantage to the new theories of trade and FDI', *NBER Working Papers* No. 11827, National Bureau of Economic Research.

Moran, Theodore H. (2001), *Parental Supervision: The New Paradigm for Foreign Direct Investment and Development*, Washington, DC: Institute for International Economics.

Morriset, Jacques and Kelly Andrews-Johnson (2003), 'The effectiveness of promotion agencies at attracting foreign direct investment', Washington, DC: *Foreign Investment Advisory Service Occasional Paper* 16.

Rasiah, Rajah (1994), 'Flexible production systems and local machine-tool subcontracting: electronics components transnationals in Malaysia', *Cambridge Journal of Economics* **18** (3), June, 279–98.

Roodman, David (2005), 'The Commitment to Development Index: 2005 Edition' Washington, DC: Center for Global Development, www.cgdev.org.

Wells, Jr., Louis T. and Alvin G. Wint (2000), *Marketing a Country: Promotion as a Tool for Attracting Foreign Investment*, Revised Edition, Washington, DC: The International Finance Corporation, the Multilateral Investment Guarantee Agency and the World Bank.

World Bank, The (2005), *Doing Business in 2004: Understanding Regulation*, Washington, DC: a co-publication of the World Bank, the International Finance Corporation and Oxford University Press, Chapter 1.

World Trade Organization (2005), *Ministerial Declaration*, Annex F (84), 18 December.

17. The most FDI-intensive economy in Europe: analysis of the Irish experience and current policy issues

Frank Barry[1]

1. INTRODUCTION

Ireland is the most FDI-intensive economy in the European Union, and the expansion in FDI inflows – in both manufacturing and services – over the course of the 1990s was an important driving force behind the remarkable boom of the 'Celtic Tiger' era. Ireland's low rate of corporation tax is one of the major factors accounting for Ireland's success in the FDI stakes. Its impact is strengthened, however, by the co-evolution of other elements of the Irish environment, such as the third-level education system and the role of the industrial development bodies within the public-sector bureaucracy. Section 2 of the chapter provides details of these various features of the Irish economy and assesses why Ireland was so successful in attracting FDI over the course of the 1990s. Section 3 presents an Irish perspective on some current issues concerning the European environment for inward FDI; specifically, the growth in offshoring of R&D functions, the implications of some recent European Court of Justice rulings, and the EU corporation tax harmonization debate. While Ireland's success in attracting inward FDI is widely known, it might come as a surprise to many to learn that in 2004, for the first time, Irish outward FDI flows exceeded inward investment. Section 4 provides some details on Irish outward direct investment and the policy issues that have arisen in tandem with its emergence.

2. INWARD FDI: THE IRISH EXPERIENCE

Ireland is the most FDI-intensive economy in Europe. As seen in Table 17.1, foreign-owned firms account for almost 50 per cent of Irish manufacturing employment. This compares to an average figure of 23 per cent for the

Table 17.1   FDI intensity of the Irish economy

	Share of foreign affiliates in manufacturing employment	Share of foreign affiliates in services employment	FDI inward stock (USD) per head of population (2004)
Ireland	49	22	57 372
EU-15	23	10	9796
CEE	33	16	2403

Notes: Affiliate employment shares (2002 or closest date) come from OECD (2005, tables E6 and E7) Science, Technology and Industry Scoreboard. CEE refers to the country average for Hungary, Poland and the Czech Republic. FDI Inward Stock data come from the UNCTAD (2005) World Investment Report.

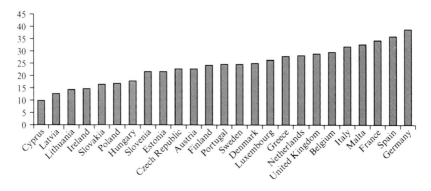

Source: Devereux (2006).

Figure 17.1   Effective average tax rates among EU member states in 2005

Western European EU member states and 33 per cent for the three largest Central and Eastern European economies. Of the 17 EU countries plus the US and Norway for which OECD (2005, Table E7) provides data, Ireland also records the highest share of services-sector employment in foreign-owned firms. These figures are reflected in the value of the FDI stock. Per head of population, the Irish inward FDI stock is a multiple of the EU average.[2]

One crucial factor in determining Ireland's success in attracting FDI has been the country's low rate of corporation tax.[3] There are various measures of the effective tax rate, which combines the tax rate and the tax base. Figure 17.1 graphs the effective average tax rate (EATR), which Devereux et al. (2002) show to be the tax rate relevant to discrete investment choices. Ireland is seen to have the fourth lowest rate among the 25 current EU member states, and by far the lowest among the Western European EU-15.

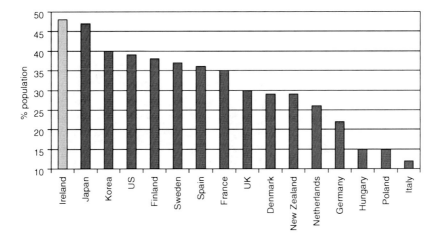

Source: OECD (2002), *Education at a Glance.*

Figure 17.2 Per cent of population aged 25–34 that has at least third-level education

Ireland has other advantages as well, however, including an English-language and common-law environment that proves attractive to US multinational corporations (MNCs). The long-established orientation of policy towards attracting FDI and the resulting FDI intensity of the economy have also helped configure Ireland's institutional structure to be able to respond rapidly to changes in the nature and the requirements of the type of global FDI that an economy with Ireland's characteristics can hope to attract. One key element of this concerns the third-level educational system. Ireland now surpasses the OECD in terms of the proportion of the cohort aged 25 to 34 with tertiary education, as seen in Figure 17.2, and, according to the data presented in Figure 17.3, has one of the highest proportions in the world of science and engineering graduates among this age group.

These outcomes, in turn, are largely responsible for the high ranking accorded to the Irish education system in the annual surveys of global executives carried out by the International Institute for Management Development. In the *World Competitiveness Yearbook* (2005), for example, global executives ranked Ireland number 2 out of a total of 60 OECD and medium-income developing countries in terms of how well the educational system is deemed to meet the needs of a competitive economy (with the UK ranked number 36), and number 5 out of 60 in terms of how university education is thought to meet the needs of a competitive economy (with the UK ranked 38th). Gunnigle and McGuire (2001), in a survey of executives of ten

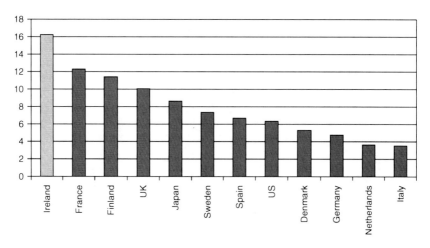

Source: European Commission, *Science and Technology Report 2003.*

*Figure 17.3   Science and engineering graduates per 1000 population aged
20–34*

major US MNCs, confirm that education and skill levels rank second in
importance to the corporation tax regime in drawing these firms to Ireland.

A factor that is more difficult to quantify is the role of the country's
Industrial Development Agency (IDA), which is widely regarded internationally as exemplary of best practice in the industrial promotion field. An
important element of governance in the agency's operations is that it is
subject to frequent external reviews, which have led to substantial changes
in structures and procedures in the 1960s, the 1980s and the 1990s. The
agency is facilitated in continuously adapting to changing circumstances
and global business trends by its 'transnational strategic network', consist-
ing of its overseas offices and its relations with investors already in Ireland.
These provide it with information about trends in targeted and newly
emerging sectors that warrant attention. The resulting feedback to headquarters not only influences the industries or sub-sectors targeted, but also
guides efforts to inform and persuade the government about required legislative changes, necessary additions to infrastructure and specific training
programmes to serve the needs of targeted sectors.[4]

Ireland's development agencies (Forfás, IDA-Ireland and Enterprise
Ireland), through the strong position they have attained in the policymaking hierarchy, have had an impact in areas not traditionally recognized
as lying within the remit of industrial promotion agencies. They played a
major role, for example, in forcing through the modernization of the
country's telecommunications infrastructure in the late 1970s and early

1980s, and in developing and upgrading human capital for the electronics sector. They were also instrumental in convincing government to reduce dramatically the rate of corporation tax on services (when the European Commission insisted that the rate be harmonized across sectors) and in driving the push for the massive increase in government spending on R&D in the National Development Plan for the period 2000–06.

Ireland's long-standing FDI orientation has also allowed agglomeration and demonstration effects to come into play.[5] As Barry and Bradley (1997) have noted, 'surveys of executives of newly arriving foreign companies . . . indicate that the presence of key market players in Ireland strongly influences the location choice of the newcomers'. Ireland hosts many such firms in its key FDI sectors: information and communications technology (ICT), the pharmaceutical-chemical industry (pharma-chem), medical instruments and international financial services. In computer hardware, such firms include IBM, Intel, Hewlett Packard, Apple and Dell; in software, Microsoft, Lotus and Oracle; in pharmaceuticals, the country hosts 9 of the top 10 companies in the world – including Glaxo, Johnson & Johnson, Pfizer, and Merck; 13 of the world's top 25 medical devices and diagnostics companies have bases in Ireland, while half of the world's top 50 banks and of the top 20 insurance companies operate out of the country. Barry and Van Egeraat (2005) show that the critical mass of companies established in related sectors facilitated the rapid adjustment of the economy as the computer hardware sector, for example, migrated eastwards out of Ireland over recent years.

Having established a reputation as a reliable location for FDI in high-tech sectors, Ireland was well placed to profit from the global high-tech boom of the 1990s. A less obvious factor behind the growth of the period is emphasized by MacSharry and White (2000). They describe how restrictive public procurement policies on the part of some of the larger EU member states used to offer a strong incentive to transnational corporations to locate there. With the outlawing of these practices under the Single Market initiative, the attractiveness of Ireland as a destination for FDI inflows increased.

3. INWARD FDI: SOME CURRENT ISSUES

3.1 Offshoring of R&D

An important new trend in global FDI concerns the offshoring of R&D functions, for which Kuemmerle (1999) provided early evidence. US Bureau of Economic Analysis data reveal a rise in European R&D employment in US affiliates from 66 500 workers in 1989 to 73 100 in 1994, up to 83 100 in

Table 17.2   Gross expenditures on R&D (GERD): Ireland, EU-15 and OECD (in per cent)

	1991	1997	2000	2002
Ireland as share of EU-15	0.35	0.69	0.70	0.73
Ireland as share of OECD	0.11	0.20	0.20	0.22

Source: OECD (2005), Science, Technology and Industry Scoreboard; Table A.2.2.

1999, while a recent National Science Foundation report (Moris, 2004), points out that between 1994 and 1999, overseas R&D employment in US MNC affiliates grew at an average annual rate of 3.9 per cent, compared with just 0.7 per cent in the parent companies – 'an indication of the increasing globalization of innovation and knowledge-based competition'.[6]

In line with these developments, Ireland's share of gross R&D expenditures in the OECD and the EU-15 increased over the 1990s and beyond, as seen in Table 17.2, while the government commitment to the issue is seen in the *five-fold* increase in expenditures on science, technology and innovation policy over the 2000–06 planning period.[7]

Nor is the increase in Ireland's share driven solely by the increased funding available from government and delivered primarily through third-level educational institutions. Business expenditures on R&D have also increased more rapidly than in the case of the EU or OECD, with the vast bulk of this (some 70 per cent) accounted for by foreign-owned multinational corporations.[8]

How does the country's corporation tax regime affect its ability to attract R&D functions? There is a strand in the Irish literature that argues that 'the tax incentives for manufacturing in Ireland . . . inhibit the performance of R&D, since R&D costs can be written off at higher tax rates in the home country' (from a report to the state agency Forfás). Hines (2003) rejects the argument that low corporation tax rates discourage R&D, but suggests that R&D *intensity ratios* may be reduced, because employment and output might be stimulated to a greater extent than R&D. Indeed, it is likely, he suggests, that low tax rates indirectly encourage local R&D activities on the part of multinational corporations eager to defend themselves against the charge that rents should not be attributed to their operations in low-tax locations.

This argument is supported by a *Wall Street Journal* analysis of Microsoft's 1997 allocation of intellectual property to an Irish subsidiary, which 'helped the computer giant shave at least USD 500 million from its annual tax bill . . . The subsidiary has . . . a thin roster of employees . . . and the software was mostly developed outside Ireland, but the subsidiary . . . controls more than

USD 16 billion in Microsoft assets' (*Wall Street Journal*, 7 November, 2005). Though the thrust of the analysis is strongly disputed both by Microsoft and the IDA, the article goes on to point out that expanding R&D operations in Ireland, by pharma-chem as well as ICT companies, is 'necessary to satisfy IRS (Internal Revenue Service) rules on moving intellectual property abroad. To do so – and thus have profits from it be taxed abroad – a company must be able to argue plausibly that its offshore unit is at least partly responsible for the innovations'.

3.2 The European Court of Justice and the Tax Harmonization Debate

Much of the running on corporation tax issues within the EU today is being made by the European Court of Justice (ECJ). A detailed study of the implications of these decisions for Ireland will be published in 2007 by the Institute of European Affairs in Dublin. The study concludes that ECJ decisions, by expanding capital mobility within the EU, will generally operate to the benefit of lower-corporation-tax environments. This may cause some EU countries to push harder for corporation tax harmonization. Since Ireland would stand to lose a substantial segment of its inward FDI were this to come about, the issue attracts a good deal of attention in the country.

One point to note is that Ireland is competing for specific multinational investments not just with other EU countries but with non-EU countries such as Switzerland and Singapore. If Ireland were forced to raise its rate of corporation tax, at least some of these investments would be likely to be lost to the EU completely. Furthermore, recent analysis suggests – perhaps surprisingly – that the Irish tax regime may in fact facilitate larger and richer EU countries in attracting FDI in spite of higher corporation tax rates: the opposite of the view enshrined in the 'race to the bottom' argument.

The formal exposition of the 'race to the bottom' argument assumes that producers will move to whichever country has the lowest tax rates, so that – in the absence of tax coordination – the attempt to attract or preserve employment will lead to tax rates being driven ever lower.[9] Baldwin and Krugman (2004) show, however, that larger, richer and less peripheral countries in Europe levy higher corporation tax rates than other countries, which suggests that these advantages can be used to extract surplus from MNCs through higher tax rates. Under these circumstances, harmonization could be detrimental to both groups of countries.

Because of the specific details of US tax law, furthermore the Irish tax regime may in fact benefit higher-tax EU economies.[10] As Hines and Rice (1994) explain, the United States taxes income on a residence basis, meaning that American corporations and individuals owe taxes to the US government on all of their worldwide income. In order to avoid subjecting American multinationals to double taxation, the US provides MNCs with a tax credit for total foreign taxes, but the tax credit is limited to US tax liability on foreign income. This strongly disincentivizes investments in countries with higher tax rates than the US, unless accompanied by investments in lower-tax jurisdictions. Thus the Irish regime reduces the disincentives that US firms face in investing in high-tax economies.[11]

More recently, Desai et al. (2006) have shown that the firms most likely to initiate operations in low-tax countries are those with growing activity in nearby high-tax countries, while a somewhat similar argument is advanced by Rose and Spiegel (2005) for low-tax offshore financial centres (OFCs). They argue that while OFCs facilitate tax avoidance, they also exert competitive pressures on home-country banking systems such that proximity to an OFC is associated with a more competitive domestic banking system and greater overall financial depth. Thus OFCs, they suggest, may increase overall welfare.

4.   OUTWARD FDI FROM IRELAND

In 2004, for the first time, the flow of outward direct investment (ODI) from Ireland exceeded the gross FDI inflow, and Ireland's outward FDI stock relative to GDP is now above the EU-15 average.

The emergence of ODI as a new and rapidly growing phenomenon in Ireland has drawn attention to the international literature on home-country effects of FDI.[12] Most of that literature identifies the effects as positive on balance. Blomström et al. (1997), for example, in a study on US firms, find that increased foreign production raises labour productivity and expands headquarters services and high-skill employment in the home base, while Desai et al. (2005) find that higher capital expenditures on the part of foreign affiliates of US MNCs are associated with higher parent-company investments in the US. The implication drawn from this is that firms combine home production with foreign production to generate final output at lower cost than would be possible without ODI. This makes each stage of the production process more profitable and ultimately raises production in both locations, suggesting that home-country production and ODI are complements rather than substitutes.

Brainard and Riker (1997a, 1997b) provide some contrary evidence for US MNCs, however, as do Braconier and Ekholm (2000) for Swedish MNCs. Such substitutability can arise if the FDI displaces exports from the firm's home base, in contrast to the type of FDI entailed in the offshoring of the labour-intensive segments of the production process.

In the Irish case, however, even though most ODI is directed towards developed countries, it does not typically entail the displacement of Irish exports. As Barry et al. (2003) point out, many of the largest Irish MNCs, which are thought to be responsible for the bulk of ODI, are in largely non-traded sectors. Of the top 10 companies, as listed by Forfás (2000), Allied Irish Banks, Bank of Ireland and Irish Life are in financial retail services; Independent Newspapers is a media company; Cement Roadstone Holdings and the Smurfit Group are in construction and packaging materials respectively. The only way these companies can expand on world markets is through FDI. This leaves only food companies Kerry and Greencore, glassware company Waterford Wedgewood and pharma company élan operating in internationally-traded sectors in which FDI might possibly substitute for exports.

Even if home-country and host-country employment were substitutes rather than complements, however, so long as the Irish economy remains at full employment the gains from ODI are likely to dominate the losses from any job displacement, even in the short term.

5. CONCLUDING COMMENTS

Already, by 1973, Ireland – with 0.6 per cent of the population of Europe and a little over 1 per cent of the EU-15 – had 1.5 per cent of the US manufacturing-sector FDI stock in Europe. At the time of writing, this figure is closer to 10 per cent. Ireland has also been very successful in attracting services FDI, with the McKinsey Global Institute (2003) identifying Ireland and India as the most popular destinations for offshored business process outsourcing (BPO) and IT business services. The present chapter went on to detail how R&D offshoring has been gathering pace in recent years, and documented the steps that Ireland has taken to ensure success in this sphere also.

Ireland's ability to attract such high volumes of FDI would be greatly hindered by any movement within the EU towards corporation tax harmonization. The chapter went on to detail some of the intricacies of the harmonization issue, pointing out that low-tax regimes such as Ireland may actually enhance the attractiveness to FDI of other higher-tax EU regimes.

Finally, recent strong growth in outward FDI has raised a new set of issues for Irish policymakers. The most difficult issues arise, however, (a) when outward FDI acts as a substitute for exports, and (b) when unemployment levels are high so that there are large adjustment costs associated with job displacement. Neither of these circumstances prevails in Ireland at present.

NOTES

1. Professor of International Business and Development, Trinity College Dublin, Ireland.
2. Luxembourg records a higher FDI stock per head of population than Ireland, but this is largely concentrated in financial services and is much less employment-intensive.
3. The low corporation tax regime has been in place since the 1950s, and facilitated the FDI-oriented evolution of the economy's institutions. The elasticity of the FDI response has been large enough to yield corporation tax receipts above the EU-15 average level when normalized by gross national product (GNP).
4. An example of the speedy implementation of legislative change is provided by the case of the UCITS Directive which established a 'single EU passport' in financial services. Ireland was the second country after Luxembourg to implement the Directive in 1989. (UCITS = undertakings for collective investment in transferable securities.)
5. See Barry et al. (2003).
6. The 2005 UNCTAD World Investment Report provides broader and more detailed evidence on the recent growth in global offshoring of R&D functions.
7. The Irish data, unfortunately, are as yet available only up to 2002.
8. OECD (2005): Sections A2 and A5.
9. Technically, the tax competition results only go through under source-based (as opposed to residence-based) taxation. Bilateral tax treaties normally give the host country the right to tax income originating within its territory, implying that the source principle is in operation. However, exemptions or tax credits for tax paid elsewhere imply that the residence principle also applies (Barba Navaretti and Venables, 2004, p. 244).
10. Note that the US accounts for around half of manufacturing-sector FDI in Ireland.
11. Nor is it necessarily true that the US tax authorities lose out from foreign tax-haven activities. As pointed out by Hines and Rice (1994), 'taking the total profitability of American multinational firms to be fixed, the US government collects the most tax revenue when American firms earn their foreign profits in tax havens, since fewer foreign tax credits are available on haven profits than on profits earned in high-tax foreign countries'. A further possibility is that profitable business operations in tax havens stimulate complementary business investment in the United States.
12. This is the topic of the 2007 UNCTAD World Investment Report, research on which is currently underway.

REFERENCES

Baldwin, R. and P. Krugman (2004), 'Agglomeration, integration and tax harmonisation', *European Economic Review*, **48** (1), 1–23.

Barba Navaretti, G. and A. Venables (2004), *Multinational Firms in the World Economy*, Princeton and Oxford: Princeton University Press.

Barry, F. and J. Bradley (1997), 'FDI and trade: the Irish host-country experience', *The Economic Journal*, **107**, 1798–811.

Barry, F. and C. Van Egeraat (2005), 'The eastward shift of computer hardware production: how Ireland adjusted', *Working Paper 27*, National Institute for Regional and Spatial Analysis, National University of Ireland, Maynooth.

Barry, F., H. Görg and A. McDowell (2003), 'Outward FDI and the investment development path of a late-industrialising economy: evidence from Ireland', *Regional Studies*, **37** (4), 341–9.

Barry, F., H. Görg and E. Strobl (2003), 'Foreign direct investment, agglomerations and demonstration effects: an empirical investigation', *Weltwirtschaftliches Archiv*, **139**, 583–600.

Blomström, M., G. Fors and R.E. Lipsey (1997), 'Foreign direct investment and employment: home country experience in the United States and Sweden', *The Economic Journal*, **107** (445), 1787–97.

Braconier, H. and K. Ekholm (2000), 'Swedish multinationals and competition from high- and low-wage locations', *Review of International Economics*, **8** (3), 448–61.

Brainard, S. and D. Riker (1997a), 'Are US multinationals exporting US Jobs?', *NBER Working Paper 5958*.

Brainard, S. and D. Riker (1997b), 'US multinationals and competition from low-wage countries', *NBER Working Paper 5959*.

Desai, M., C. Foley and J. Hines (2005), 'Foreign direct investment and the domestic capital stock', *NBER Working Paper 11075*.

Desai, M., C.F. Foley and J.R. Hines Jr. (2006), 'Do tax havens divert economic activity?', *Economics Letters*, **90** (2), 219–24.

Devereux, M., R. Griffith and A. Klemm (2002), 'Corporate income tax reforms and international tax competition', *Economic Policy*, **17**, 451–95.

Devereux, Michael P. (2006), 'Taxes in the EU new member states and the location of capital and profit', paper delivered to an IMF-Joint Vienna Institute-National Bank of Poland conference on 'Labour and Capital Flows in Europe Following Enlargement'.

European Commission (2003), *Third European Report on Science and Technology Indicators*.

Forfás (2000), *International Trade and Investment Report*, Dublin: Forfás.

Forfás (2005), *International Trade and Investment Report*, Dublin: Forfás.

Gunnigle, P. and D. McGuire (2001), 'Why Ireland? A qualitative review of the factors influencing the location of US multinationals in Ireland with particular reference to the impact of labour issues', *Economic and Social Review*, **32**, 43–67.

Hines, J.R. (2003), 'Sensible tax policies in open economies', *Journal of the Statistical and Social Inquiry Society of Ireland*, **33**, pp. 1–36.

Hines, J.R. and E.M. Rice (1994), 'Fiscal paradise: foreign tax havens and American business', *Quarterly Journal of Economics*, **109** (1), 149–82.

Kuemmerle, W. (1999), 'Foreign direct investment in industrial research in the pharmaceuticals and electronics industries – results of a survey of multinational firms', *Research Policy*, **28**, 179–93.

MacSharry, R. and P. White (2000), *The Making of the Celtic Tiger: the Inside Story of Ireland's Booming Economy*, Dublin, Ireland: Mercier Press.

McKinsey Global Institute (2003), *Offshoring: Is it a win–win game?*, San Francisco: McKinsey and Company.

Moris, F. (2004), *Industrial R&D Employment in the United States and in US Multinational Corporations*, InfoBrief 05-302, National Science Foundation.

OECD (2002), *Education at a Glance*, Paris: OCED.

OECD (2005), *Science, Technology and Industry Scoreboard*, Paris: OCED.

Rose, A. and M. Spiegel (2005), 'Offshore financial centers: parasites or symbionts?', unpublished manuscript, University of California, Berkeley.

UNCTAD (2005), *World Investment Report: Transnational Corporations and the Internationalization of R&D*, New York and Geneva: United Nations.

IMD (2005), *World Competitiveness Yearbook*, Lausanne: International Institute for Management Development.

18. Attracting sustainable FDI and building a knowledge-based economy: the case of CzechInvest

Jakub Mikulasek

While specifically representing the Czech economic development agency in this chapter, I presume that my views are valid for all investment promotion agencies in Central and Eastern Europe, given that we share many things with countries such as Hungary, Poland or Slovakia. My contribution is divided into three parts. After describing very briefly the significance of foreign investment for the Czech Republic, I focus on how the environment has changed since the early 1990s. To conclude, I share our views of how to attract the right kind of investment – sustainable investment.

THE CHANGING LANDSCAPE OF FDI IN THE CZECH REPUBLIC

The density of foreign companies in Central and Eastern Europe was basically close to zero at the beginning of the 1990s. In the case of the Czech Republic, foreign direct investment (FDI) inflows started to take off in 1998 (see Figure 18.1) – later than in Hungary, but earlier than in other countries in the area. By 2006, foreign investors in the Czech Republic were already representing as much as 45 per cent of industrial employment, 55 per cent of its industrial production and 65 per cent of its industrial exports.

The role of foreign investors in services, one of the key subjects in the investment policies of all countries in this region, is neatly summarized by a poster Siemens used in the Czech Republic, which says: 'We like being in the Czech Republic. We have high-end technologies for the Czech Republic, 14 000 jobs and charity activities, beneficial for Czech society'. I might add that the Czech society, or the Czech Republic, is very thankful for foreign investment in general.

By 2006, the Czech Republic had attracted 400+ US companies, 165 Japanese companies, 20 Taiwanese companies and 15 Korean companies.

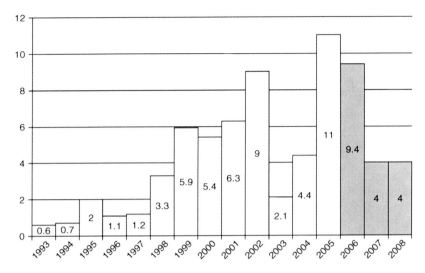

Source: Czech National Bank, 2/2006; 2006–2008 prediction, Economist Intelligence Unit.

Figure 18.1   FDI inflows into the Czech Republic (USD billion)

Obviously, Germany, Austria, the Netherlands and other European countries represent the main investors in Central and Eastern Europe. However,
there appears to be a difference between European investment and overseas
investment. What we see is that while many European companies invest in
existing businesses through acquisitions and through privatizations of the
national giants in the Eastern European countries, US or Asian businesses
usually set up greenfield operations, because they need production facilities.
Their basic need is to access the European market, which they will typically
do from one of the Eastern European countries today.

THE CHANGING ROLE OF CZECHINVEST

The company history of CzechInvest, the Czech Republic's Investment and
Business Development Agency, is another excellent case in point regarding
the changes that we have experienced in investment promotion in the
decade up to 2005. Basically, one can identify four different stages. When
CzechInvest was first established, in 1993, it was set up purely as an investment promotion agency, with nothing but a marketing agenda. Our job was
to market the Czech Republic and simply to try to get as many big names
from industry as possible, with certain services. In 1998, when FDI inflows

started to take off, it became evident that to attract the names we wanted we needed to prepare the infrastructure – in other words, we needed to enhance our product. So CzechInvest also became involved in product development. We started to administer public money that went into the development of the industrial zones, for example. This helped us attract foreign investors.

Early in the new millennium, in 2003, the government recognized the need to tailor investment promotion to the dual economy structure, that is to help local small- and medium-sized companies (SMEs) gain access to FDI companies, and to use structural funds to keep attracting foreign investors. In 2005, finally, we started to consolidate the two policies, the development of local SMEs and local suppliers and the technological development policies that are linked to the attraction of FDI.

CZECHINVEST'S CHANGING VISION OF A KNOWLEDGE-BASED ECONOMY

Let me illustrate with Figure 18.2 what CzechInvest was doing as an investment promotion agency in 2001 or 2002. At the time, we were purely taking care of foreign companies because this was what we had been set up to do, and we were pretty much welcoming anyone who had a large name in manufacturing. The overlapping area between the two circles in the figure represents our target: innovation, good and sustainable investment. You can

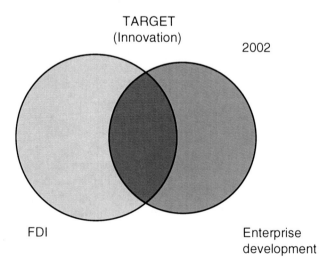

Figure 18.2   CzechInvest's scope of activities in 2002

Toyoda Gosei, Groundbreaking ceremony, April 2001

Figure 18.3   CzechInvest ad run in the Financial Times *(2001)*

see that we attracted that part of FDI which coincided with our wish list, and the rest was out. Note that enterprise development, that is the development of local companies that we are now trying to link to the foreign companies, was not even on our radar screen at the time.

To serve these foreign investors, or to reach this target of attracting these foreign investors, we have offices around the world in the countries that can generate, or that are most likely to generate, investment names for the Czech Republic. Specifically, we have foreign offices in the east and the west of the US, in the UK and Ireland, the Benelux countries, France and Germany, and in Japan and Southeast Asia. As marketing departments do, we also rely on advertising campaigns in our effort to attract as many foreign companies with large names as possible. Figure 18.3 shows an advertisement that we used in the *Financial Times* back in 2001.

Figure 18.4, marking the evolution up to 2004 when CzechInvest was already involved in supporting local companies, shows an increase in the FDI volume compared with that in 2002 (Figure 18.2). More important, a major part of the FDI volume already overlaps with our desired circle. Moreover, local business and structural foreign aids are starting to overlap.

Let me give two examples for first examples of cooperation between local companies and foreign aid. First, by 2004, CzechInvest had already started

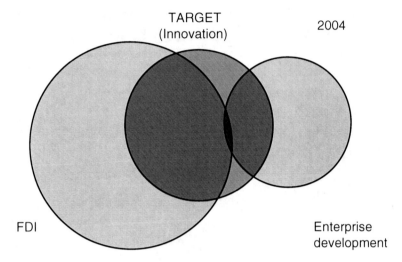

Figure 18.4   CzechInvest's scope of activities in 2004

to try and boost Czech suppliers to foreign companies as much as possible, so that they could gain business from them and also gain insight into what kind of supplies or services these companies and large names would be needing. Second, and as a case in point for the growing high-tech product, high-tech intersection, we are supporting projects like 'Medipark' on the Czech side. Medipark is a project launched by Masaryk University in Brno and the South Moravian region. The project is a 15-hectare development containing incubators, a spin-off centre and technology transfer units focusing on medicine, biology and chemistry. CzechInvest is promoting this project abroad but, unlike in the past, when CzechInvest told foreign companies 'Come to the Czech Republic, no matter where, we are the best', we are offering a certain product, saying: 'Look, if you are doing this and that, this park should be something for you'. And we have already been able to win a few foreign partners for Medipark.

To support both local companies and foreign companies, we needed to set up a regional network, so now we have 14 offices across the Czech Republic. These are basically marketing branches, so they can talk to local businesses. They can also promote the structural funds that CzechInvest administers, and they can link foreign companies in their regions.

Around 2003 to 2004 we recognized that we were no longer in the business alone, that other countries were also pushing very hard, that is, Slovakia or Poland, but also, above all in services, China, Mauritius, India and the like. As a case in point, a US company looking to establish a service centre in 2002 was telling me: 'Well, we think that it's either Prague or

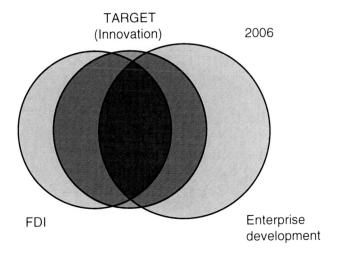

Figure 18.5   CzechInvest's scope of activities in 2006

Budapest'. And we had to start convincing them that the Czech Republic is not only about Prague, that there are other regions, and finally convinced them to consider Brno, the number two city in the Czech Republic. After a year, finally, Brno was selected, but the project was frozen on the US side because of internal problems immediately thereafter. In 2005, the project was re-launched, and we had to repeat the whole exercise, supply the data, supply the comparative advantages. But we were no longer competing in the league of Prague or Budapest: our proposition was now Olomouc, which is even smaller than Brno, because Brno was no longer competitive with one location in China, so we were urging the local authorities in Olomouc: 'It's either Olomouc or China. You have to try fast'.

As is evident from Figure 18.5, the FDI circle and the enterprise development circle had by 2006 become more closely aligned with each other and above all with our target (innovation) list.

A case in point is a high-end project supported by CzechInvest: a joint venture of a top American clinic and medical research institution, Mayo Clinic, with a university hospital in Brno. Together, they have set up a clinical research/educational centre focusing on cardio and neurovascular diseases, internal medicine, neurology and oncology. The deal got its final approval from the Czech government in 2006, and contracts have been signed with major partners, including IBM, GE Healthcare, Johnson & Johnson and Pfizer. In other words, the Czech Republic has come a long way, moving from low-wage, low-tag assemblies to much higher wage and higher value added investment deals.

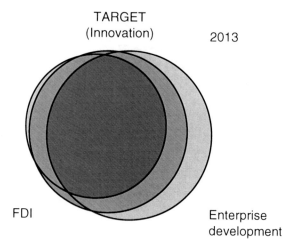

Figure 18.6   CzechInvest's vision of a knowledge-based economy for 2013

Our vision for 2013, finally, is that the FDI and the business development sides of our mission will have merged together, and that this will create as many innovative projects as possible.

ATTRACTING SUSTAINABLE INVESTMENT

To conclude, when or where can we make a difference in promoting sustainable investment? Let me start by questioning the meaning of the term 'sustainable'. Take for instance the case of Flextronics, which left the Czech Republic several years ago. Politicians were asking us, 'How come we supported this project and now they are going even further east?' Several weeks later we offered the vacated facility to another company, Honeywell, which today employs several hundred engineers. And Flextronics in fact kept its design centre in the Czech Republic. So was the investment of Flextronics back in 2001 sustainable or not, even though it left? I think it was.

So how can we attract sustainable investment? I would like to mention five points. First, and most importantly, you have to target the right partners or potential investors. You have to use your limited resources and really focus on specific groups and allocate your resources accordingly. Second, you have to develop and innovate your product, at the macro level, at the micro level and at the institutional level; and for these efforts to be successful, you need to cooperate with all the ministries. Third, you have to be flexible. You may need to change your strategy and your tools. Back in

2003, for instance, CzechInvest saw the need to start attracting more services, so we set up special incentives for services and R&D projects, pushing up the services share to 30 per cent of all our projects by 2006. Fourth, it is important not to neglect 'relationship marketing', that is you have to keep supporting the existing investors, continue to work with them, and try to upgrade their investment in your country. Usually we use our foreign offices to interlink with the existing investors, so we can talk to their parent companies and convince them that we are able to manage and upgrade their investment. Finally, it is important to integrate the positive effects of foreign direct investment, and of the foreign investors in the local economy. In my opinion, this is exactly what CzechInvest has been doing, and I have tried to illustrate this with the increasing alignment of the three circles depicted in Figures 18.2 and 18.4 to 18.6.

Index